# Table of Contents

# Chapter 1: Introduction to Unreal Engine

## 1.1. Understanding the Unreal Engine Ecosystem

In this section, we will delve into the Unreal Engine ecosystem, which serves as the foundation for your journey into game development. Unreal Engine, often referred to simply as Unreal, is a powerful and versatile game engine that has been instrumental in the creation of numerous high-quality games and immersive experiences.

### Unreal Engine's Origin

Unreal Engine's roots trace back to the early 1990s when it was initially developed by Tim Sweeney, the founder of Epic Games. The engine has come a long way since then, evolving and adapting to the changing landscape of game development.

### Core Components

Unreal Engine comprises several core components that work together to empower developers in creating stunning and interactive worlds. These components include:

1. **Unreal Editor**: This is the primary interface where you will design and build your game worlds, create assets, and script gameplay.

2. **Blueprint Visual Scripting**: Unreal's unique visual scripting system allows you to create game logic without extensive coding knowledge, making it accessible to developers of various skill levels.

3. **Rendering Engine**: Unreal's rendering engine is renowned for its ability to deliver photorealistic visuals, making it a top choice for creating visually impressive games.

4. **Physics Simulation**: Unreal Engine includes a robust physics simulation system that enables the creation of realistic interactions and environments.

5. **Audio Engine**: Sound is a crucial aspect of game immersion, and Unreal Engine provides tools for implementing high-quality audio and sound effects.

6. **Asset Pipeline**: Managing 3D models, textures, and other assets is made easier with Unreal's asset pipeline, which streamlines the importing and organization of resources.

### Versatility and Applications

Unreal Engine is not limited to game development; it has found applications in various industries, including architecture, film production, virtual reality, and more. Its real-time rendering capabilities have made it a valuable tool for creating architectural visualizations, interactive simulations, and even virtual production in the film industry.

## Community and Resources

One of the strengths of Unreal Engine is its vibrant and supportive community. Online forums, tutorials, and official documentation provide a wealth of resources to help you navigate the engine and troubleshoot issues.

## Licensing Options

Unreal Engine offers flexible licensing options, including a free version for non-commercial use and royalty-based licensing for commercial projects. Understanding these options is crucial when considering your project's scope and goals.

In conclusion, understanding the Unreal Engine ecosystem is the first step in your journey as a game developer. Whether you are aiming to create games, simulations, or other interactive experiences, Unreal Engine provides a robust and versatile platform to bring your ideas to life. This section has provided an overview, but as you delve deeper into the subsequent chapters, you will gain hands-on experience and expertise in using Unreal Engine to build your projects.

---

## 1.2. The Evolution of Unreal Engine: A Historical Perspective

Unreal Engine's journey through the years has been marked by significant milestones and innovations that have shaped the world of game development. Understanding its evolution provides valuable insights into its current capabilities and the industry's progress.

## Early Beginnings

Unreal Engine's origins can be traced back to the late 1980s when Tim Sweeney, the visionary behind it, began experimenting with game development. His early work led to the creation of ZZT, a text-based adventure game. This laid the foundation for his future endeavors.

## Unreal Engine 1 (Unreal Engine 1.0 - 1.5)

The first official version of Unreal Engine, released in 1998, brought 3D graphics and real-time rendering to the forefront. It powered the groundbreaking game "Unreal," known for its stunning visuals and gameplay. Unreal Engine 1 introduced the UnrealEd level editor, which set a new standard for level design tools.

## Unreal Engine 2 (Unreal Engine 2.0 - 2.5)

Unreal Engine 2, released in 2000, continued to push the boundaries of graphics and physics in gaming. It powered notable titles like "Tom Clancy's Splinter Cell" and "Deus Ex: Invisible War." The introduction of the UnrealScript language allowed for greater flexibility in game scripting.

### Unreal Engine 3 (Unreal Engine 3.0 - 3.5)

Unreal Engine 3, released in 2006, marked a significant leap in graphics quality and performance. It became the engine of choice for many developers, including Epic Games' "Gears of War" series and the critically acclaimed "Bioshock." Unreal Engine 3 introduced powerful features like the Kismet visual scripting system.

### Unreal Engine 4 (Unreal Engine 4.0 - 4.27)

Unreal Engine 4, unveiled in 2012 and made available to the public in 2015, was a game-changer. It introduced a subscription-based model and made the engine's full source code accessible. This democratized game development and led to an explosion of creativity. Unreal Engine 4 has powered countless games, from indie gems to AAA blockbusters.

### Unreal Engine 5 (Unreal Engine 5.0 - Present)

Unreal Engine 5, introduced in 2021, focuses on next-gen graphics and unprecedented levels of detail. The Nanite virtualized geometry system and Lumen global illumination technology redefine what's possible in real-time rendering. UE5 empowers developers to create incredibly detailed and immersive worlds.

### Industry Impact

Unreal Engine's impact extends beyond gaming. It has been used in film and television production, architectural visualization, automotive design, and more. Its real-time capabilities have transformed industries, enabling real-time previews, interactive simulations, and virtual production techniques.

### Open-Source and Community

Epic Games' commitment to the community led to the release of Unreal Engine's source code on GitHub. This open approach fosters collaboration, innovation, and a wealth of community-created plugins and assets.

In conclusion, Unreal Engine's evolution has been a remarkable journey, driven by a passion for pushing the boundaries of what's possible in interactive entertainment. As you explore the engine's capabilities in this book, keep in mind the rich history and innovation that has brought us to where we are today in the world of game development.

---

## 1.3. Key Features and Capabilities of Unreal Engine

Unreal Engine is renowned for its extensive set of features and capabilities that empower game developers to create immersive and visually stunning experiences. In this section, we'll explore some of the key features that make Unreal Engine a top choice for game development.

### High-Quality Graphics and Realism

Unreal Engine is synonymous with high-quality graphics and realism. It boasts a cutting-edge rendering engine that supports advanced rendering techniques such as physically-based rendering (PBR), dynamic global illumination (Lumen), and real-time ray tracing. These features enable developers to create visually stunning environments, realistic lighting, and lifelike characters, pushing the boundaries of visual fidelity in games.

### Blueprints Visual Scripting

Unreal Engine's Blueprints visual scripting system is a standout feature that simplifies game development, making it accessible to both programmers and non-programmers. With Blueprints, you can create complex gameplay mechanics, character behaviors, and interactive elements using a node-based graph. This intuitive approach allows for rapid prototyping and iteration, reducing the need for extensive coding.

```
// Example Blueprint Node
On Event Begin Play
    |--> Spawn Actor from Class (Spawn a character)
          |--> Set Actor Location (Set character's initial position)
          |--> Play Animation (Start character's animation)
```

### Robust Physics Simulation

Unreal Engine incorporates a robust physics simulation system that enables realistic interactions within the game world. Whether it's simulating the behavior of objects, character movements, or environmental physics, Unreal Engine provides the tools to create immersive and dynamic gameplay experiences.

### Cross-Platform Development

Unreal Engine supports cross-platform development, allowing you to target a wide range of platforms, including PC, console, mobile, virtual reality (VR), and augmented reality (AR). This flexibility is invaluable for reaching a broad audience and maximizing the reach of your game.

### Asset Management and Workflow

Efficient asset management is crucial in game development, and Unreal Engine excels in this aspect. It offers a streamlined asset pipeline for importing, organizing, and managing 3D models, textures, audio files, and other resources. This makes it easier for artists and developers to collaborate seamlessly.

### Blueprint Marketplace and Community Support

Unreal Engine's marketplace and community support provide a wealth of assets, plugins, and resources created by developers from around the world. Whether you need pre-built assets, code plugins, or guidance from experienced developers, the Unreal community has you covered.

### Real-Time Collaboration

Unreal Engine's collaboration features enable multiple team members to work on the same project simultaneously. This real-time collaboration streamlines the development process, allowing artists, designers, and programmers to see changes instantly and collaborate effectively.

### Virtual Production

Unreal Engine has gained popularity in the film and television industry for its use in virtual production. It enables filmmakers to create virtual sets and environments, visualizing scenes in real-time and capturing them on camera. This innovative approach has revolutionized filmmaking.

### Continuous Updates and Support

Epic Games, the company behind Unreal Engine, consistently provides updates, bug fixes, and new features to keep the engine at the forefront of technology. This commitment ensures that developers have access to the latest tools and capabilities.

In conclusion, Unreal Engine's key features and capabilities make it a formidable choice for game development and various other industries. Its focus on high-quality graphics, accessibility through Blueprints, physics simulation, cross-platform support, asset management, and a thriving community contribute to its reputation as a powerhouse in the world of game engines. As you embark on your journey with Unreal Engine, these features will become valuable tools in your development toolkit.

---

## 1.4. Setting Up Your Development Environment

Before you can start using Unreal Engine to create your games or projects, you need to set up your development environment. This involves installing the necessary software and configuring your system to work seamlessly with Unreal Engine. In this section, we'll guide you through the steps to set up your development environment.

### Supported Platforms

Unreal Engine is versatile and supports a variety of platforms, including Windows, macOS, and Linux. However, the primary development platform for Unreal Engine is Windows. While macOS and Linux are supported for building projects, some features and tools may be limited or require workarounds.

### Hardware Requirements

To run Unreal Engine efficiently, you'll need a capable computer with sufficient hardware resources. Unreal Engine 4 and later versions have higher system requirements due to their advanced graphics capabilities. Here are some basic hardware requirements:

- **Operating System**: Windows 10 (64-bit), macOS 10.14, or a Linux distribution that Unreal Engine supports.
- **Processor**: Quad-core Intel or AMD processor.
- **Memory (RAM)**: 16 GB or more.
- **Graphics Card**: DirectX 11 compatible graphics card.
- **Storage**: 100 GB of free space on your hard drive or SSD.

## Unreal Engine Installation

1. **Download Unreal Engine**: Visit the Epic Games website and download the Epic Games Launcher, which includes Unreal Engine. Create an Epic Games account if you don't have one.

2. **Install the Launcher**: Run the Epic Games Launcher installer and follow the on-screen instructions. After installation, launch the Epic Games Launcher.

3. **Install Unreal Engine**: In the Epic Games Launcher, go to the "Unreal Engine" tab. Click "Install Engine" and choose a directory where you want to install Unreal Engine.

## Epic Games Account

To access Unreal Engine and its features, you'll need an Epic Games account. This account is free and provides you with access to the engine, marketplace, and community resources. You can create an account during the installation process or on the Epic Games website.

## Engine Version

Unreal Engine often receives updates and new releases. When starting a new project, it's essential to select the appropriate engine version for your needs. You can choose the latest stable version or an older version if your project requires compatibility with specific features or plugins.

## Plugins and Extensions

Unreal Engine supports a wide range of plugins and extensions created by the community and third-party developers. These can enhance your workflow and add functionality to the engine. Explore the marketplace and Unreal Engine's documentation to find and install plugins that suit your project requirements.

## Integrated Development Environment (IDE)

While Unreal Engine provides a built-in code editor called "Blueprints" for visual scripting, you may want to use an external integrated development environment (IDE) for C++ programming. Common choices include Visual Studio and Visual Studio Code. Ensure you have the necessary tools and extensions installed for Unreal Engine development.

## Conclusion

Setting up your development environment is the first step toward creating games and interactive experiences with Unreal Engine. Pay close attention to the system requirements, keep your engine version up-to-date, and explore the available plugins and extensions to streamline your workflow. With the right environment in place, you'll be ready to start building your projects using Unreal Engine's powerful tools and features.

---

## 1.5. Navigating the Unreal Engine Interface

Once you have set up your development environment, it's time to familiarize yourself with the Unreal Engine interface. Navigating the interface is essential for efficiently creating and managing your projects. In this section, we will explore the main components of the Unreal Engine interface.

### Unreal Editor

The Unreal Editor is the central hub for creating and editing your projects. When you open Unreal Engine, you'll be greeted by the Unreal Editor interface. Let's take a look at its key components:

1. **Viewport**: The viewport is where you'll see your game world or level. It provides a real-time preview of your scene and allows you to navigate and interact with it.

2. **Toolbar**: The toolbar contains various tools and options for manipulating objects, adding actors, and accessing common commands. It includes options for moving, rotating, scaling objects, as well as tools for landscape editing, rendering, and more.

3. **Modes Panel**: The modes panel houses a set of modes that allow you to perform specific actions or tasks in your scene. For example, you can switch to "Placement Mode" to add new objects to your level.

4. **World Outliner**: The World Outliner displays a hierarchical list of all the actors and objects in your level. You can use it to select and organize elements within your scene.

5. **Details Panel**: The Details panel provides a comprehensive set of properties and settings for the currently selected object. You can adjust an object's properties here, such as its location, rotation, and materials.

6. **Content Browser**: The Content Browser is where you manage and organize your project's assets, including 3D models, textures, materials, and blueprints. You can create folders, import assets, and search for resources.

7.  **Viewport Controls**: In the viewport, you can use controls like the mouse and keyboard shortcuts to navigate and manipulate the camera, objects, and the scene itself.

## Viewport Navigation

Navigating the viewport is essential for inspecting and editing your game world. Here are some common viewport navigation controls:

- **Mouse Look**: Right-click and drag to rotate the camera's view.
- **Mouse Pan**: Middle-click and drag to pan the camera.
- **Mouse Zoom**: Scroll the mouse wheel to zoom in and out.
- **Fly Mode**: Press F to enter Fly Mode, allowing you to move freely in 3D space.
- **Viewport Shading**: You can switch between different viewport shading modes, such as wireframe, unlit, and lit, to view your scene in various ways.

## Customizing the Interface

Unreal Engine offers a high degree of customization for its interface. You can rearrange and resize panels, create custom layouts, and save them for different tasks or workflows. To customize the interface, go to the "Window" menu and explore the options for managing and arranging panels.

## Conclusion

Navigating the Unreal Engine interface is a crucial skill for efficient game development. Familiarize yourself with the various panels and tools available in the Unreal Editor, and practice viewport navigation to explore your game world. As you work on your projects, you'll discover additional interface features and shortcuts that streamline your workflow and help you bring your creative ideas to life within the Unreal Engine environment.

# Chapter 2: Conceptualizing Your Game

## 2.1. Generating Game Ideas: Finding Inspiration

Generating game ideas is the initial spark that sets your creative process in motion. Whether you're a seasoned game developer or just starting, finding inspiration for your game concept is a crucial step. In this section, we'll explore various methods and sources for generating game ideas.

### 1. Personal Interests and Hobbies

Your personal interests and hobbies can be a goldmine for game ideas. Consider what you're passionate about, whether it's a particular genre of music, a historical period, a sport, or a hobby like cooking. These interests can serve as a foundation for your game concept, adding a personal touch to your project.

### 2. Classic Literature and Mythology

Classic literature, mythology, and folklore are rich sources of inspiration. You can draw upon timeless stories and characters to create a unique game world. Adaptations of myths and legends have been the basis for many successful games, providing a familiar yet fresh narrative.

### 3. Popular Media and Pop Culture

Movies, TV shows, books, and other forms of media can inspire game ideas. For example, science fiction novels have led to the creation of iconic sci-fi games. Be mindful of copyright and intellectual property rights when drawing inspiration from popular media.

### 4. Environmental Themes

The environment and nature can provide themes for your game. Consider exploring ecosystems, weather phenomena, or the beauty of landscapes. Games like "Journey" and "Firewatch" showcase the potential of environmental themes.

### 5. Social and Political Issues

Games can be a powerful medium for addressing social and political issues. Think about the topics that matter to you and how they can be integrated into your game's narrative or mechanics. These games can raise awareness and provoke meaningful discussions.

### 6. Historical Events and Settings

History is a treasure trove of stories and settings. You can transport players to different time periods and immerse them in historical events. Games like "Assassin's Creed" and "Red Dead Redemption" exemplify the possibilities of historical settings.

## 7. Dreams and Imagination

Your own dreams and imagination can be fertile ground for game ideas. Dreams often feature surreal and fantastical elements that can be woven into a unique gaming experience. Let your creativity flow without constraints.

## 8. Collaboration and Brainstorming

Don't hesitate to collaborate with others or engage in brainstorming sessions. Discussing ideas with friends, colleagues, or fellow developers can lead to unexpected and innovative concepts. A fresh perspective can be invaluable.

## 9. Problem Solving and Mechanics

Sometimes, game ideas emerge from solving a specific problem or exploring new gameplay mechanics. Start with a gameplay mechanic or puzzle concept, and build your game's theme and narrative around it.

## 10. Personal Experiences and Emotions

Your personal experiences and emotions can be the foundation for emotionally engaging games. Games like "That Dragon, Cancer" are powerful examples of how personal stories can be transformed into interactive experiences.

## Conclusion

Generating game ideas is a creative and exploratory process. You can find inspiration in a wide range of sources, from personal interests to historical events, and even within your own dreams and imagination. Keep an open mind, embrace collaboration, and be willing to experiment with different concepts. The journey of conceptualizing your game is an exciting one, and the ideas you generate will lay the foundation for your game development journey.

---

## 2.2. Defining Your Game's Genre and Style

Once you have a collection of potential game ideas, the next step in conceptualizing your game is to define its genre and style. These choices will shape the overall experience and gameplay mechanics. In this section, we'll explore how to determine your game's genre and style effectively.

### Understanding Game Genres

Game genres categorize games based on their gameplay mechanics and overall experience. Here are some common game genres to consider:

1. **Action**: These games focus on physical challenges, reflexes, and hand-eye coordination. Examples include "Super Mario," "Devil May Cry," and "Tomb Raider."

2. **Adventure**: Adventure games emphasize storytelling, exploration, and puzzle-solving. Notable titles are "The Legend of Zelda," "Monkey Island," and "Life is Strange."

3. **Role-Playing Game (RPG)**: RPGs center on character development, decision-making, and immersive worlds. Well-known RPGs include "The Elder Scrolls," "Final Fantasy," and "The Witcher."

4. **Simulation**: Simulation games replicate real-world activities and scenarios. They can range from life simulations like "The Sims" to city-building games like "SimCity."

5. **Strategy**: Strategy games require careful planning and decision-making. Subgenres include real-time strategy (RTS) and turn-based strategy (TBS). Examples are "StarCraft" (RTS) and "Civilization" (TBS).

6. **Puzzle**: Puzzle games challenge players with logic, pattern recognition, and problem-solving. "Tetris," "Portal," and "Candy Crush" fall into this category.

7. **Horror**: Horror games aim to scare and unsettle players. Notable horror games include "Resident Evil," "Silent Hill," and "Amnesia: The Dark Descent."

8. **Sports and Racing**: These games simulate real sports or racing events. Popular titles include "FIFA," "NBA 2K," and "Gran Turismo."

9. **Platformer**: Platformers involve precise jumping and navigation. Classic platformers like "Super Mario Bros." and "Sonic the Hedgehog" are iconic examples.

10. **Shooter**: Shooter games focus on combat and firearms. Subgenres include first-person shooters (FPS) like "Call of Duty" and third-person shooters (TPS) like "Gears of War."

Choosing the Right Genre

Selecting the right genre for your game idea is crucial. Consider the following factors:

- **Audience**: Who is your target audience? Some genres appeal more to specific demographics.

- **Gameplay Mechanics**: Does your game idea align with the gameplay mechanics associated with a particular genre?

- **Theme and Story**: Does your narrative fit well within a particular genre? Different genres lend themselves to distinct themes and storytelling approaches.

- **Competitive Landscape**: Research existing games in your chosen genre to understand the competition and opportunities for innovation.

Beyond genre, your game's style encompasses its visual and auditory elements, as well as its overall atmosphere. Here are some elements of game style to consider:

1. **Art Style**: Choose an art style that complements your game's theme. Options range from realistic to cartoony and everything in between.

2. **Graphics**: Determine the level of graphical fidelity you aim to achieve. Consider factors like texture quality, lighting, and special effects.

3. **Sound and Music**: Music and sound effects play a significant role in setting the mood. Decide whether your game will have an orchestral score, electronic music, or other soundscapes.

4. **Narrative Style**: Define the narrative style, including whether your game will have voice acting, written dialogue, or a silent protagonist.

5. **Atmosphere**: Consider the overall atmosphere you want to create. Is it a lighthearted and humorous game, a dark and gritty experience, or something in between?

6. **UI and HUD**: Design the user interface (UI) and heads-up display (HUD) elements to match your game's style and provide a seamless user experience.

Iterate and Refine

The process of defining your game's genre and style may involve iteration and refinement. Don't be afraid to experiment and adjust your choices as your game concept evolves. Feedback from peers and playtesting can also help you fine-tune your decisions.

Conclusion

Defining your game's genre and style is a critical step in the conceptualization process. It sets the tone for your game's development and helps you make informed decisions about gameplay mechanics, visual design, and narrative direction. By carefully considering your options and staying open to adjustments, you'll lay a strong foundation for your game's development journey.

## 2.3. Creating a Game Design Document

A Game Design Document (GDD) is a fundamental blueprint for your game development project. It serves as a comprehensive reference that outlines the game's concept, mechanics, objectives, and overall vision. In this section, we'll explore the importance of creating a GDD and the key elements it should contain.

A well-crafted GDD is a crucial tool that serves multiple purposes throughout the game development process:

1. **Clear Vision**: It provides a clear and shared vision of the game for the entire development team, ensuring everyone is on the same page regarding the game's goals and design.

2. **Reference Guide**: Team members can refer to the GDD for guidance on mechanics, levels, and features. It helps maintain consistency throughout development.

3. **Communication**: It serves as a communication tool between team members, stakeholders, and potential collaborators, making it easier to convey ideas and concepts.

4. **Project Management**: The GDD assists in project management by defining milestones, tasks, and deadlines. It helps track progress and ensures that the project stays on course.

5. **Documentation**: It serves as a historical record of the game's development, making it easier to review design decisions and track changes over time.

## Key Elements of a Game Design Document

While the specific content of a GDD may vary based on the project's scope and requirements, there are essential elements that every GDD should include:

### 1. Title and Overview
- **Game Title**: The title should reflect the game's theme and style.

- **Overview**: Provide a concise overview of the game's concept and what sets it apart from other games. Describe the core experience players can expect.

### 2. Game Mechanics
- **Core Mechanics**: Explain the fundamental gameplay mechanics that define the player's interactions with the game world.

- **Progression Systems**: Describe how players advance in the game, earn rewards, and experience character growth.

### 3. Story and Narrative
- **Story Synopsis**: Provide an overview of the game's narrative, including the setting, main characters, and central plot.

- **Dialogue and Narrative Flow**: Outline how the story is presented to players, including dialogue systems, cutscenes, and branching narratives.

### 4. Gameplay and Level Design
- **Level Layout**: Describe the layout and design of key game levels or areas.

- **Puzzles and Challenges**: Detail any puzzles, challenges, or obstacles that players will encounter.

- **Player Progression**: Explain how players will progress through the game, including the order of levels and any gating mechanisms.

## 5. Art and Visuals
- **Art Style**: Define the game's art style, including character designs, environments, and visual effects.

- **Concept Art**: Include concept art or references to convey the visual direction.

## 6. Audio and Music
- **Sound Effects**: Describe the types of sound effects used in the game.

- **Music**: Specify the style and mood of the game's music and provide examples if possible.

## 7. User Interface (UI)
- **HUD Elements**: Detail the elements of the heads-up display (HUD), including health bars, minimaps, and inventory screens.

- **Menus**: Describe menu screens, navigation, and user interactions.

## 8. Monetization (if applicable)
- **Business Model**: Outline the monetization strategy, whether it's a one-time purchase, in-app purchases, ads, or a subscription model.

- **Economy Design**: If applicable, describe the in-game economy, virtual goods, and pricing.

## 9. Technical Requirements
- **Platforms**: Specify the target platforms (e.g., PC, consoles, mobile devices).

- **Technology Stack**: Identify the game engine and any external tools or libraries used.

## 10. Project Management and Timeline
- **Milestones**: List key project milestones and their deadlines.

- **Team Roles**: Define the roles and responsibilities of team members.

### Iterate and Update

A GDD is not a static document; it should evolve as the project progresses. Regularly review and update the GDD to reflect design changes, new ideas, and lessons learned during development. This ensures that the document remains a valuable resource throughout the project's lifecycle.

## Conclusion

Creating a Game Design Document is a foundational step in game development that helps you define your game's vision, mechanics, and content. It serves as a reference guide, communication tool, and project management aid. By carefully crafting and maintaining your GDD, you provide clarity and direction for your development team, setting the stage for a successful game development journey.

---

## 2.4. Planning Gameplay Mechanics

Planning gameplay mechanics is a crucial aspect of game design that directly influences how players interact with your game world. Gameplay mechanics define the rules, actions, and systems that govern the player's experience. In this section, we'll delve into the process of planning and designing gameplay mechanics effectively.

### Understanding Gameplay Mechanics

Gameplay mechanics encompass a wide range of elements that collectively shape the player's experience. These elements include:

1. **Player Actions**: Define the actions players can perform, such as movement, jumping, attacking, and interacting with objects.

2. **Game Systems**: Create systems that govern core gameplay elements, such as combat, inventory management, and character progression.

3. **Rules and Constraints**: Establish rules and limitations that shape the game's challenges and difficulty level. These rules define what is possible within the game world.

4. **Feedback and Rewards**: Implement feedback mechanisms to inform players about their progress and provide rewards for their achievements. This includes visual and auditory cues, as well as in-game rewards like points or items.

5. **Puzzles and Challenges**: Design puzzles, challenges, and obstacles that engage players' problem-solving skills and contribute to the overall gameplay experience.

6. **User Interface (UI)**: Create an intuitive UI that allows players to access essential information and interact with game systems seamlessly.

### Steps for Planning Gameplay Mechanics

Effective planning of gameplay mechanics involves several key steps:

## 1. Define Core Mechanics

Start by defining the core gameplay mechanics that are central to your game's experience. These mechanics will be the foundation upon which the rest of your gameplay is built. For example, if you're creating a platformer, core mechanics might include jumping and running.

## 2. Design Systems

Identify and design the game systems that support your core mechanics. For instance, if your game involves combat, you'll need to design combat systems, including attack animations, hitboxes, and damage calculations.

## 3. Create Prototypes

Prototyping is a crucial step in gameplay design. Build small, functional prototypes to test your core mechanics and systems. Prototyping helps you identify what works and what needs refinement early in the development process.

```
// Example Unity script for player movement
public class PlayerController : MonoBehaviour
{
    public float moveSpeed = 5.0f;

    void Update()
    {
        float horizontalInput = Input.GetAxis("Horizontal");
        float verticalInput = Input.GetAxis("Vertical");

        Vector3 movement = new Vector3(horizontalInput, 0, verticalInput) * m
oveSpeed * Time.deltaTime;

        transform.Translate(movement);
    }
}
```

## 4. Balance and Iterate

Balance is crucial in gameplay design. Continuously playtest and iterate on your mechanics to ensure that the game offers a satisfying and enjoyable experience. Adjust rules, difficulty, and feedback based on player feedback and testing.

## 5. Player Progression

Consider how players will progress in your game. Define the mechanics and systems related to character development, leveling up, or acquiring new abilities. This adds depth to the gameplay and motivates players to continue.

Create opportunities for player engagement by designing compelling challenges and puzzles. Players should feel challenged and rewarded as they progress through the game. Ensure a good balance between difficulty and fun.

## 7. Accessibility

Consider accessibility options to make your game inclusive to a broader audience. Provide options for adjusting difficulty, controlling input methods, and accommodating players with different abilities.

## Documentation and Communication

As you plan gameplay mechanics, document your decisions and communicate them clearly with your development team. Use visual diagrams, flowcharts, and written descriptions to convey how mechanics work together and how they align with the overall game design.

## Conclusion

Planning gameplay mechanics is a critical step in game design that directly impacts the player's experience. By defining core mechanics, designing supporting systems, and continuously iterating, you can create engaging and enjoyable gameplay. Effective documentation and communication ensure that your development team shares a clear vision of the game's mechanics, leading to a cohesive and well-designed gaming experience.

---

## 2.5. Storyboarding and Visual Planning

Storyboarding and visual planning are essential components of game development that help you convey the narrative, level design, and overall vision of your game. In this section, we'll explore the significance of storyboarding and visual planning and provide guidance on how to effectively use these techniques in your game development process.

## The Importance of Storyboarding

Storyboarding is the process of creating a visual representation of your game's narrative, scenes, and events. It involves drawing or sketching key moments and sequences, much like a comic book or graphic novel. Storyboarding offers several benefits:

1. **Narrative Clarity**: It helps you visualize and refine the game's storyline, ensuring that it is coherent and engaging.
2. **Scene Planning**: Storyboarding assists in planning the layout and composition of individual game scenes and levels.

3. **Visual References**: It provides visual references for artists, animators, and level designers, helping them understand the intended look and feel of the game.

4. **Communication**: Storyboards serve as a communication tool, allowing you to convey your ideas and vision to the development team, including artists, designers, and writers.

Creating a Storyboard

Here are steps to create an effective storyboard for your game:

*1. Outline the Narrative*

Begin by outlining the main narrative of your game. Identify key plot points, character arcs, and significant events. This serves as the foundation for your storyboard.

*2. Break Down Scenes*

Divide the game into individual scenes or levels. Each scene should represent a distinct moment in the game's story or gameplay. Decide what each scene aims to achieve in terms of storytelling and player experience.

*3. Sketch the Scenes*

For each scene, create rough sketches or drawings that depict the key events, characters, and environments. You don't need to be a professional artist; simple sketches that convey the ideas will suffice.

```
[Scene 1: Protagonist's Arrival]
- Sketch: Protagonist entering a mysterious forest.
- Description: The player's character arrives in the enchanted forest, settin
g the stage for the adventure.

[Scene 2: Encounter with a Companion]
- Sketch: Protagonist meeting a friendly forest creature.
- Description: The protagonist encounters a helpful companion who provides gu
idance and assistance.
```

*4. Add Descriptions*

Include descriptions or notes alongside each sketch to provide context and details about what's happening in the scene. Explain the significance of the scene in the game's narrative.

*5. Iterate and Refine*

Review and iterate on your storyboard. Seek feedback from team members to ensure that the narrative and visual elements align with the overall game design. Make adjustments as needed.

## Visual Planning for Level Design

Visual planning goes beyond storyboarding and focuses on creating detailed visual representations of game levels and environments. It helps level designers and artists understand the layout, aesthetics, and gameplay elements of each level. Use tools like concept art, mood boards, and level sketches to convey your vision effectively.

```
[Level 1: Enchanted Forest]
- Concept Art: A lush and vibrant forest with towering trees and bioluminesce
nt plants.
- Mood Board: Colors inspired by nature, with a magical and mysterious ambian
ce.
- Level Sketch: Layout of the forest, showing paths, obstacles, and points of
interest.
```

## Conclusion

Storyboarding and visual planning are integral to game development, enabling you to shape your game's narrative and level design. These techniques facilitate communication with your team, ensuring that everyone shares a common vision. By creating clear and visually engaging storyboards and level plans, you lay a strong foundation for the development process and enhance the overall quality of your game.

# Chapter 3: Basic Level Design

## 3.1. Introduction to Level Design in Unreal

Level design is a fundamental aspect of game development, responsible for creating the spaces and environments in which players will experience your game. In this section, we'll explore the basics of level design in Unreal Engine, one of the industry-standard game engines known for its powerful level design capabilities.

### What Is Level Design?

Level design involves crafting the playable areas, levels, and environments within a video game. It encompasses various elements, including layout, architecture, lighting, gameplay mechanics, and storytelling. Effective level design contributes to player immersion, engagement, and enjoyment.

### Key Principles of Level Design

Successful level design relies on several key principles:

*1. Flow and Pacing*
- **Flow**: Level layouts should guide players naturally through the game, ensuring a smooth and intuitive progression. Players should feel a sense of purpose and direction as they navigate the environment.

- **Pacing**: Balance action-packed sequences with moments of respite to maintain player engagement. Pacing varies depending on the game's genre and narrative.

*2. Clear Communication*
- **Visual Clarity**: Environments should convey information visually. Players should understand the rules, objectives, and hazards without the need for excessive text or tutorials.

- **Signposting**: Use visual cues, landmarks, and level design elements to guide players toward their goals and objectives.

*3. Gameplay Mechanics Integration*
- **Gameplay Spaces**: Design levels that accommodate the game's core mechanics. Different gameplay elements should seamlessly fit into the environment.

- **Challenges**: Create opportunities for players to apply their skills and engage with the game's mechanics. Introduce challenges that progressively increase in complexity.

*4. Immersion and Atmosphere*
- **Immersive Environments**: Craft environments that immerse players in the game's world and narrative. Attention to detail, ambiance, and storytelling elements contribute to immersion.

- **Aesthetics**: Consider the visual style, color palette, and theme of the level to evoke specific emotions and atmosphere.

## 5. Player Agency

- **Choice and Exploration**: Allow players to make meaningful choices and explore the environment. Offer alternative routes, secrets, and hidden areas to reward exploration.

- **Consequences**: Ensure that player actions have consequences within the level and impact the narrative or gameplay.

## Unreal Engine and Level Design

Unreal Engine provides a robust set of tools and features to support level design:

- **Level Editor**: Unreal Engine's Level Editor is a powerful tool for building and editing game levels. It offers a real-time 3D viewport, brushes for creating geometry, and a range of editing tools.

- **Lighting**: Unreal Engine's advanced lighting system allows you to create dynamic and realistic lighting scenarios, enhancing the visual quality and atmosphere of your levels.

- **Blueprints**: Blueprint visual scripting enables you to create interactive objects, gameplay mechanics, and events within your levels without extensive coding.

- **Asset Library**: Unreal Engine's extensive asset library provides a wide range of 3D models, textures, and materials to use in your level designs.

## Conclusion

Level design is a critical aspect of game development that shapes the player experience. Effective level design requires a deep understanding of game mechanics, player psychology, and storytelling. Unreal Engine offers a comprehensive set of tools and features to empower level designers and bring their creative visions to life. In the following sections, we will dive deeper into specific aspects of level design in Unreal Engine, including the use of the Level Editor and the implementation of textures and lighting.

---

## 3.2. Working with Unreal's Level Editor

Unreal Engine's Level Editor is a powerful and versatile tool that allows game developers to create, modify, and design game levels and environments. In this section, we will explore the basics of working with Unreal's Level Editor, including its interface, fundamental features, and best practices.

Getting Started with the Level Editor

When you open Unreal Engine, you can access the Level Editor by selecting a project or creating a new one. Here are the key components of the Level Editor interface:

1. **Viewport**: The main area where you visualize and manipulate your game level in 3D. You can navigate the viewport using the camera controls, including pan, orbit, and zoom.

2. **Modes Panel**: This panel contains various modes and tools for adding and editing objects, lights, and other elements in your level. Common modes include Placement Mode, Landscape Mode, and Geometry Editing.

3. **Toolbar**: The toolbar provides quick access to essential tools and commands, such as selecting objects, moving, rotating, scaling, and more.

4. **Details Panel**: This panel displays properties and settings for selected objects in your level. You can use it to fine-tune object parameters, materials, and lighting.

5. **World Outliner**: The World Outliner lists all the objects in your level, making it easy to select, organize, and manage them. You can group objects into folders and hierarchies.

6. **Content Browser**: The Content Browser allows you to access and manage assets, materials, and meshes for your level. You can drag and drop assets directly into the level.

Basic Level Editing Tasks

Here are some fundamental tasks you can perform in Unreal's Level Editor:

1. *Adding Objects to the Level*
- Select the desired mode (e.g., Placement Mode).
- Choose an object or asset from the Content Browser.
- Click in the viewport to place the object.

2. *Transforming Objects*
- Select one or more objects in the viewport.
- Use the toolbar or gizmo to move, rotate, or scale the objects.

3. *Creating and Editing Geometry*
- Use the Geometry Editing mode to create and modify basic shapes and brushes.
- Adjust parameters in the Details Panel to refine geometry properties.

4. *Lighting and Materials*
- Add lights to illuminate your level.
- Assign materials to objects by dragging and dropping materials from the Content Browser.

- Use the camera controls to navigate and explore your level.
- Use the Play button to test your level in the Unreal Editor.

## Best Practices for Level Design in Unreal

Effective level design is essential for creating immersive and engaging gameplay experiences. Consider the following best practices:

- **Optimization**: Keep an eye on performance by using the built-in optimization tools in Unreal Engine. Efficiently use assets, reduce unnecessary geometry, and apply level streaming where needed.

- **Consistency**: Maintain a consistent visual style, lighting, and scale throughout your level to ensure a cohesive player experience.

- **Iteration**: Level design often involves multiple iterations. Don't be afraid to make changes and improvements based on playtesting and feedback.

- **Player Flow**: Pay attention to player flow and ensure that your level guides players naturally from one area to another without confusion.

- **Documentation**: Document your level design decisions, asset usage, and lighting setups for future reference and collaboration with the development team.

## Conclusion

Unreal Engine's Level Editor is a versatile and powerful tool for creating game levels and environments. Whether you are designing a sprawling open world or a confined indoor space, understanding the basics of the Level Editor and following best practices in level design will help you create compelling and visually appealing game levels. In the following sections, we will explore more advanced aspects of level design in Unreal Engine, including texturing, lighting, and level testing and iteration.

---

## 3.3. Designing Your First Level: Basic Principles

Designing your first game level in Unreal Engine is an exciting step in the game development process. In this section, we'll explore the fundamental principles and considerations for creating a well-designed game level that engages players and aligns with your game's vision.

## Define Your Level's Purpose

Before diving into level design, it's essential to define the purpose and objectives of your level:

1.  **Narrative Context**: Understand how your level fits into the game's overall narrative. What is the story or goal that players should experience or achieve in this level?

2.  **Gameplay Focus**: Determine the primary gameplay elements and challenges your level will feature. Is it focused on combat, exploration, puzzle-solving, or a combination of these?

3.  **Player Experience**: Envision the type of experience you want to provide to players. Consider the emotions, tension, and excitement you want them to feel.

## Layout and Flow

A well-structured level layout contributes to player engagement. Here are some layout and flow considerations:

1.  **Guided Exploration**: Create a level that guides players naturally, using environmental cues, lighting, and level geometry. Lead them toward key points of interest and objectives.

2.  **Variety**: Incorporate a variety of spaces and areas within your level. Include open areas for combat, tight corridors for tension, and interactive hubs for storytelling.

3.  **Pacing**: Control the pacing by balancing moments of action with moments of relaxation. This ensures players have time to absorb the environment and narrative.

4.  **Looping and Backtracking**: Design levels with logical paths that allow for looping and backtracking. This can lead to discoveries, alternate routes, and a sense of interconnectedness.

## Environmental Storytelling

Use environmental storytelling techniques to convey narrative elements without relying solely on dialogue or cutscenes:

1.  **Visual Clues**: Place objects, props, and environmental details that hint at the level's backstory or upcoming challenges. For example, a damaged barricade suggests recent combat.

2.  **World Building**: Create a believable game world by integrating elements like posters, signs, and graffiti that provide context and flavor.

3.  **Hidden Details**: Reward observant players with hidden lore or easter eggs that enhance the game's depth.

## Challenges and Puzzles

If your level includes challenges or puzzles, consider the following:

1. **Progressive Difficulty**: Start with simpler challenges and gradually increase the complexity as players advance through the level.

2. **Clear Objectives**: Ensure that players understand their objectives and how to solve puzzles. Use visual and audio cues to guide them.

3. **Feedback**: Provide feedback when players interact with objects or make progress. Visual or audio cues can confirm successful actions.

## Testing and Iteration

Testing your level is crucial to identify and address issues:

1. **Playtesting**: Have others play your level and gather feedback. Pay attention to how players navigate, react to challenges, and perceive the narrative.

2. **Iteration**: Be prepared to make changes and improvements based on playtest feedback. Iteration is a fundamental part of level design.

## Documentation

Document your level design decisions, including layout, enemy placement, and narrative context. Clear documentation helps with communication within your development team and future reference.

## Conclusion

Designing your first game level is both an art and a science. By defining your level's purpose, focusing on layout and flow, incorporating environmental storytelling, and testing and iterating, you can create a compelling and immersive experience for players. Remember that level design is an ongoing process, and continuous improvement is key to creating memorable game levels. In the following sections, we will explore more advanced level design concepts and techniques in Unreal Engine.

---

## 3.4. Implementing Textures and Lighting

Texturing and lighting are crucial elements of level design in Unreal Engine that significantly impact the visual quality and atmosphere of your game levels. In this section, we'll explore the process of implementing textures and lighting to enhance your level's aesthetics and storytelling.

## Texturing Your Game Level

Texturing involves applying textures, materials, and surfaces to the geometry of your level to give it a realistic and visually appealing look. Here's how to approach texturing in Unreal Engine:

1. **Materials and Shaders**: Unreal Engine uses a node-based material editor that allows you to create complex materials and shaders. These materials define how surfaces react to light and interact with the environment.

2. **Texture Maps**: Utilize texture maps, including diffuse maps (for base color), normal maps (for surface detail and depth), specular maps (for surface reflectivity), and more. These maps add realism to materials.

3. **Material Instances**: Create material instances to make variations of existing materials without duplicating shaders. This is useful for creating different surface types (e.g., concrete, wood, metal) with the same base material.

4. **UV Mapping**: Properly unwrap and map UV coordinates for your 3D models. This ensures that textures are applied correctly and don't appear distorted.

5. **Seamless Textures**: Use seamless textures to avoid visible seams or tiling artifacts when textures repeat across surfaces. Seamless textures create a cohesive look.

6. **Layered Materials**: Combine multiple materials or textures in layers to create complex surfaces. This is useful for terrain or organic objects.

7. **Detail Texturing**: Add detail textures to enhance surface detail. Detail textures are often used in conjunction with normal maps to simulate fine surface features.

Example Material Node (Unreal Engine Material Editor):

```
[Base Color] -> Texture Sample (Diffuse Map)
[Normal] -> Texture Sample (Normal Map)
[Specular] -> Texture Sample (Specular Map)
```

## Lighting Your Game Level

Lighting plays a critical role in establishing the mood and atmosphere of your game level. Unreal Engine provides various lighting techniques and tools to achieve realistic lighting scenarios:

1. **Dynamic Lighting**: Unreal Engine supports dynamic lighting, allowing lights to move and change in real-time. This is essential for dynamic gameplay and interactive environments.

2. **Static Lighting**: For more complex scenes, static lighting can be used. It bakes lighting information into textures to improve performance but is less flexible than dynamic lighting.

3. **Light Types**: Utilize different types of lights, including point lights, spotlights, directional lights, and skylights, to achieve specific lighting effects.

4. **Lighting Scenarios**: Implement different lighting scenarios for day and night cycles, interior and exterior scenes, and special events within your level.

5. **Light Probes**: Use light probes to capture and reproduce real-world lighting conditions, especially in outdoor environments or architectural visualization.

6. **Light Functions**: Implement light functions to create custom lighting patterns and effects, such as animated or patterned lights.

Example Blueprint (Unreal Engine Blueprint Editor):

```
- [Event Begin Play]
  - [Set Light Color] -> Point Light (Light Actor)
    - [Color] -> (R: 1.0, G: 0.75, B: 0.5)
```

## Optimization and Performance

While textures and lighting enhance visual quality, it's essential to consider performance optimization:

1. **Texture Resolution**: Adjust texture resolutions based on the distance from the camera. Lower resolution textures can be used for distant objects to save memory and improve performance.

2. **Lightmap Resolution**: When using static lighting, optimize lightmap resolutions to balance quality and performance.

3. **Level Streaming**: Implement level streaming to load and unload parts of the level dynamically based on the player's location, reducing memory usage.

4. **Lighting Complexity**: Be cautious with the number of dynamic lights and overlapping shadow casters in a scene, as excessive lighting complexity can impact performance.

## Conclusion

Texturing and lighting are essential elements of level design in Unreal Engine that significantly impact the visual appeal and atmosphere of your game levels. By carefully applying materials, textures, and lighting techniques, you can create immersive and visually stunning environments that enhance the player's experience. Balancing aesthetics with performance optimization is key to creating compelling and responsive game levels. In the following sections, we will delve into more advanced aspects of level design, including level testing and iteration.

---

## 3.5. Level Testing and Iteration

Testing and iteration are integral parts of the level design process in Unreal Engine. Thorough testing helps identify issues, fine-tune gameplay, and improve the overall quality of your game levels. In this section, we'll explore the importance of level testing and provide guidance on effective iteration.

## The Importance of Level Testing

Testing your game level is essential for several reasons:

1. **Gameplay Experience**: Testing allows you to experience the level from a player's perspective and assess how enjoyable and engaging it is.

2. **Bug Detection**: It helps identify and address bugs, glitches, or unintended behaviors that could disrupt gameplay.

3. **Balancing**: Testing helps you fine-tune difficulty, pacing, and balance to ensure that the level provides a satisfying challenge to players.

4. **Narrative Flow**: You can evaluate how well the level conveys the narrative and if it aligns with the overall story.

5. **Player Feedback**: Gathering feedback from playtesters provides valuable insights that can lead to improvements in level design.

## Playtesting and Feedback

Effective playtesting involves the following steps:

1. **Select Playtesters**: Choose playtesters who represent your target audience or player demographic. This can include team members, alpha testers, or external testers.

2. **Clear Instructions**: Provide clear instructions to playtesters, including the objectives and goals of the level. Encourage them to provide feedback and report any issues they encounter.

3. **Observation**: Observe playtesters as they navigate the level. Pay attention to their actions, reactions, and interactions with the environment.

4. **Feedback Collection**: Gather feedback through surveys, interviews, or feedback forms. Ask playtesters about their overall experience, any frustrations, and areas they enjoyed.

5. **Bug Reports**: Encourage playtesters to report any bugs, glitches, or technical issues they encounter during gameplay.

6. **Iterative Process**: Use the feedback collected to make iterative changes to the level. Address issues, improve gameplay, and refine the level's design based on playtester input.

## Testing Tools in Unreal Engine

Unreal Engine provides several tools and features to facilitate level testing:

1. **PIE (Play In Editor)**: You can quickly test your level by playing it directly in the Unreal Editor. This allows for rapid testing and iteration.

2. **Spectator Mode**: Spectator mode enables you to observe gameplay from different angles and perspectives, helping you identify level design issues.

3. **Debugging Tools**: Use Unreal Engine's debugging tools to track gameplay elements, monitor performance, and identify errors or bottlenecks.

4. **Console Commands**: Unreal Engine offers a range of console commands that can be used for testing, debugging, and modifying gameplay parameters in real-time.

Example Console Command (Unreal Engine Console):

- [ToggleDebugCamera]: Toggles the debug camera mode, allowing you to fly thr ough the level and observe gameplay.

## Iteration and Improvement

Iteration is a fundamental aspect of level design:

1. **Feedback Analysis**: Carefully analyze the feedback received from playtesters. Identify common issues and areas that require improvement.

2. **Prioritization**: Prioritize feedback based on its impact on gameplay and the level's overall quality.

3. **Iterative Changes**: Implement iterative changes to the level, addressing issues, enhancing gameplay, and refining the design.

4. **Testing Phases**: Conduct multiple rounds of testing and iteration to ensure that improvements are effective and don't introduce new issues.

5. **Documentation**: Document the changes made during each iteration, including the rationale behind the changes.

## Conclusion

Level testing and iteration are essential steps in the level design process that contribute to the overall quality and player experience of your game levels. By engaging playtesters, collecting feedback, and making iterative improvements, you can create engaging and polished levels that captivate players and align with your game's vision. The testing and iteration process is ongoing, and continuous improvement is key to achieving exceptional level design. In the following chapters, we will explore more advanced topics in game development and level design.

# Chapter 4: Working with Blueprints

## 4.1. Blueprint Basics: Visual Scripting in Unreal

Blueprints are a powerful visual scripting system in Unreal Engine that allows game developers to create interactive gameplay elements, define behaviors, and implement game logic without writing traditional code. In this section, we'll delve into the basics of Blueprint visual scripting, exploring its interface and fundamental concepts.

### Understanding Blueprint Visual Scripting

Blueprints are a node-based visual scripting system in Unreal Engine, designed to make game development more accessible to a wide range of developers, including those without extensive programming experience. With Blueprints, you can create and modify game logic, objects, and interactions through a visual interface.

### Blueprint Editor Interface

Before diving into Blueprint scripting, let's familiarize ourselves with the Blueprint Editor interface:

1. **Graph Panel**: The central area where you build your visual script using nodes and connections.

2. **My Blueprint Panel**: This panel contains settings and properties specific to the Blueprint you are editing. You can define variables, assign default values, and configure various options here.

3. **Palette**: The Palette on the left side of the editor provides a library of nodes and functions that you can use to build your Blueprint scripts. These nodes represent different actions, events, and functions.

4. **Details Panel**: Similar to the My Blueprint panel, the Details panel displays information and settings for selected nodes and objects within your Blueprint.

### Nodes and Connections

In Blueprints, you construct scripts by connecting nodes to define the flow of logic. Here are some essential types of nodes:

- **Event Nodes**: Triggered by specific events or interactions in the game, such as "Begin Play" or "On Actor Hit."

- **Execution Nodes**: Control the flow of logic by determining the order in which nodes are executed. For example, "Sequence" nodes execute actions in sequence, while "Branch" nodes implement conditional logic.

- **Variable Nodes**: Represent variables that store data or values. You can get, set, or manipulate these variables using various nodes.

- **Function Nodes**: Encapsulate reusable logic and can be called from multiple parts of your Blueprint. You can create custom functions to simplify complex logic.

- **Action Nodes**: Perform actions within the game world, such as spawning actors, playing sounds, or moving objects.

## Creating a Simple Blueprint

Let's create a basic Blueprint to illustrate the process:

1. **Create a New Blueprint**: In the Blueprint Editor, click on "File" and select "New Blueprint Class." Choose the base class that suits your needs, such as "Actor" for interactive objects.

2. **Add Components**: In the My Blueprint panel, you can add components like static meshes, collision boxes, or audio components to your Blueprint.

3. **Event Graph**: Open the Event Graph tab in the Graph Panel. Here, you can define the logic for your Blueprint.

4. **Add Nodes**: Drag and drop nodes from the Palette to the Event Graph. Connect nodes to create logic flow. For example, you can use an "Event Begin Play" node to trigger actions when the game starts.

```
Example Blueprint (Visual Script):

[Event Begin Play]
    |
[Spawn Actor]
    | \
[Set Actor Location] [Play Sound]
```

## Testing and Debugging

Blueprints offer built-in tools for testing and debugging:

- **Simulation**: You can simulate Blueprint behavior within the editor to see how it functions in different scenarios.

- **Debugging**: Unreal Engine provides debugging tools to track node execution, variable values, and error messages.

## Conclusion

Blueprints are a versatile and user-friendly way to create game logic and interactivity in Unreal Engine. With their visual scripting approach, even developers with limited coding experience can craft intricate gameplay elements. In the following sections, we will delve deeper into Blueprint concepts, explore advanced scripting techniques, and learn how to debug and optimize Blueprint scripts.

## 4.2. Creating Simple Gameplay Elements with Blueprints

Blueprints in Unreal Engine empower developers to create gameplay elements, interactions, and behaviors without the need for traditional coding. In this section, we'll explore how to use Blueprints to create simple gameplay elements, such as interactive objects, triggers, and character actions.

### Interactive Objects

Interactive objects are essential for creating engaging gameplay experiences. With Blueprints, you can make objects in your game world interactive by defining their behavior. Here's a basic example of creating an interactive door:

1.  **Create an Interactive Object Blueprint**: Create a new Blueprint, and add a Static Mesh component to represent the door.

2.  **Variables**: Define variables within the Blueprint to store information about the door's state, such as whether it's open or closed.

3.  **Events**: Use events like "On Interact" or "On Toggle" to trigger actions when the player interacts with the door.

4.  **Logic**: In the Blueprint's Event Graph, implement logic to handle the door's behavior. For example, you can use a "Branch" node to check if the door is open or closed. If closed, trigger an animation to open it.

```
Example Blueprint Logic:

[On Interact]
   |
[Branch]
   /        \
[Is Door Closed?] [Is Door Locked?]
   |                |
[Open Door] [Display Locked Message]
```

### Triggers and Events

Triggers are commonly used to detect when a player or object enters a specific area and trigger events accordingly. Here's how to create a trigger using Blueprints:

1.  **Create a Trigger Volume**: Add a "Box Collision" or "Sphere Collision" component to your level to define the trigger area.

2.  **Blueprint Setup**: Create a new Blueprint for the trigger, and in the Event Graph, use "On Actor Begin Overlap" or "On Component Begin Overlap" to detect when a player enters the trigger.

3.  **Events**: Define events or actions that should occur when the trigger is activated. This can include opening a door, triggering an enemy spawn, or displaying a message.

```
Example Trigger Blueprint Logic:

[On Actor Begin Overlap]
      |
[Play Sound]
      |
[Spawn Enemy]
```

Character Actions

Blueprints can also control character actions and behaviors. For example, you can create a Blueprint to define character movement, abilities, or interactions. Here's how to create a simple character action:

1.  **Character Blueprint**: Create a Blueprint for your character and define input controls, such as pressing a key to perform an action.

2.  **Input Events**: In the Blueprint's Event Graph, use "Input Key" events to detect when the player presses the designated key.

3.  **Logic**: Implement the logic for the character action. For example, if the player presses the "Spacebar," you can make the character jump using a "Launch Character" node.

```
Example Character Blueprint Logic:

[Input Key (Spacebar)]
      |
[Launch Character]
```

Testing and Debugging

Testing your Blueprint-driven gameplay elements is crucial for ensuring they function as intended. Unreal Engine provides tools for testing and debugging Blueprints:

-   **Play in Editor (PIE)**: Use PIE to test your game within the editor, allowing you to interact with and evaluate the behavior of your Blueprints.

-   **Print String Nodes**: Insert "Print String" nodes into your Blueprint graphs to display messages or variable values for debugging purposes.

-   **Breakpoints**: Set breakpoints in your Blueprints to pause execution and inspect the state of variables and nodes at specific points in your script.

## Conclusion

Blueprints empower game developers to create interactive gameplay elements, triggers, and character actions with ease and without traditional coding. By defining events, variables, and logic within Blueprint scripts, you can bring your game to life with engaging interactions and behaviors. In the following sections, we will explore more advanced Blueprint concepts and techniques for debugging and optimizing your Blueprint scripts.

---

## 4.3. Debugging and Optimizing Blueprints

Debugging and optimizing Blueprints are crucial steps in ensuring your game functions smoothly and efficiently. In this section, we'll explore techniques for identifying and resolving issues in your Blueprint scripts and optimizing their performance.

### Debugging Blueprints

Debugging is the process of identifying and fixing errors, unexpected behavior, or issues in your Blueprint scripts. Unreal Engine provides several tools and techniques for effective Blueprint debugging:

1. **Print String Nodes**: These nodes allow you to print messages and variable values to the screen or log, making it easier to track the flow of your Blueprint logic.

Example Blueprint Debugging with Print String:

```
[On Player Death]
    |
[Print String] -> "Player has died."
    |
[Respawn Player]
```

2. **Breakpoints**: Set breakpoints in your Blueprint graphs to pause script execution at specific points. This enables you to inspect variables and the state of nodes during runtime.

3. **Watch Window**: The Watch Window allows you to monitor the values of specific variables in real-time as your Blueprint runs. You can add variables to the Watch Window for easy tracking.

4. **Error Messages**: Pay attention to error messages and warnings generated by Unreal Engine. These messages often provide valuable information about the cause of issues.

### Common Debugging Scenarios

Here are some common scenarios where Blueprint debugging is essential:

- **Logic Errors**: When your Blueprint's logic isn't behaving as expected, such as incorrect branching conditions or unexpected outcomes.

- **Runtime Issues**: Identifying issues that occur during gameplay, such as objects not spawning or characters behaving unpredictably.

- **Variable Mismatch**: Debugging when variables are not getting set or updated correctly.

- **Event Flow**: Ensuring that events and actions trigger in the correct order and at the right times.

## Optimizing Blueprints

Optimizing Blueprints is crucial for maintaining good game performance. Inefficient Blueprint scripts can lead to framerate drops and performance issues. Here are some optimization techniques:

1. **Minimize Tick Events**: Tick events are executed every frame and can be resource-intensive. Use them sparingly and consider alternative methods like events triggered by specific conditions.

2. **Function Calls**: Limit the number of function calls and expensive operations within your Blueprints. Complex calculations should be kept to a minimum.

3. **Variable Usage**: Avoid creating unnecessary variables. Unused variables consume memory and can clutter your Blueprints.

4. **Replication**: If you're creating multiplayer games, optimize replication by minimizing the data that needs to be replicated across the network. Only replicate essential information.

5. **Switches vs. Branches**: Use "Switch" nodes instead of multiple "Branch" nodes when dealing with multiple options. "Switch" nodes are more efficient.

Example Blueprint Optimization with Switch Node:

```
[Switch on Enum]
     |
[Option 1] -> [Action 1]
     |
[Option 2] -> [Action 2]
```

6. **Object Pooling**: When dealing with frequently spawned and destroyed objects (e.g., bullets or enemies), consider implementing object pooling to reuse existing objects instead of creating new ones.

7. **Profile and Profiling Tools**: Use Unreal Engine's profiling tools to identify performance bottlenecks in your Blueprints. This can help pinpoint areas that require optimization.

### Testing and Validation

After making optimizations to your Blueprints, it's essential to thoroughly test and validate your changes. Test your game under various conditions and scenarios to ensure that optimizations haven't introduced new issues or altered gameplay behavior.

### Conclusion

Debugging and optimizing Blueprints are vital steps in game development, ensuring that your game functions correctly and performs well. By using debugging tools, addressing common issues, and applying optimization techniques, you can create smoother and more efficient gameplay experiences. In the following sections, we will delve into advanced Blueprint concepts and explore advanced scripting techniques to enhance your game development skills further.

---

## 4.4. Blueprint Best Practices

When working with Blueprints in Unreal Engine, adhering to best practices can help maintain a clean and efficient project. In this section, we'll explore some essential Blueprint best practices to ensure the quality, maintainability, and performance of your game development projects.

### Organizing Blueprints

1. **Naming Conventions**: Use clear and consistent naming conventions for your Blueprints, variables, functions, and assets. Descriptive names make it easier to understand and manage your project.

2. **Comments and Documentation**: Add comments and documentation to explain the purpose and functionality of your Blueprints. This helps other team members understand your work and is invaluable for troubleshooting.

### Efficient Blueprint Design

3. **Modular Design**: Break complex Blueprints into smaller, reusable functions or components. Modular Blueprints are easier to maintain and can be used across multiple parts of your project.

4. **Event Dispatchers**: Use event dispatchers to decouple Blueprints. This allows one Blueprint to broadcast events that other Blueprints can listen to, promoting clean communication between components.

5. **Variable Scope**: Keep variable scope limited to where they are needed. Avoid using global variables unless necessary.

6. **Function Parameters**: Minimize the number of function parameters. Excessive parameters can make Blueprints hard to use and understand.

## Performance Optimization

7. **Tick Function**: Be cautious with the use of the Tick function, as it runs every frame and can impact performance. If a Blueprint doesn't require frequent updates, consider alternatives like timers or event-based triggering.

8. **Replication**: When working with multiplayer games, carefully consider which variables and events need replication. Over-replication can strain network bandwidth and affect gameplay.

9. **Lightweight Collisions**: Use simple collision shapes for objects where complex collisions are not necessary. Complex collision shapes can be resource-intensive.

## Debugging and Testing

10. **Debugging Messages**: Remove or disable debugging messages and print nodes before packaging your game. These messages are valuable during development but can clutter the final build.

11. **Regression Testing**: After making significant changes to your Blueprints, perform regression testing to ensure that existing functionality has not been affected.

## Version Control

12. **Version Control**: Utilize version control systems (e.g., Git) to track changes to your Blueprints and collaborate with team members. This helps prevent conflicts and allows you to roll back to previous versions if needed.

## Backup and Recovery

13. **Regular Backups**: Create regular backups of your project, including Blueprints. This safeguards your work against unexpected data loss or corruption.

## Blueprint Optimization Tools

14. **Blueprint Profiling**: Use Unreal Engine's profiling tools to identify performance bottlenecks in your Blueprints. Profiling helps you pinpoint areas that require optimization.

15. **Blueprint Nativization**: For performance-critical Blueprints, consider using Blueprint Nativization to convert them into C++ code, which can run faster in some cases.

## Community and Resources

16. **Community Support**: Take advantage of the Unreal Engine community and resources. Online forums, documentation, and tutorials can provide solutions to common Blueprint challenges.

## Conclusion

Adhering to Blueprint best practices is essential for maintaining a well-organized, efficient, and reliable game development project. By following these guidelines, you can enhance collaboration with your team, improve the maintainability of your Blueprints, and optimize the performance of your game. While these practices are valuable, remember that they can evolve over time, so staying up-to-date with the latest Unreal Engine developments is also crucial for success in game development. In the following sections, we will explore advanced Blueprint concepts and delve deeper into Unreal Engine's capabilities.

## 4.5. Advanced Blueprint Concepts

In this section, we will delve into advanced Blueprint concepts that can help you take your game development skills to the next level. These concepts include more complex scripting techniques, advanced debugging, and practical examples of Blueprint usage in game development.

### Custom Blueprint Nodes

Unreal Engine allows you to create custom Blueprint nodes using C++. This advanced feature enables you to extend the functionality of Blueprints by defining your own node types. Custom nodes can encapsulate complex logic, making your Blueprints more readable and efficient.

Creating custom Blueprint nodes involves:

1. **C++ Development**: Writing C++ code to define the behavior of your custom node.

2. **Blueprint Node Graph**: Defining the visual representation of your node in the Blueprint Editor.

3. **Integration**: Registering and integrating your custom node into Unreal Engine.

Custom Blueprint nodes are particularly useful for implementing specialized gameplay mechanics, AI behaviors, or intricate calculations that would be cumbersome to handle solely within Blueprints.

### Blueprint Interfaces

Blueprint interfaces provide a way to define a contract or set of functions that Blueprint classes can implement. They enable communication between different types of Blueprints without requiring direct inheritance or shared parent classes.

Key benefits of Blueprint interfaces include:

- **Polymorphism**: You can design systems that work with various Blueprints that adhere to the same interface, promoting flexibility and modularity.

- **Efficient Communication**: Interfaces provide a standardized way for Blueprints to communicate, reducing the need for custom event dispatchers or casting.

- **Encapsulation**: Interface functions define what should be done but not how. Implementing classes decide how to fulfill the interface contract.

Blueprint Function Libraries (BFLs) are collections of reusable functions that you can access from multiple Blueprints. They are excellent for consolidating common logic, such as math calculations, string manipulation, or utility functions, into a single location.

Creating a Blueprint Function Library involves:

1. **C++ Implementation**: Writing the C++ code for your functions.

2. **Blueprint Expose**: Using the UFUNCTION() macro to expose the functions to Blueprints.

3. **Blueprint Usage**: Accessing and using these functions in your Blueprint graphs.

BFLs simplify Blueprint development by centralizing frequently used functionality and promoting code reusability.

Replication is essential for multiplayer games, ensuring that game state changes are synchronized across all connected players. While replication often involves C++ code, Unreal Engine provides tools to handle replication within Blueprints.

Key concepts related to replication in Blueprints include:

- **Replicated Variables**: Marking variables as "Replicated" allows their values to be synchronized across the network automatically.

- **Remote Function Calls**: Blueprint nodes like "Run on Server" and "Run on Owning Client" enable you to call functions on specific network roles.

- **Replicated Events**: Use "Replicated" event nodes to trigger events across all clients and the server.

Effective use of replication in Blueprints requires a solid understanding of networking concepts and best practices for multiplayer game development.

Debugging becomes more critical as your Blueprints become more complex. Advanced debugging techniques include:

- **Custom Debug Messages**: Creating custom debugging messages with detailed information about Blueprint execution and variable values.

- **Structured Debugging**: Using the "Break" and "Breakpoint" nodes to pause execution at specific points in your Blueprints for in-depth inspection.

- **Execution Pin Data**: Examining the execution pin data to understand the flow of Blueprint execution.

- **Advanced Profiling**: Utilizing Unreal Engine's advanced profiling tools to identify and resolve performance bottlenecks in complex Blueprint graphs.

## Conclusion

Advanced Blueprint concepts open up new possibilities for game development in Unreal Engine. Whether you're creating custom nodes, defining interfaces, using Blueprint Function Libraries, handling replication, or mastering debugging techniques, these advanced concepts empower you to create more complex and sophisticated gameplay experiences. As you continue to refine your Blueprint skills and combine them with C++ programming, you'll be well-equipped to tackle ambitious game projects and create compelling interactive experiences. In the upcoming chapters, we will explore additional aspects of game development, including asset creation, game marketing, and legal considerations.

# Chapter 5: Incorporating 3D Models

## 5.1. Basics of 3D Modeling for Unreal

Incorporating 3D models is a fundamental aspect of game development in Unreal Engine. 3D models bring life to your virtual worlds, from characters and creatures to environments and props. In this section, we'll explore the basics of 3D modeling for Unreal, including essential concepts, software tools, and best practices.

### What is 3D Modeling?

3D modeling is the process of creating three-dimensional digital representations of objects or characters. These models are used in games, animations, simulations, and various other digital media. In Unreal Engine, 3D models are the building blocks of your game's visuals and play a crucial role in defining the look and feel of your virtual world.

### Types of 3D Models

There are several types of 3D models commonly used in game development:

1. **Static Meshes**: These are non-animated 3D objects that make up the environment, architecture, and props within your game world. Static meshes are typically used for buildings, rocks, trees, and other stationary objects.

2. **Skeletal Meshes**: Skeletal meshes are 3D models that support animation through a skeletal rig. They are used for characters and creatures and allow for animations like walking, running, and jumping.

3. **Particle Systems**: While not traditional 3D models, particle systems are used to create dynamic effects such as fire, smoke, explosions, and magical spells. They add visual complexity and realism to your game.

4. **Decals**: Decals are 3D models used to project textures onto surfaces in the game world. They are often used for adding details like dirt, graffiti, or bullet holes.

### 3D Modeling Software

To create 3D models, you'll need specialized software. Some popular 3D modeling software options include:

- **Autodesk Maya**: A comprehensive modeling and animation software used for creating characters, animations, and environments.

- **Blender**: An open-source 3D modeling tool with a wide range of features, suitable for both beginners and experienced modelers.

- **Autodesk 3ds Max**: A professional 3D modeling and animation software, often used for architectural visualization and game development.

- **ZBrush**: Primarily used for sculpting highly detailed 3D models, particularly character models.

- **Cinema 4D**: Known for its ease of use and motion graphics capabilities, it's used in animation, motion graphics, and game development.

Modeling Workflow

The typical workflow for creating 3D models involves several stages:

1. **Conceptualization**: Begin by defining the concept and design of your 3D model. Sketch out ideas or create concept art to guide your modeling process.

2. **Modeling**: Use your chosen 3D modeling software to create the basic shape of your model. Depending on the type of model, you'll use different techniques such as polygon modeling, sculpting, or parametric modeling.

3. **UV Mapping**: UV mapping involves flattening the 3D model onto a 2D surface to apply textures accurately. This step is crucial for texturing.

4. **Texturing**: Apply textures to your model to give it color, detail, and realism. Textures can include diffuse (color), normal maps (surface details), and specular maps (specular highlights).

5. **Rigging and Animation**: For skeletal meshes, rigging involves creating a skeleton and assigning weights to vertices. Animations are created by manipulating the skeleton.

6. **Exporting**: Export your 3D model in a compatible file format such as FBX or OBJ for use in Unreal Engine.

Optimizing 3D Models

Optimizing 3D models is essential for maintaining good game performance:

- **Polygon Count**: Keep polygon counts reasonable. Excessive polygons can impact performance. Use LODs (Level of Detail) for objects that vary in distance from the camera.

- **Texture Resolution**: Use appropriate texture resolutions. High-resolution textures can consume memory and slow down loading times.

- **Collision Meshes**: Create simplified collision meshes for static objects. Complex collision meshes can affect physics calculations.

Conclusion

Incorporating 3D models into Unreal Engine is a fundamental skill for game developers. Understanding the types of 3D models, the software tools for creating them, and the modeling workflow will enable you to bring your game world to life with visually appealing and interactive elements. As you continue your journey in game development, you'll explore more advanced techniques for 3D modeling, texturing, and character rigging, allowing you to create increasingly complex and immersive games.

---

## 5.2. Importing 3D Models into Unreal Engine

Once you've created or obtained 3D models using 3D modeling software, the next step is to import them into Unreal Engine. In this section, we'll explore the process of importing 3D models, setting up materials and textures, and preparing them for use in your game.

### Supported File Formats

Unreal Engine supports a variety of 3D file formats for importing models. Some common formats include:

- **FBX**: Autodesk's FBX format is widely used for transferring 3D models between different software applications. It supports geometry, materials, animations, and skeletal rigs.

- **OBJ**: OBJ files are simple 3D geometry files that can be imported into Unreal Engine. While they lack some advanced features, they are suitable for static objects.

- **Alembic (ABC)**: Alembic files are used for complex animations and simulations. Unreal Engine can import Alembic files to support dynamic animations and simulations.

- **Collada (DAE)**: The Collada format is another option for transferring 3D models. It supports geometry, materials, animations, and skeletal rigs.

- **Datasmith**: Unreal Engine's Datasmith format is designed for seamless integration with software like Autodesk 3ds Max and Autodesk Revit. It provides enhanced support for materials and scene hierarchy.

### Importing 3D Models

To import a 3D model into Unreal Engine, follow these steps:

1. **File Selection**: In the Unreal Editor, navigate to the Content Browser. Right-click in the Content Browser, choose "Import," and select the 3D model file you want to import.

2. **Import Options**: Unreal Engine will display import options based on the selected file format. Adjust these options to match the requirements of your project, including scale, rotation, and animation settings.

3. **Materials and Textures**: If the model has associated materials and textures, make sure to import them as well. Unreal Engine will create material instances for imported textures.

4. **Import Destination**: Specify the destination folder in the Content Browser where you want to import the model and its assets.

5. **Import**: Click the "Import" button to initiate the import process. Unreal Engine will create assets in the specified folder.

## Materials and Textures

Materials and textures are essential for adding realism and visual detail to your 3D models in Unreal Engine. Here's an overview of how materials and textures work:

- **Materials**: Materials define how light interacts with the surface of an object. They control properties like color, reflectivity, and transparency. Unreal Engine uses a node-based material editor, enabling you to create complex materials by connecting nodes representing various properties and textures.

- **Textures**: Textures are images applied to the surfaces of 3D models to add detail and realism. Common types of textures include diffuse (color), normal maps (surface details), specular maps (specular highlights), and roughness maps (surface roughness).

To apply materials and textures to your 3D models:

1. **Material Creation**: Create materials in Unreal Engine's Material Editor. Define their properties and connect textures as needed.

2. **Material Assignment**: Assign the created materials to the corresponding parts of your 3D model using the Static Mesh Editor.

3. **Texture Import**: Import textures into Unreal Engine and assign them to the appropriate material slots. Configure texture properties such as compression settings and mipmaps.

## Collision Setup

To enable collision detection for your 3D models, Unreal Engine provides several collision generation methods:

- **Automatic Convex Collision**: Unreal Engine can automatically generate a simplified convex collision shape for static meshes. This collision shape is used for physics and collision detection.

- **Complex Collision**: For complex collision shapes, you can create custom collision meshes within your 3D modeling software and import them alongside the model. These are especially useful for characters or objects with irregular shapes.

To optimize performance, Unreal Engine allows you to create multiple levels of detail (LOD) for your 3D models. Each LOD represents a simplified version of the model, reducing polygon count for objects at a distance from the camera. Unreal Engine can automatically switch between LODs based on the model's distance from the camera, improving performance without sacrificing visual quality.

## Conclusion

Importing 3D models into Unreal Engine is a crucial step in game development. Understanding the supported file formats, importing process, materials and textures, collision setup, and LODs will help you integrate 3D assets seamlessly into your game world. As you work with more complex models and scenes, mastering these aspects becomes increasingly important for creating visually stunning and optimized games. In the following sections, we will explore texturing, animating 3D models, and optimizing model performance in Unreal Engine.

---

## 5.3. Texturing and Material Basics

Texturing and materials play a crucial role in making 3D models in Unreal Engine visually appealing and realistic. In this section, we will explore the fundamentals of texturing and materials, including how to apply textures to 3D models and create materials using Unreal Engine's Material Editor.

### Understanding Textures

Textures are 2D images that are applied to the surfaces of 3D models to add detail, color, and realism. They are used to simulate various surface characteristics, such as:

- **Diffuse Texture**: This texture defines the base color of the surface. It gives the object its primary color and appearance.

- **Normal Map**: Normal maps simulate surface details and bumps by affecting how light interacts with the model. They create the illusion of depth and detail without adding geometry.

- **Specular Map**: Specular maps control the intensity and color of specular highlights on the surface. They determine where the surface is shiny or reflective.

- **Roughness Map**: Roughness maps define the surface's roughness or smoothness. A rougher surface scatters light in many directions, creating a diffuse reflection.

- **Metallic Map**: Metallic maps determine whether a surface is metallic or non-metallic. Metallic surfaces reflect light differently, and this map controls that behavior.

Before you can use textures in Unreal Engine, you need to import them into your project. Follow these steps to import textures:

1. **Navigate to Content Browser**: In the Unreal Editor, open the Content Browser.

2. **Right-click and Select "Import"**: Right-click in the Content Browser, choose "Import," and select the texture files you want to import. Unreal Engine supports various image formats like PNG, JPG, TGA, and more.

3. **Set Texture Properties**: Unreal Engine will display options for importing textures, such as compression settings, texture group, and mipmaps. Configure these settings based on your project's requirements.

4. **Import**: Click the "Import" button to bring the textures into your project.

## Creating Materials

Materials in Unreal Engine define how light interacts with the surfaces of 3D models. To create a material:

1. **Right-click in Content Browser**: In the Content Browser, right-click and choose "Materials & Textures" > "Material."

2. **Name the Material**: Give your material a descriptive name.

3. **Open Material Editor**: Double-click the newly created material to open the Material Editor.

4. **Add Textures**: In the Material Editor, you can add textures by creating nodes. For example, to add a diffuse texture, right-click, search for "Texture Sample," and connect it to the Base Color input of the material node.

5. **Connect Nodes**: Use nodes to control various material properties, such as roughness, metallic, normal, and more. You can blend textures, apply mathematical operations, and create complex effects.

6. **Apply Material**: Save your material, and you can now apply it to 3D models in the scene. In the Static Mesh Editor, select the model and assign the material in the Details panel.

## UV Mapping

UV mapping is a critical step in texturing 3D models. It involves flattening the 3D model's surface onto a 2D plane to apply textures accurately. UV maps define how textures are wrapped around the model.

You can create and edit UV maps using 3D modeling software like Blender, Maya, or 3ds Max. Once you import the model into Unreal Engine, it will use the existing UV maps to apply textures.

Material instances are variations of materials that share the same parent material. They allow you to tweak specific properties of a material without duplicating the entire material. This is useful for creating variations of a material, such as different colors or textures.

Understanding texturing and materials is essential for creating visually appealing 3D models in Unreal Engine. By grasping the concepts of textures, importing them, creating materials, and applying UV mapping, you can enhance the visual quality of your game. Experimenting with Unreal Engine's Material Editor and exploring advanced material features will enable you to create a wide range of realistic surfaces and effects for your 3D models. In the next section, we will explore animating 3D models, allowing them to come to life in your game world.

---

## 5.4. Animating Models in Unreal

Animating 3D models brings life and interactivity to your game world. Unreal Engine provides powerful tools and workflows for creating animations for characters, creatures, objects, and more. In this section, we will explore the basics of animating models in Unreal Engine.

### Types of Animation

Unreal Engine supports several types of animations:

- **Skeletal Animation**: This type of animation is commonly used for characters and creatures with articulated skeletons. It involves creating a rig that defines the bone structure and then animating the bones to achieve movement.

- **Vertex Animation**: Vertex animations manipulate the actual vertices of a 3D model to create deformation or morphing effects. This is useful for animating non-skeletal objects like cloth or facial expressions.

- **Particle Systems**: While not traditional animations, particle systems create dynamic effects like fire, smoke, and explosions. They add visual complexity and realism to your game.

- **Matinee and Sequencer**: Unreal Engine provides visual tools like Matinee (in older versions) and Sequencer (in newer versions) for creating cinematic and scripted animations. These tools are useful for cutscenes and storytelling.

## Skeletal Animation

Skeletal animation is widely used for character animation in games. Here's an overview of the process:

1. **Character Rigging**: Rigging involves defining the skeleton and attaching it to the character model. Each bone in the skeleton corresponds to a part of the character.

2. **Animation Keyframes**: Animation is created by setting keyframes at different points in time. Keyframes define the position, rotation, and scale of each bone at a specific frame.

3. **Inverse Kinematics (IK)**: Unreal Engine supports IK solvers, which allow you to create more natural movements by manipulating end-effectors (e.g., hands and feet) and having the rest of the body adapt accordingly.

4. **Blend Trees**: Blend trees are used to mix and blend animations smoothly. For example, you can blend between a character's idle and running animations based on their movement speed.

5. **Animation Blueprints**: Animation Blueprints are used to control the logic and behavior of animations. You can create complex animation behaviors by scripting in Blueprint.

## Vertex Animation

Vertex animation is suitable for non-skeletal objects or effects. It involves deforming the vertices of a 3D model directly over time. Unreal Engine supports tools like the Morph Target system for creating vertex animations.

1. **Morph Targets**: Morph targets (also known as blend shapes) define different states of a 3D model's vertices. You can create various morph targets representing different expressions or deformations. Animations are created by blending between these targets.

2. **Cloth Simulation**: Unreal Engine has built-in cloth simulation tools that allow you to create realistic cloth animations for characters or objects.

## Particle Systems

Particle systems are used to create dynamic and procedural animations, such as fire, smoke, sparks, and more. Unreal Engine provides a robust particle system editor for creating and fine-tuning these effects.

1. **Emitter Modules**: Particle systems consist of emitter modules, each responsible for a specific aspect of the effect, such as spawn rate, lifetime, velocity, and color.

2. **Cascade (Older Versions)**: In older versions of Unreal Engine, Cascade was used for particle system creation.

3. **Niagara (Newer Versions)**: In newer versions, Niagara has replaced Cascade as the preferred tool for creating complex particle systems with more flexibility and control.

## Matinee and Sequencer

Matinee (in older versions) and Sequencer (in newer versions) are visual tools for creating cinematic and scripted animations. They are used for cutscenes, camera animations, and scripted sequences.

1. **Keyframes and Tracks**: In Matinee and Sequencer, you create animations by placing keyframes on tracks. Each track represents an animated property, such as camera position or object visibility.

2. **Timeline and Sequences**: You can sequence multiple animations and shots in a timeline to create complex cinematic sequences.

3. **Cinematic Camera**: These tools allow you to create cinematic camera movements and effects, enhancing storytelling in your game.

## Conclusion

Animating 3D models in Unreal Engine is a versatile and creative process. Whether you're animating characters with skeletal animation, creating dynamic effects with particle systems, or crafting cinematic sequences with Matinee or Sequencer, Unreal Engine provides the tools and flexibility you need to bring your game world to life. As you delve deeper into animation, you can explore more advanced techniques such as inverse kinematics, animation blending, and procedural animation to create captivating and interactive experiences for players.

## 5.5. Optimizing Model Performance

Optimizing the performance of 3D models in Unreal Engine is crucial to ensure that your game runs smoothly on a wide range of hardware configurations. In this section, we will explore various techniques and best practices for optimizing model performance.

## Polygon Count and LODs

One of the primary considerations for model optimization is managing the polygon count. High-poly models can lead to performance issues, especially in complex scenes with many objects. Unreal Engine provides Level of Detail (LOD) systems to address this.

1. **LOD Creation**: Create multiple LODs for your 3D models. These LODs are simplified versions of the model with reduced polygon counts. Unreal Engine automatically switches between LODs based on the distance between the camera and the model.

2. **Simplified Geometry**: When creating LODs, focus on reducing the polygon count while preserving the model's visual quality. You can remove small details that won't be noticeable at a distance.

3. **Distance-Based Switching**: Configure the LOD switching distances appropriately. For example, a model might use a high-poly LOD when close to the camera and switch to a lower-poly LOD at a certain distance.

## Texture Resolution and Compression

Textures play a significant role in model performance. Unreal Engine provides tools and settings to optimize texture usage:

1. **Texture Size**: Use appropriate texture resolutions for your models. High-resolution textures can consume significant memory and impact loading times.

2. **Texture Compression**: Enable texture compression settings to reduce memory usage. Unreal Engine supports various compression formats that balance quality and performance.

3. **Mipmaps**: Mipmaps are pre-scaled versions of textures for different viewing distances. Enabling mipmaps improves rendering performance and reduces aliasing artifacts.

## Material Optimization

Materials can also affect performance, so it's essential to optimize them:

1. **Material Instances**: Use material instances for variations of a material instead of creating entirely new materials. Material instances share the same parent material, saving memory.

2. **Shader Complexity**: Unreal Engine provides tools to visualize shader complexity. Avoid complex shader networks that can slow down rendering.

3. **Material Parameters**: Use material parameters to expose values that can be adjusted in real-time, allowing for dynamic material changes without the need for new materials.

## Collision Simplification

Collision meshes should be simplified to improve physics calculations:

1. **Automatic Collision**: Unreal Engine can generate automatic convex collision for static meshes. Ensure that the collision mesh is simple but accurate enough for physics interactions.

2. **Custom Collision**: For complex objects or characters, create custom collision meshes within your 3D modeling software. These should be optimized for physics calculations.

## Culling and Occlusion

Culling techniques help reduce rendering load:

1. **Frustum Culling**: Unreal Engine performs frustum culling by default, only rendering objects within the camera's view frustum.

2. **Occlusion Culling**: Consider implementing occlusion culling techniques to skip rendering objects that are entirely hidden by others. This can significantly improve performance in complex scenes.

## Level Streaming

For large environments or open-world games, use level streaming to load and unload portions of the game world dynamically. This reduces memory usage and optimizes performance by focusing resources on the player's current location.

## Conclusion

Optimizing model performance in Unreal Engine is a critical step in game development. By managing polygon counts, texture usage, materials, and collision meshes, you can ensure that your game runs smoothly on a variety of hardware configurations. Leveraging LODs, texture compression, and culling techniques helps strike a balance between visual quality and performance. As you continue to develop your game, testing and profiling will be essential to identify and address performance bottlenecks and deliver a polished and enjoyable player experience.

# Chapter 6: Adding Audio and Sound Effects

## Section 6.1: Audio Basics in Unreal Engine

Audio plays a crucial role in enhancing the overall gaming experience. Unreal Engine provides a comprehensive set of tools and features for handling audio and sound effects in your game. In this section, we'll explore the fundamental concepts of audio in Unreal Engine.

### Audio Components

In Unreal Engine, audio is managed using Audio Components. These components can be attached to various in-game objects to emit sounds from specific locations in the game world. To create an Audio Component, you can do so programmatically in C++ or through the Unreal Engine's Blueprint visual scripting system.

Here's an example of creating an Audio Component in C++:

```
UAudioComponent* MyAudioComponent = CreateDefaultSubobject<UAudioComponent>(TEXT("MyAudioComponent"));
```

### Sound Waves

Sound Waves are the building blocks of audio in Unreal Engine. They represent the actual audio data and can be imported into your project. Unreal Engine supports various audio formats, such as WAV, MP3, and OGG. Once imported, you can use Sound Waves to create sound cues and trigger them in your game.

### Sound Classes

Sound Classes are used to categorize and control the properties of audio assets in Unreal Engine. You can define properties like volume, pitch, and attenuation settings for a Sound Class, which can then be applied to multiple Sound Waves. This allows for consistent audio management across your game.

Here's an example of creating a Sound Class in Unreal Engine:

```
USoundClass* MySoundClass = CreateDefaultSubobject<USoundClass>(TEXT("MySound Class"));
```

### Attenuation

Attenuation settings control how the sound fades with distance from the listener. Unreal Engine provides various attenuation curves and settings that allow you to customize how a sound's volume decreases as the listener moves away from the source.

### Spatialization

Spatialization is the process of making sounds appear to come from specific locations in the game world. Unreal Engine uses spatialization techniques to provide a realistic audio experience, where sounds are perceived as coming from their corresponding in-game objects.

### Audio Concurrency

Concurrency settings control how multiple instances of the same sound asset are handled simultaneously. Unreal Engine allows you to define rules for prioritizing and limiting the number of concurrent instances of a particular sound.

### Sound Mixes

Sound Mixes are used to balance and control the overall audio experience in your game. You can adjust the volume levels of different audio classes and apply effects like reverb and EQ to create the desired audio atmosphere.

### Real-Time Audio Effects

Unreal Engine supports real-time audio effects through Audio Sound Modulators (ASMs). ASMs allow you to apply dynamic effects to audio in response to gameplay events, providing a more immersive experience.

### Audio in Blueprints

If you prefer visual scripting, Unreal Engine's Blueprint system provides nodes for working with audio components, sound cues, and various audio-related functionalities. This allows designers and non-programmers to create complex audio interactions.

In summary, understanding the basics of audio in Unreal Engine is essential for creating immersive and engaging games. With the knowledge of audio components, sound waves, sound classes, attenuation, spatialization, and other audio-related concepts, you can enhance the audio experience for players in your game.

---

## Section 6.2: Importing and Managing Sound Files

In Unreal Engine, importing and managing sound files is a crucial part of the audio development process. This section will guide you through the steps of importing sound files into your project, managing them efficiently, and optimizing your audio assets for your game.

### Importing Sound Files

To import sound files into your Unreal Engine project, follow these steps:

1. **Locate the Content Browser:** Open the Content Browser in Unreal Engine, which is typically found in the "Window" menu under "Content Browser."

2. **Navigate to the Desired Folder:** Choose the folder within your project where you want to import the sound file. You can create a new folder by right-clicking in the Content Browser and selecting "New Folder."

3. **Import Sound File:** Right-click within the chosen folder, select "Import," and then choose the sound file you wish to import. Unreal Engine supports various audio formats, including WAV, MP3, and OGG. After selecting the file, click "Open."

4. **Set Import Options:** Unreal Engine will provide you with import options for the sound file. You can adjust settings like compression quality, sound group, and import type according to your needs. Make sure to review these options before proceeding.

5. **Import:** Click the "Import" button to bring the sound file into your project. Unreal Engine will process the file and make it available for use in your game.

Managing Sound Assets

Effective management of sound assets is essential for keeping your project organized and maintaining performance. Here are some best practices:

- **Naming Conventions:** Use clear and consistent naming conventions for your sound assets. This makes it easier to locate and identify them later.

- **Asset Folders:** Organize your sound assets into folders within the Content Browser. For example, you can create folders for music, sound effects, and voiceovers.

- **Sound Classes:** Assign sound assets to appropriate sound classes to control their behavior. Sound classes help you manage properties like volume and pitch.

- **Attenuation:** Adjust attenuation settings for individual sound assets to control how they fade with distance. This is particularly important for 3D positional audio.

- **Sound Cues:** Create Sound Cues to encapsulate complex audio logic and behavior. Sound Cues allow you to trigger, modify, and manipulate sound assets dynamically during gameplay.

Optimizing Sound Assets

Optimizing sound assets is crucial for maintaining performance in your game. Here are some optimization techniques:

- **File Formats:** Choose the appropriate audio format for your needs. WAV files provide high quality but may be larger in size, while compressed formats like OGG or MP3 can save space but may sacrifice some quality.

- **Sound Quality:** Adjust compression settings to balance audio quality and file size. Higher quality settings result in larger files, so find the right balance for your project.

- **Streaming:** For large sound files, consider using sound streaming to load portions of the audio as needed, reducing memory usage.

- **Sound Classes:** Use sound classes to control the overall audio mix in your game. Adjusting volume levels and applying effects can help create a balanced audio experience.

- **Concurrency:** Set concurrency settings to manage how many instances of a sound can play simultaneously. This helps prevent audio clutter and maintains clarity.

By following these steps and best practices, you can effectively import, manage, and optimize sound files in Unreal Engine, ensuring a high-quality audio experience for your players while keeping your project organized and performant.

---

## Section 6.3: Creating Ambient Soundscapes

Creating immersive ambient soundscapes is an essential aspect of game audio design in Unreal Engine. These soundscapes can set the mood, enhance the atmosphere, and make your game world come alive. In this section, we'll explore the process of creating ambient soundscapes using Unreal Engine's tools and features.

### Ambient Sound Actors

Unreal Engine provides Ambient Sound Actors, which are used to emit ambient audio into the game world. These actors can be placed in your levels to generate continuous background sounds. To create an Ambient Sound Actor, follow these steps:

6. In the level, right-click to bring up the context menu.
7. Under "Actor Classes," select "Ambient Sound."
8. Place the Ambient Sound Actor in your level.

You can then configure the properties of the Ambient Sound Actor to define the audio it emits, such as the sound wave to use, volume, pitch, and attenuation settings.

### Sound Cue for Ambience

To create complex ambient soundscapes, you can use Sound Cues. Sound Cues allow you to combine multiple sound assets and apply various effects and modifications to create dynamic and evolving audio environments.

9. In the Content Browser, right-click and select "Sound Cue."
10. Name the Sound Cue and double-click it to open the Sound Cue Editor.

11. Inside the Sound Cue Editor, you can add audio nodes, such as Sound Wave Player nodes, to play individual sound assets.
12. You can use Sound Modulator nodes to apply real-time effects like reverb, modulation, or pitch modulation to your audio.
13. Connect nodes and adjust parameters to create your desired ambient soundscape.

### Triggered Ambience

In addition to continuous ambient audio, you can also create triggered ambient sounds that play in response to in-game events. For example, you can use Blueprint scripting to trigger ambient sounds when the player enters a specific area or performs certain actions. Here's a simple example using Blueprints:

```
// In your Blueprint script
PlaySoundAtLocation(AmbientSoundCue, GetActorLocation());
```

This code snippet plays the specified Sound Cue at the location of the actor executing the script.

### Randomization and Variation

To make your ambient soundscapes more natural and less repetitive, consider using randomization and variation techniques. Unreal Engine allows you to add random pitch and volume modulation to your ambient sounds, creating a more organic audio experience. You can do this within the Sound Cue Editor or through Blueprint scripting.

### Layered Ambience

Layering multiple ambient soundscapes can add depth to your game's audio. You can have different layers for various environmental elements, such as wind, birds, and water, and control their playback and volume dynamically to match the game's context and player's location.

### Optimization

Optimizing your ambient soundscapes is important to ensure smooth performance. You can use attenuation settings to control how ambient sounds fade with distance, reducing CPU load and memory usage. Additionally, managing concurrency settings helps prevent too many simultaneous ambient sounds from playing, preventing audio clutter.

In conclusion, creating ambient soundscapes in Unreal Engine is a powerful way to enhance the immersive quality of your game world. By using Ambient Sound Actors, Sound Cues, triggered ambience, randomization, and layering techniques, you can craft captivating audio environments that immerse players in your game's world. Proper optimization ensures that these soundscapes contribute to the overall gaming experience without sacrificing performance.

## Section 6.4: Implementing Dynamic Sound Effects

Dynamic sound effects play a crucial role in making your game world feel responsive and immersive. In this section, we'll explore how to implement dynamic sound effects in Unreal Engine, allowing you to create realistic and engaging auditory experiences for your players.

### Sound Cue Modulation

One powerful technique for adding dynamism to sound effects is modulation within Sound Cues. Unreal Engine's Sound Cue system allows you to modulate various parameters of a sound in real-time, creating variations that respond to in-game events. For example, you can modulate the pitch, volume, or filter settings of a gunshot sound effect when a gun is fired, resulting in a more realistic and dynamic auditory experience.

Here's an example of how you can modulate the pitch of a sound in a Sound Cue using Blueprint scripting:

```
// In your Blueprint script
PlaySoundCueWithModulation(GunshotSoundCue, ModulationSettings);
```

### Spatialized Sound Effects

In a 3D game world, spatialized sound effects are essential for creating a sense of space and location. Unreal Engine handles spatialization automatically based on the 3D position of the sound source and the listener. However, you can fine-tune spatialization settings, such as attenuation and reverb, to match your game's requirements.

For example, you can adjust the attenuation settings to control how quickly a sound's volume decreases with distance from the listener, simulating real-world audio behavior. Here's an example in C++:

```
GunshotSound->AttenuationSettings = GunshotAttenuationSettings;
```

### Dynamic Mixing

Dynamic mixing allows you to adjust the mix of sound effects and music in response to in-game events. Unreal Engine provides tools to create dynamic sound mixes that change based on gameplay conditions. For instance, you can increase the volume of intense music when a player enters a combat situation or adjust the balance of different sound classes to maintain audio clarity.

Here's an example of how you can change the sound mix using Blueprint scripting:

```
// In your Blueprint script
SetSoundMixClassOverride(DynamicSoundMix, SoundClass, Volume);
```

### Interactive Sound Environments

Unreal Engine supports interactive sound environments, which enable sound effects to respond to in-game factors like weather, time of day, or player actions. You can use

Blueprint scripting to trigger changes in environmental soundscapes, making your game world feel alive and responsive.

## Real-Time DSP Effects

Unreal Engine allows you to apply real-time DSP (Digital Signal Processing) effects to sound effects. This can be used to simulate effects like echo, reverb, and filtering. By altering these effects based on in-game conditions, you can create dynamic and realistic soundscapes.

## Blueprint Scripting

Blueprint scripting is a powerful tool for implementing dynamic sound effects in Unreal Engine. You can create scripts that respond to in-game events and trigger sound effects accordingly. For example, you can play footstep sounds when a character moves, adjust the pitch of an engine sound as a vehicle accelerates, or trigger environmental audio based on player interactions.

```
// In your Blueprint script
PlaySoundAtLocation(FootstepSoundCue, GetActorLocation());
```

## Optimization

While implementing dynamic sound effects, it's essential to consider optimization. Unreal Engine provides tools to manage concurrency, prioritize important sound effects, and control the number of simultaneous sound instances. Proper optimization ensures that dynamic audio enhancements don't negatively impact performance.

In summary, implementing dynamic sound effects in Unreal Engine involves a combination of modulating Sound Cues, spatialization, dynamic mixing, interactive sound environments, real-time DSP effects, and Blueprint scripting. These techniques allow you to create immersive and responsive auditory experiences that enhance your game's overall immersion and engagement. Proper optimization ensures that dynamic audio enhancements are delivered efficiently without compromising performance.

---

## Section 6.5: Audio Testing and Balancing

Audio testing and balancing are critical aspects of game development that ensure the audio experience is enjoyable, immersive, and free from issues. In this section, we'll explore various techniques and best practices for testing and balancing audio in your Unreal Engine project.

### Testing Audio Assets

Thoroughly testing audio assets is essential to identify any issues or anomalies in the audio experience. Here are some key testing considerations:

- **Functional Testing:** Ensure that sound effects play as intended and are triggered by the correct in-game events. Verify that music and ambient sounds follow the expected cues and transitions.

- **Spatialization Testing:** Test spatialized sound effects to ensure they accurately reflect in-game locations and positions. Verify that 3D sound positioning is realistic and consistent.

- **Environmental Testing:** Check how audio responds to changes in the game environment, such as weather, time of day, or location. Ensure that dynamic soundscapes adapt appropriately to these changes.

- **Performance Testing:** Monitor system performance while playing the game with audio enabled. Ensure that audio processing doesn't significantly impact frame rate or cause performance issues.

## Sound Quality Assurance

Sound quality assurance involves evaluating the overall quality of audio assets to ensure they meet the desired standards. Here are some quality assurance practices:

- **Audio Clarity:** Verify that sounds are clear and distinguishable, even in complex or noisy situations. Ensure that dialogue and important audio cues are easily understood.

- **Balancing:** Balance the volume levels of different sound classes, sound effects, and music tracks to create a cohesive and enjoyable audio mix. Pay attention to the balance between dialogue and other audio elements.

- **Consistency:** Ensure a consistent audio experience across different platforms and hardware configurations. Test on various devices to catch any inconsistencies in sound quality or performance.

- **Audio Compression:** Review the compression settings of audio assets to strike the right balance between file size and audio quality. Avoid noticeable artifacts or degradation in sound due to heavy compression.

## Usability Testing

Usability testing involves gathering feedback from players to evaluate the overall audio experience. This can help identify issues that may not be apparent during development. Here are some usability testing strategies:

- **Player Feedback:** Encourage players to provide feedback on audio quality, clarity, and immersion. Listen to their suggestions and concerns to make improvements.

- **Beta Testing:** Conduct beta tests with a focus on audio. Collect data on how players perceive the audio experience and use this feedback to refine sound assets and settings.

- **Accessibility:** Ensure that audio cues are accessible to all players, including those with hearing impairments. Implement subtitles or visual cues when necessary.

Tools for Audio Testing

Unreal Engine provides tools and features to facilitate audio testing and balancing:

- **Audio Profiler:** Use the built-in Audio Profiler to analyze audio performance and identify potential issues. The profiler provides valuable data on resource usage, sound concurrency, and more.

- **Real-Time Debugging:** Unreal Engine allows for real-time debugging of audio. You can use the editor's debugging tools to inspect sound cues, attenuation settings, and sound classes while the game is running.

- **Sound Mixes:** Continuously adjust sound mixes based on player feedback and testing results. Fine-tune the balance between sound classes and effects to create an optimal audio experience.

- **Playback Testing:** Frequent playtesting with audio enabled is crucial. Test the game on different platforms and hardware configurations to ensure audio quality and performance consistency.

Balancing Audio for Immersion

Balancing audio elements is a key part of audio design. Achieving a good balance between sound effects, music, and dialogue is essential for creating an immersive experience. Here are some tips for balancing audio:

- **Priority:** Assign priorities to different sound classes and elements. Important sounds should have higher priorities to ensure they are always audible.

- **Dynamic Mixing:** Utilize dynamic mixing techniques to adjust the audio mix based on in-game events or player actions. For example, increase the intensity of music during action sequences.

- **Dialogue Clarity:** Ensure that dialogue remains clear and audible even when other audio elements are present. Use volume adjustments and attenuation settings to achieve this.

- **Environmental Audio:** Use ambient sounds and environmental audio to enhance immersion. Match the audio to the visual environment to create a cohesive experience.

- **Player Control:** Allow players to adjust audio settings, including volume levels for music, sound effects, and dialogue. Provide options for audio customization to cater to individual preferences.

In conclusion, audio testing and balancing are essential steps in game development to ensure a high-quality audio experience. Thoroughly test audio assets, assess sound quality, gather player feedback, and use Unreal Engine's tools to optimize and balance audio elements for immersion and enjoyment. Balancing audio elements and allowing player control over audio settings contribute to a more engaging and immersive gaming experience.

# Chapter 7: Implementing UI and Menus

## Section 7.1: Designing User Interfaces in Unreal

Designing user interfaces (UI) is a crucial aspect of game development, as it directly impacts how players interact with your game. Unreal Engine provides powerful tools and features for creating visually appealing and functional UI elements. In this section, we'll delve into the process of designing user interfaces within Unreal Engine.

### UMG (Unreal Motion Graphics)

Unreal Engine offers the Unreal Motion Graphics (UMG) system for designing user interfaces. UMG is a robust visual UI design and layout tool that allows you to create and customize UI elements using a combination of widgets, animation, and scripting.

To create a new UMG Widget Blueprint, follow these steps:

14. In the Content Browser, right-click and select "User Interface" > "Widget Blueprint."
15. Name your Widget Blueprint and double-click it to open the UMG Designer.

### Canvas Panel and Widgets

UMG utilizes a Canvas Panel as the primary container for UI elements. Within the Canvas Panel, you can add various widgets like buttons, text, images, and more. These widgets can be dragged and dropped onto the canvas, and their properties can be customized in the Details panel.

For example, you can create a button widget by dragging and dropping a Button widget onto the canvas. You can then customize its appearance, text, and behavior.

### Anchors and Alignment

UMG allows you to specify how UI elements behave and adapt to different screen sizes and resolutions. You can use anchors and alignment settings to control the positioning and scaling of widgets. This ensures that your UI elements look and function correctly on various devices and screen ratios.

### Widget Blueprint Scripting

Widget Blueprints can include scripting to add functionality to your UI elements. You can use Blueprint nodes to define event-driven behavior, such as button clicks or input interactions. For example, you can create a button that triggers a specific action when clicked by adding scripting to the button's "OnClicked" event.

```
// Example Blueprint scripting in UMG
OnClicked.AddDynamic(this, &UMyWidget::ButtonClicked);
```

### Styling and Theming

Unreal Engine allows you to style and theme your UI elements to match the visual aesthetics of your game. You can create custom styles, define color schemes, and use materials and textures to achieve the desired look and feel for your UI. This flexibility ensures that your UI aligns with your game's artistic direction.

### Localization and Text Handling

If your game targets a global audience, Unreal Engine provides localization support for UI text. You can manage localized text through localization files and easily switch between different languages and regions.

### Testing and Debugging

Testing your UI is essential to ensure that it functions correctly and looks good on various devices and screen resolutions. Unreal Engine offers tools for testing and debugging UI elements during development. You can use the PIE (Play In Editor) mode to interact with your UI in a real-time game environment and identify any issues or glitches.

In conclusion, designing user interfaces in Unreal Engine using UMG offers a powerful and flexible way to create visually appealing and interactive UI elements. With the Canvas Panel, widgets, anchors, alignment, scripting, styling, localization support, and testing tools, you can craft intuitive and engaging interfaces that enhance the player's experience in your game.

---

## Section 7.2: Creating Menus and HUDs

Menus and Heads-Up Displays (HUDs) are integral parts of most games, providing players with essential information and options. In Unreal Engine, you can create menus and HUDs using the Unreal Motion Graphics (UMG) system, allowing you to design custom interfaces for your game's menus, settings, and in-game displays. In this section, we'll explore the process of creating menus and HUDs in Unreal Engine.

### Creating Main Menus

Main menus are the first point of interaction for players when they start your game. You can design main menus using UMG widgets and Blueprints to handle menu functionality. Here are the basic steps to create a main menu:

16. **Create a UMG Widget Blueprint:** Start by creating a new UMG Widget Blueprint and designing your main menu interface. Add buttons for options like "New Game," "Load Game," "Settings," and "Quit."

17. **Widget Blueprint Scripting:** Use Blueprint scripting to add functionality to your main menu buttons. For example, you can create an event in your Widget Blueprint to start a new game when the "New Game" button is clicked.

```
// Example Blueprint scripting for starting a new game
OnClicked.AddDynamic(this, &UMainMenuWidget::StartNewGame);
```

7. **Level Streaming:** Configure level streaming to load the game level when the "New Game" button is clicked. Unreal Engine's level streaming system allows you to seamlessly transition between different game levels and menus.

## Options and Settings Menus

Options and settings menus allow players to customize their gaming experience. These menus can include options for adjusting graphics settings, audio settings, controls, and more. Here's how to create options and settings menus:

18. **Design UMG Widgets:** Create separate UMG widgets for each section of your options menu, such as graphics, audio, and controls. Design the widgets with sliders, checkboxes, and input fields to adjust settings.

19. **Blueprint Logic:** Implement Blueprint logic to handle the functionality of the settings. For example, you can adjust the game's volume based on the audio slider's position or remap controls based on player input.

20. **Save and Load Settings:** Use Blueprint scripting to save and load player settings. Unreal Engine provides ways to store and retrieve player preferences, such as graphics quality or keybindings.

## Heads-Up Displays (HUDs)

HUDs are essential for displaying real-time information to players during gameplay. Unreal Engine allows you to create custom HUDs using UMG widgets. Here's how to design and implement HUDs:

21. **Create a UMG Widget Blueprint:** Similar to menus, start by creating a UMG Widget Blueprint for your HUD. Design the HUD elements you want to display during gameplay, such as health bars, minimaps, or score counters.

22. **Blueprint Scripting:** Use Blueprint scripting to update and control the HUD elements in real-time. For example, you can update a player's health bar based on their current health status or display a countdown timer.

```
// Example Blueprint scripting to update a health bar
UpdateHealthBar(PlayerHealth);
```

3. **HUD Activation:** Configure when and how the HUD should be displayed. You can activate the HUD when the game starts and deactivate it during cutscenes or menu screens.

## Transitioning Between Menus and Gameplay

Seamless transitions between menus and gameplay are crucial for a smooth player experience. Unreal Engine provides tools for managing these transitions:

- **Level Streaming:** Use level streaming to switch between different menu and game levels.
- **Game Mode and Game State:** Unreal Engine's Game Mode and Game State classes help manage the game's current state, allowing you to determine whether the player is in a menu or in-game.
- **Widget Switching:** You can use Blueprint scripting to switch between different UMG widgets, allowing you to transition between menus and HUDs.

```
// Example Blueprint scripting to switch between menus
ShowMainMenu();
```

In summary, creating menus and HUDs in Unreal Engine involves designing UMG widgets, adding Blueprint scripting for functionality, and using Unreal Engine's systems to manage transitions between menus and gameplay. By customizing your interfaces and providing players with intuitive and interactive menus and HUDs, you can enhance the overall gaming experience and make your game more engaging and user-friendly.

---

## Section 7.3: Integrating UI with Gameplay

Integrating user interfaces (UI) with gameplay is a fundamental aspect of game development. In Unreal Engine, you have the tools and flexibility to seamlessly blend UI elements with the game world, enhancing player immersion and interaction. In this section, we'll explore the process of integrating UI with gameplay in Unreal Engine.

### Widgets in 3D Space

Unreal Engine allows you to position UI widgets in 3D space within the game world. This feature is particularly useful for creating interactive in-game interfaces, such as control panels, holographic displays, or character status indicators. Here's how you can integrate widgets into the 3D world:

23. **Create a Widget Component:** To display a UI widget in 3D space, you'll use a Widget Component. Add a Widget Component to an actor in your level.

24. **Assign the Widget:** In the Widget Component properties, assign the UMG widget you want to display.

25. **Set World Location and Rotation:** Position and orient the Widget Component in 3D space to determine where the UI will appear within the game world.

26. **Blueprint Logic:** Use Blueprint scripting to control the visibility and behavior of the UI widget. For example, you can trigger a widget to appear when the player approaches a specific object in the game world.

```
// Example Blueprint scripting to show a 3D UI widget
if (PlayerIsNearControlPanel)
{
    WidgetComponent->SetVisibility(true);
}
```

### In-Game Menus

In-game menus are an essential part of many games, allowing players to access settings, inventory, and other game-related information while playing. Integrating in-game menus with Unreal Engine involves the following steps:

27. **Create a Widget Blueprint:** Design your in-game menu as a UMG Widget Blueprint. Include buttons and elements for various menu options.

28. **Blueprint Logic:** Add Blueprint scripting to control menu functionality. For instance, you can create functions to handle saving the game, adjusting settings, or navigating through the menu.

29. **HUD Integration:** To display the in-game menu, you can either create a HUD widget that overlays the game screen or integrate the menu into the game world as a 3D widget component.

30. **Input Handling:** Implement input handling in Blueprints to open and close the in-game menu in response to player actions, such as pressing a designated key or button.

```
// Example Blueprint scripting to toggle an in-game menu
if (PlayerPressesMenuKey)
{
    ToggleInGameMenu();
}
```

### Interaction Prompts

To provide players with guidance and feedback, you can integrate interaction prompts into your game. These prompts can be displayed when the player approaches interactive objects or encounters in-game events. Here's how you can implement interaction prompts:

31. **Design UI Prompts:** Create UI prompts using UMG widgets, such as text or icons, to convey information to the player.

32. **Blueprint Logic:** Use Blueprint scripting to control when and where the interaction prompts appear. You can trigger prompts based on the player's proximity to objects or game events.

33. **Visibility Control:** Set the visibility of the UI prompts dynamically to ensure they appear and disappear at the appropriate times.

```
// Example Blueprint scripting to show an interaction prompt
if (PlayerIsNearInteractiveObject)
{
    InteractionPromptWidget->SetVisibility(true);
}
```

### Health Bars and Status Indicators

Health bars, stamina indicators, and other status displays are commonly integrated UI elements in games. Unreal Engine allows you to create and update these indicators in real-time to provide players with essential feedback. Here's how to implement status indicators:

34. **Design Status Widgets:** Create UMG widgets that represent health bars, stamina meters, or any other status indicators relevant to your game.

35. **Blueprint Logic:** Use Blueprint scripting to update the values of these indicators based on in-game events. For example, decrease the health bar when the player takes damage.

```
// Example Blueprint scripting to update a health bar
void UpdateHealthBar(float HealthValue)
{
    HealthBarWidget->SetPercent(HealthValue);
}
```

3. **Real-Time Updates:** Continuously update the status indicators to reflect changes in the game, ensuring that players receive up-to-date information about their character's status.

In conclusion, integrating UI with gameplay in Unreal Engine offers a wide range of possibilities for creating immersive and interactive game experiences. Whether you're positioning widgets in 3D space, designing in-game menus, providing interaction prompts, or updating status indicators, Unreal Engine's flexibility and Blueprint scripting capabilities empower you to craft engaging and dynamic user interfaces that enhance your game's overall quality and player engagement.

---

## Section 7.4: UI Animation and Effects

UI animation and effects play a vital role in enhancing the visual appeal and interactivity of your game's user interface (UI). In Unreal Engine, you can create captivating UI animations and effects using the Unreal Motion Graphics (UMG) system and various animation tools. In this section, we'll explore how to bring life to your UI through animation and effects.

## Keyframe Animation

Keyframe animation is a fundamental technique for animating UI elements in Unreal Engine. With keyframes, you can define specific points in time where UI properties, such as position, size, rotation, and opacity, change. Here's how to create keyframe animations in UMG:

36. **Design Your UI:** Start by designing your UI elements in a UMG Widget Blueprint.

37. **Add Keyframes:** Within the UMG Designer, select the widget you want to animate, and open the timeline. Add keyframes at different points on the timeline, specifying the desired property values at each keyframe.

38. **Easing Curves:** Customize the animation's ease-in and ease-out behaviors by adjusting the easing curves between keyframes. This controls the acceleration and deceleration of the animation.

39. **Trigger Animations:** Use Blueprint scripting to trigger the animations based on in-game events or player interactions. You can start animations when a button is clicked, a certain condition is met, or at predefined moments in your game.

```
// Example Blueprint scripting to trigger a UI animation
if (PlayerClicksButton)
{
    PlayAnimation(YourAnimation);
}
```

## Particle Effects

Integrating particle effects with your UI can add a dynamic and visually appealing dimension to your game. Unreal Engine provides a robust particle system that allows you to create various particle effects and integrate them into your UI. Here's how to do it:

40. **Create Particle Systems:** Design your particle systems using Unreal Engine's Cascade particle editor. You can create effects like fire, smoke, sparks, or magical particles.

41. **UMG Integration:** In your UMG Widget Blueprint, add an Image widget where you want the particle effect to appear.

42. **Blueprint Logic:** Use Blueprint scripting to play and control the particle system within the Image widget. You can start the particle system when specific events occur or based on player interactions.

```
// Example Blueprint scripting to start a particle effect
if (PlayerActivatesPower)
{
    ParticleComponent->ActivateSystem();
}
```

## Transitions and Screen Effects

UI transitions and screen effects are often used to create smooth transitions between different UI screens or game states. These effects can include fades, wipes, screen shakes, and more. Here's how to implement transitions and screen effects:

43. **Design Transition Animations:** Create animations or UI elements that represent transitions between screens or states. For example, a fade-in/out effect can be achieved by animating an overlay with a changing opacity.

44. **Blueprint Logic:** Use Blueprint scripting to trigger these transition animations when needed. For instance, when transitioning from a menu to gameplay, you can fade out the menu UI and fade in the game UI.

```
// Example Blueprint scripting for a screen transition
if (PlayerStartsGame)
{
    StartScreenTransition(FadeOutDuration, FadeInDuration);
}
```

## Sound Integration

Adding sound effects to UI animations and interactions enhances the overall experience. You can integrate sound cues to complement UI actions like button clicks, transitions, or animations. Here's how to integrate sound with your UI:

45. **Create Sound Cues:** Design sound cues in Unreal Engine's audio system to represent different UI actions or events, such as button clicks, transitions, or UI animations.

46. **Blueprint Logic:** Use Blueprint scripting to trigger sound cues in response to UI interactions or animations. You can trigger sounds when a button is pressed, an animation starts, or a screen transition occurs.

```
// Example Blueprint scripting to play a sound on button click
if (PlayerClicksButton)
{
    PlaySoundCue(ButtonClickSound);
}
```

## Performance Considerations

While adding UI animations and effects, it's crucial to consider performance optimization. Excessive or complex animations can impact frame rates and overall gameplay experience. To optimize UI animation performance:

- **Use Efficient Animations:** Keep animations concise and efficient. Avoid overcomplicating them with unnecessary keyframes or effects.

- **Culling and Occlusion:** Implement culling and occlusion techniques to ensure that UI elements and animations are only processed and rendered when they are visible to the player.

- **Sound Management:** Carefully manage sound cues to prevent audio clutter and excessive resource usage. Consider using concurrency settings to limit the number of simultaneous sounds.

In conclusion, UI animation and effects in Unreal Engine allow you to create visually engaging and interactive user interfaces that enhance the overall gaming experience. By incorporating keyframe animations, particle effects, transitions, sound integration, and considering performance optimization, you can elevate your game's UI to a professional level, providing players with a more immersive and enjoyable gameplay journey.

---

## Section 7.5: Usability Testing for UI

Usability testing is a critical step in game development that ensures your user interface (UI) is intuitive, user-friendly, and meets the expectations of your player base. Conducting usability tests helps identify issues, gather valuable feedback, and make informed improvements to enhance the overall user experience. In this section, we'll explore the importance of usability testing for UI in Unreal Engine game development.

### Testing Scenarios

Usability testing involves creating specific testing scenarios that simulate how players would interact with your game's UI. These scenarios should cover a range of common actions and tasks within the UI, such as:

- Navigating the main menu and submenus
- Adjusting settings and preferences
- Interacting with in-game menus and HUD elements
- Using interactive UI components like buttons, sliders, and checkboxes
- Accessing inventory, maps, or character information screens
- Resolving common UI-related issues, such as troubleshooting connection problems in multiplayer menus

By designing relevant testing scenarios, you can evaluate the effectiveness of your UI in providing a smooth and intuitive experience for players.

### Participant Selection

Usability testing requires participants who represent your target audience. It's essential to select a diverse group of participants with varying levels of gaming experience, from novice to experienced gamers. This diversity allows you to gather feedback from different perspectives and skill levels.

## Testing Environment

Set up a controlled testing environment where participants can focus on the UI without distractions. Ensure that the hardware and software configurations match those of your intended player base. Consider using screen recording and eye-tracking software to capture participant interactions and gaze patterns for in-depth analysis.

## Usability Test Execution

During usability testing, observe participants as they complete the predefined testing scenarios. Encourage them to think aloud and express their thoughts, feelings, and frustrations while interacting with the UI. Pay attention to common issues such as:

- Difficulty locating specific UI elements
- Confusion regarding the purpose of certain buttons or icons
- Challenges in navigating through menus
- Frustration with unresponsive or unintuitive controls
- Suggestions for improvements or features they would like to see

Take notes and record observations to document usability issues and areas for improvement.

## Analyzing Results

After conducting usability tests, analyze the collected data and feedback. Identify recurring issues and prioritize them based on severity and impact on the user experience. Usability testing can reveal critical insights that may lead to UI redesign, improved user guidance, or enhanced visual clarity.

## Iterative Design

Usability testing is an iterative process. Implement changes and improvements based on the feedback and insights gathered from each testing session. Continue testing and refining the UI until it meets the desired usability standards and provides a seamless user experience.

## Remote Usability Testing

In addition to in-person usability testing, consider remote usability testing. This approach allows you to gather feedback from a broader and geographically diverse participant pool. Remote testing can be conducted using screen-sharing software, remote monitoring tools, or specialized usability testing platforms.

## Accessibility Testing

Include accessibility testing as part of your usability testing process. Ensure that players with disabilities, such as visual or hearing impairments, can effectively use and interact with your UI. Address any accessibility issues and make necessary adjustments to improve inclusivity.

## Beta Testing and Player Feedback

Beta testing is an opportunity to gather usability feedback from a larger player base before the game's official release. Encourage beta testers to provide feedback on the UI, and consider implementing changes based on their suggestions. Additionally, engage with your community and player base through forums, surveys, and social media to continuously gather feedback and address UI-related concerns.

In summary, usability testing for UI in Unreal Engine game development is a crucial step in creating a user-friendly and enjoyable gaming experience. By designing relevant testing scenarios, selecting appropriate participants, analyzing results, and conducting iterative design improvements, you can refine your game's UI to meet the needs and expectations of your players. Incorporating accessibility testing, beta testing, and ongoing player feedback ensures that your UI remains responsive and user-centric throughout the development process.

# Chapter 8: Scripting Gameplay Mechanics

## Section 8.1: Introduction to Gameplay Scripting

Gameplay scripting is a fundamental aspect of Unreal Engine game development that empowers you to define and control various game mechanics, player interactions, and AI behaviors. In this section, we'll introduce you to the world of gameplay scripting within Unreal Engine and the importance of scripting in shaping your game's unique experience.

### Role of Gameplay Scripting

Gameplay scripting serves as the backbone of interactivity in your game. It enables you to:

- Define player movements and actions: From character movement to combat mechanics, gameplay scripting allows you to specify how players can interact with your game world.

- Create AI behaviors and pathfinding: Scripting AI behaviors is essential for making non-player characters (NPCs) and enemies react realistically and intelligently within the game environment.

- Implement game rules and logic: Scripting game rules and logic determines how your game functions, including win/lose conditions, scoring, and progression.

- Scripting Challenges and Solutions: Create puzzles, challenges, and dynamic scenarios that engage players and test their skills.

### Unreal Engine's Blueprint System

Unreal Engine offers a powerful visual scripting system known as Blueprints. Blueprints allow you to create gameplay scripts using a node-based interface without writing code. This visual approach simplifies the process of defining behaviors, interactions, and mechanics.

For instance, you can use Blueprints to:

- Control character movement and animations.
- Define how objects interact with each other, such as switches, doors, and levers.
- Implement combat systems, including attacks, damage calculation, and enemy AI.
- Design interactive puzzles and challenges by scripting logic and triggers.
- Handle game events and progression, such as cutscenes and level transitions.

### Introduction to Blueprint Nodes

Blueprints consist of nodes that represent various functions, variables, and events. You connect these nodes to create a visual script that defines the behavior you want. Key components of Blueprint scripting include:

- **Event Graph:** This is where you define what happens in response to specific events, such as a player input or a collision.

- **Functions and Macros:** You can create custom functions and macros to encapsulate logic and reuse it throughout your project.

- **Variables:** Define and manipulate variables to store and manage information, such as player health, score, or quest progress.

- **Flow Control:** Use flow control nodes like branches and loops to create conditional logic and repetitive actions.

## Combining Blueprints and C++

Unreal Engine offers a flexible approach that allows you to use both Blueprints and C++ for gameplay scripting. While Blueprints provide an intuitive visual scripting environment, C++ offers greater control and performance optimization. Many developers use a combination of both approaches to leverage the strengths of each.

You can create C++ classes that interact with Blueprints, making it possible to implement complex game mechanics in C++ while exposing them to Blueprints for customization. This combination of Blueprints and C++ empowers you to achieve a balance between ease of use and performance.

## Scripting Best Practices

To create efficient and maintainable gameplay scripts, consider the following best practices:

- **Modularity:** Break down complex scripts into smaller, reusable components and functions. This simplifies debugging, testing, and updates.

- **Comments and Documentation:** Provide clear comments and documentation for your scripts to make them understandable for other team members and yourself in the future.

- **Testing and Debugging:** Regularly test and debug your scripts to catch errors and ensure they function as intended.

- **Optimization:** Optimize your scripts for performance, especially in resource-intensive areas, by identifying and resolving bottlenecks.

- **Version Control:** Use version control systems to track changes and collaborate with team members effectively.

In conclusion, gameplay scripting is a foundational element of Unreal Engine game development that allows you to define and control the interactive and dynamic aspects of your game. Unreal Engine's Blueprint system provides an accessible and versatile tool for visual scripting, while the integration of C++ offers additional flexibility and performance optimization. By following best practices and continually refining your scripting skills, you can create engaging and immersive gameplay experiences for your players.

---

## Section 8.2: Scripting Player Movements and Actions

Scripting player movements and actions is a fundamental aspect of gameplay scripting in Unreal Engine. It involves defining how the player character can move, interact with the game world, and perform various actions. In this section, we'll explore how to script player movements and actions using Unreal Engine's Blueprint system.

### Character Movement

The movement of the player character is a crucial aspect of gameplay. Unreal Engine provides a Character class that comes with built-in movement components and functions. To script player movement:

47. **Character Blueprint:** Create a Character Blueprint for your player character if you haven't already.

48. **Input Handling:** Use Blueprint scripting to handle player inputs, such as keyboard or controller inputs, to determine the character's movement direction.

```
// Example Blueprint scripting to handle player movement input
InputAxis MoveForward
InputAxis MoveRight
```

3. **Add Movement Input:** Use the "Add Movement Input" node to apply movement to the character based on the input direction. You can control the character's speed, acceleration, and jump height through this node.

```
// Example Blueprint scripting to add movement input
Add Movement Input
```

4. **Collision and Physics:** Consider collision and physics interactions to ensure that the character can navigate the game world smoothly and interact with objects realistically.

### Player Actions

Player actions include a wide range of interactions, such as jumping, attacking, picking up items, and more. Scripting player actions allows you to define how the player character responds to various inputs and triggers. Here's how to script player actions:

49. **Input Mapping:** Set up input mappings in your project settings to define action names and associate them with specific keys or buttons.

50. **Action Handling:** Use Blueprint scripting to detect input events related to player actions. For example, you can detect when the player presses the "Jump" button.

```
// Example Blueprint scripting to handle player jumping
InputAction Jump
```

3. **Action Implementation:** Define the behavior for each player action in response to the corresponding input event. For instance, when the "Jump" input is detected, use Blueprint scripting to make the character jump.

```
// Example Blueprint scripting to make the character jump
Character Jump
```

4. **Interaction with Game Objects:** Player actions often involve interacting with in-game objects or entities. Use Blueprint scripting to handle interactions like opening doors, picking up items, or attacking enemies.

Animation and Feedback

Player movements and actions are closely tied to animations and feedback. Unreal Engine allows you to integrate animations seamlessly with gameplay scripting to provide visual and audio cues that enhance the player experience. To script animations and feedback:

51. **Animation Blueprints:** Create Animation Blueprints to define how the character's animations change based on their movements and actions.

52. **Animation States:** Use animation state machines to transition between different animation states, such as idle, walking, running, and attacking, based on the character's actions.

53. **Audio and Visual Feedback:** Implement audio cues, particle effects, and UI elements to provide feedback to the player when they perform actions. For example, play a sound effect when the character jumps or show a health bar when the character takes damage.

Advanced Movements and Actions

Depending on your game's complexity, you may need to implement advanced movements and actions, such as double jumping, wall running, or combo attacks. Unreal Engine's Blueprint system allows you to extend and customize player movements and actions to suit your game's requirements.

In conclusion, scripting player movements and actions in Unreal Engine is a foundational skill for creating engaging and interactive gameplay experiences. By using Blueprint scripting, you can define how the player character moves, interacts with the game world, and performs various actions. This scripting process involves input handling, character movement, collision and physics interactions, animation integration, and feedback mechanisms. Whether you're creating a platformer, an action-adventure game, or any other genre, mastering player movement and action scripting is essential for delivering a satisfying gaming experience.

## Section 8.3: Creating AI Behaviors and Pathfinding

Creating AI behaviors and implementing pathfinding for non-player characters (NPCs) and enemies is a critical aspect of gameplay scripting in Unreal Engine. AI behaviors define how NPCs and enemies interact with the game world and make decisions, while pathfinding allows them to navigate the environment intelligently. In this section, we'll delve into the process of creating AI behaviors and implementing pathfinding using Unreal Engine's Blueprint system.

### AI Behaviors

AI behaviors determine how NPCs and enemies respond to various stimuli and make decisions based on their objectives. Unreal Engine's Blueprint system enables you to script complex AI behaviors using visual scripting. Here's an overview of the steps involved:

54. **Behavior Tree:** Unreal Engine provides a Behavior Tree system, which is a graphical representation of AI behaviors. Create a Behavior Tree for your NPC or enemy AI.

55. **AI Controller:** Attach an AI Controller to your NPC or enemy character. The AI Controller is responsible for executing the behavior tree and making decisions for the AI.

56. **Blackboard:** Use a Blackboard to store and share data between the behavior tree and the AI Controller. You can define key variables and values in the blackboard that influence AI decisions.

57. **Tasks and Decorators:** In the Behavior Tree, use tasks to define specific actions the AI should take, such as moving to a location, attacking a target, or patrolling. Decorators can be used to apply conditions or filters to tasks.

```
// Example Blueprint scripting for AI behavior tasks
Move To
Attack
```

5. **Conditional Logic:** Implement conditional logic within the behavior tree to make decisions based on the current game state, the player's actions, or other environmental factors.

```
// Example Blueprint scripting for conditional AI behavior
if (PlayerIsVisible)
{
    AttackPlayer
}
```

## Pathfinding

Pathfinding is a crucial component of AI behavior, enabling NPCs and enemies to navigate the game world intelligently. Unreal Engine provides a built-in navigation system that supports pathfinding. Here's how to implement pathfinding in your AI behavior:

58. **Navigation Mesh:** Configure the navigation mesh in your level to represent walkable areas for characters. Unreal Engine's NavMesh system automatically generates navigation data based on the level geometry.

59. **AI Move To:** Use the "AI Move To" node in Blueprints to instruct the AI to move to a specific location. The AI Controller handles pathfinding automatically.

```
// Example Blueprint scripting for AI movement using pathfinding
AI Move To
```

3. **Dynamic Navigation:** For dynamic environments where obstacles can change, use Blueprint scripting to update the AI's destination dynamically to avoid obstacles or follow the player.

```
// Example Blueprint scripting for dynamic pathfinding
Find Path to Location Synchronously
```

4. **Custom Pathfinding:** In some cases, you may need custom pathfinding logic. You can use Blueprint scripting to implement custom pathfinding algorithms or modify the AI's behavior based on specific conditions.

## Advanced AI Behaviors

Depending on your game's complexity, you may need to implement advanced AI behaviors such as state machines, decision trees, or finite state machines (FSMs). Unreal Engine's Blueprint system provides the flexibility to create and manage these advanced AI behaviors effectively.

Additionally, Unreal Engine offers tools for behavior debugging and visualization, allowing you to monitor and fine-tune your AI behaviors during development.

In conclusion, creating AI behaviors and implementing pathfinding in Unreal Engine using the Blueprint system is essential for bringing your game's NPCs and enemies to life. AI behaviors define how characters interact with the game world and make decisions, while pathfinding enables them to navigate intelligently. By leveraging the Behavior Tree system, Blackboards, tasks, decorators, and conditional logic, you can create sophisticated AI behaviors that enhance gameplay and provide challenging experiences for players. Whether you're creating a single-player adventure or a multiplayer shooter, mastering AI scripting and pathfinding is crucial for delivering engaging and immersive gaming experiences.

## Section 8.4: Implementing Game Rules and Logic

Implementing game rules and logic is a critical aspect of gameplay scripting in Unreal Engine. Game rules define the core mechanics, win/lose conditions, scoring, and progression of your game. Logic scripting ensures that the game functions as intended and provides an enjoyable player experience. In this section, we'll explore how to implement game rules and logic using Unreal Engine's Blueprint system.

### Core Game Mechanics

Core game mechanics are the fundamental rules and interactions that define how players engage with your game. These mechanics vary widely depending on the game genre but can include movement, combat, resource management, puzzle-solving, and more. Here's how to implement core game mechanics:

60. **Blueprint Scripting:** Use Blueprint scripting to define the rules and behaviors associated with core game mechanics. For example, you can script the movement controls for a platformer or the combat mechanics for an action game.

```
// Example Blueprint scripting for character movement
InputAxis MoveForward
InputAxis MoveRight
```

5. **Feedback and Visuals:** Implement visual and audio feedback to make core mechanics more engaging and intuitive. For instance, display on-screen prompts for actions or play sound effects when specific events occur.

6. **Testing and Balancing:** Continuously test and balance core game mechanics to ensure that they provide a satisfying player experience. Adjust variables, such as movement speed or damage values, based on player feedback and testing results.

### Win/Lose Conditions

Win and lose conditions define the outcomes of the game and determine when the player succeeds or fails. Implementing win/lose conditions involves scripting events and checks to determine the game's conclusion. Here's how to do it:

61. **Victory Conditions:** Use Blueprint scripting to define the conditions that lead to victory. This can include reaching a specific goal, defeating a boss, or completing a set of objectives.

```
// Example Blueprint scripting for victory condition
if (AllObjectivesCompleted)
{
    Victory
}
```

2. **Defeat Conditions:** Similarly, script defeat conditions, such as the player's health reaching zero, running out of time, or failing specific challenges.

```
// Example Blueprint scripting for defeat condition
if (PlayerHealth <= 0)
```

```
{
    Defeat
}
```

3. **Game State Management:** Manage the game's state and transitions between victory, defeat, and ongoing gameplay. You can implement level transitions, cutscenes, or end-of-game sequences using Blueprint scripting.

## Scoring and Progression

Scoring and progression systems add depth and replayability to your game. Implementing these systems allows players to track their performance and feel a sense of accomplishment. Here's how to script scoring and progression:

62. **Score Tracking:** Use Blueprint scripting to track player scores based on in-game actions, achievements, or objectives completed.

```
// Example Blueprint scripting for scoring
if (EnemyDefeated)
{
    AddScore(10)
}
```

2. **Progression Systems:** Implement progression systems that unlock new levels, abilities, or content as players achieve specific milestones or reach predefined goals.

```
// Example Blueprint scripting for unlocking content
if (PlayerScore >= 1000)
{
    UnlockNewLevel(Level2)
}
```

3. **UI Integration:** Display player scores, progress, and unlocked content through the user interface (UI). Use Blueprint scripting to update and manage UI elements accordingly.

## Game Events and Triggers

Game events and triggers are scripted events that occur based on specific conditions or player actions. These events can include cutscenes, scripted sequences, or dynamic challenges. Here's how to implement game events and triggers:

63. **Event Scripting:** Create Blueprint scripts for events and triggers that respond to player actions or predefined conditions in the game world.

```
// Example Blueprint scripting for triggering an event
if (PlayerEntersTriggerZone)
{
    StartCutscene
}
```

2. **Sequencing:** Sequence events and triggers to create dynamic and engaging gameplay experiences. Use Blueprint scripting to control the order and timing of events.

```
// Example Blueprint scripting for sequencing events
StartEvent1
Delay(3 seconds)
StartEvent2
```

3. **Interaction:** Implement interactions between the player character and the game world, such as pressing buttons, solving puzzles, or triggering scripted sequences through player actions.

### Debugging and Testing

Thoroughly test and debug your game rules and logic to ensure that they function correctly and provide a balanced gameplay experience. Use Unreal Engine's debugging tools, such as breakpoints and print statements, to identify and resolve issues in your Blueprint scripts.

In conclusion, implementing game rules and logic using Unreal Engine's Blueprint system is essential for creating engaging and immersive gameplay experiences. Whether you're defining core game mechanics, win/lose conditions, scoring and progression systems, or scripting game events and triggers, mastering gameplay scripting is crucial for game development. By combining these elements and continually iterating based on player feedback and testing results, you can create a compelling and enjoyable gaming experience that keeps players coming back for more.

---

## Section 8.5: Scripting Challenges and Solutions

Scripting challenges and solutions is an integral part of gameplay scripting in Unreal Engine. Challenges add depth and excitement to your game, while scripting solutions allows you to design puzzles, obstacles, and dynamic scenarios that engage players and test their skills. In this section, we'll explore how to script challenges and their solutions using Unreal Engine's Blueprint system.

### Challenge Design

Challenges are gameplay segments that require players to overcome obstacles, solve puzzles, or demonstrate specific skills. To design effective challenges, follow these steps:

64. **Define the Objective:** Clearly define the goal of the challenge. What should the player achieve or overcome? This could be reaching a distant platform, solving a puzzle, defeating enemies, or completing a timed task.

65. **Create Obstacles:** Design obstacles or hurdles that impede the player's progress. These can include physical barriers, environmental hazards, or enemies that pose a threat.

66. **Puzzle Elements:** If the challenge involves puzzles, incorporate puzzle elements such as switches, levers, keys, and locks. Blueprint scripting allows you to create interactive puzzle mechanics.

```
// Example Blueprint scripting for puzzle interaction
if (PlayerInteractsWithSwitch)
{
    ActivateBridge
}
```

4. **Dynamic Elements:** Consider adding dynamic elements that change the challenge's conditions, creating variation and unpredictability. Blueprint scripting can control these dynamic elements.

```
// Example Blueprint scripting for dynamic challenge elements
if (RandomEventOccurs)
{
    ModifyChallengeConditions
}
```

## Scripting Solutions

Scripting solutions involves defining the conditions and actions required to successfully overcome challenges. Here's how to script solutions using Unreal Engine's Blueprint system:

67. **Objective Check:** Implement Blueprint scripts to check whether the player has met the challenge's objective. This may involve proximity checks, item collection, or specific actions.

```
// Example Blueprint scripting to check if the challenge objective is met
if (PlayerReachesObjective)
{
    ChallengeCompleted
}
```

2. **Feedback and Rewards:** Provide feedback to the player when they successfully complete a challenge. This could include visual effects, sound cues, and UI updates. Additionally, reward the player with items, points, or progress.

```
// Example Blueprint scripting for providing feedback and rewards
PlayVictoryEffects
IncreasePlayerScore(100)
```

3. **Failure Conditions:** Define what happens if the player fails to complete the challenge. This could result in the player character taking damage, respawning at a checkpoint, or triggering a game over sequence.

```
// Example Blueprint scripting for handling failure conditions
if (PlayerFailsChallenge)
{
    PlayerTakeDamage
    RespawnAtCheckpoint
}
```

4. **Progression Integration:** Ensure that challenge completion contributes to the overall game progression. This may involve unlocking new areas, granting access to abilities, or advancing the story.

```
// Example Blueprint scripting for progression integration
if (ChallengeCompleted)
{
    UnlockNextLevel
    AdvanceStory
}
```

## Iterative Design

Designing challenges and scripting solutions is an iterative process. Playtest your challenges and gather feedback from players to refine the difficulty, pacing, and overall experience. Use Blueprint scripting to make adjustments based on playtest results.

## Multiplayer Challenges

If your game includes multiplayer functionality, consider how challenges and solutions will work in a multiplayer context. Blueprint scripting can handle multiplayer-specific interactions and ensure that challenges are balanced and fair for all players.

## Tutorial and Learning Curve

Challenges can serve as opportunities to teach players new mechanics and concepts. Script tutorial sequences that guide players through the challenges, gradually introducing them to the game's mechanics and complexities.

In conclusion, scripting challenges and solutions is a creative and essential aspect of Unreal Engine gameplay scripting. Challenges add depth and excitement to your game, while scripting solutions allows you to create engaging obstacles, puzzles, and dynamic scenarios. By carefully designing challenges, scripting their solutions, and iterating based on player feedback, you can create a balanced and rewarding gaming experience that keeps players engaged and motivated to overcome the obstacles you've designed.

# Chapter 9: Multiplayer Aspects

## Section 9.1: Basics of Multiplayer Game Design

Multiplayer game design is a complex and dynamic field within game development. It involves creating games that allow multiple players to interact and compete, either locally or online. In this section, we'll explore the basics of multiplayer game design, including the key concepts, challenges, and considerations that developers need to address when creating multiplayer experiences.

### Understanding Multiplayer Game Types

Multiplayer games come in various forms, each offering a unique player experience. Here are some common multiplayer game types:

68. **Local Multiplayer:** In local multiplayer games, players share the same physical space and typically use the same screen or device to play. Examples include split-screen racing games or party games.

69. **Online Multiplayer:** Online multiplayer games connect players over the internet, allowing them to compete or cooperate from different locations. This category includes massively multiplayer online games (MMOs), online shooters, and cooperative online adventures.

70. **Asynchronous Multiplayer:** Asynchronous multiplayer games don't require players to be online simultaneously. Players take turns, often receiving notifications when it's their time to play. Mobile word games and turn-based strategy games are common examples.

71. **Cooperative and Competitive:** Multiplayer games can be cooperative, where players work together towards a common goal, or competitive, where players compete against each other. Some games combine both elements.

### Key Considerations in Multiplayer Game Design

Designing multiplayer games presents unique challenges and considerations compared to single-player experiences. Here are some fundamental aspects to keep in mind:

72. **Networking:** Implementing robust networking code is essential for online multiplayer games. This includes handling player connections, synchronizing game state across clients, and minimizing latency.

73. **Game Balance:** Balancing gameplay becomes more complex when multiple players are involved. Game designers must ensure that the game remains fair and enjoyable for all participants.

74. **Player Interaction:** Consider how players interact with each other. Communication tools, such as chat or voice chat, can enhance the multiplayer experience but also introduce challenges like toxic behavior.

75. **Cheating and Security:** Preventing cheating is crucial in multiplayer games. Implement anti-cheat measures and secure your game's data and communication channels to maintain fair play.

76. **Scalability:** Plan for scalability to accommodate different player counts. Ensure that the game works well whether there are two players or hundreds in a single match.

77. **Server Infrastructure:** For online multiplayer, you'll need server infrastructure to host game sessions. Decide whether to use dedicated servers, peer-to-peer connections, or a hybrid approach.

## Player Progression and Rewards

Many multiplayer games incorporate progression systems that reward players for their achievements and encourage continued play. Consider implementing features such as:

- **Experience Points (XP):** Award players with XP for their in-game actions, which can lead to leveling up and unlocking new content.

- **Unlockables:** Provide players with cosmetic items, character skins, or in-game currency that they can earn and use to customize their experience.

- **Leaderboards:** Implement leaderboards to display the rankings of top players, fostering competition and motivation.

- **Seasons and Events:** Run limited-time events and seasons that introduce new content and challenges, keeping the game fresh.

## Player Matchmaking

Effective player matchmaking is crucial for providing balanced and enjoyable multiplayer experiences. Matchmaking algorithms aim to pair players of similar skill levels or experience to ensure fair competition. Unreal Engine provides tools and libraries for implementing matchmaking systems tailored to your game's needs.

## Testing and Balancing

Thorough testing and balancing are essential for multiplayer games. Organize playtesting sessions with a diverse group of players to gather feedback and make adjustments to gameplay, balance, and network performance. Frequent updates and patches can help maintain a healthy and engaging multiplayer community.

In summary, multiplayer game design is a multifaceted field that requires careful consideration of player interaction, networking, fairness, and progression. Whether you're creating a local party game or a large-scale online multiplayer experience, understanding these fundamental concepts and addressing the associated challenges is essential for delivering a successful and enjoyable multiplayer gaming experience.

---

## Section 9.2: Setting Up a Multiplayer Environment

Setting up a multiplayer environment is a critical step in the development of online multiplayer games. This section will guide you through the key aspects and considerations when configuring your game for multiplayer functionality in Unreal Engine.

### Game Architecture

Before diving into the technical aspects, it's essential to understand the overall architecture of your multiplayer game. Unreal Engine supports various multiplayer architectures, including:

78. **Client-Server Model:** In this model, one player's device (the server) hosts the game session, while others (clients) connect to it. The server manages game logic, and clients send inputs and receive updates from the server. This approach offers centralized control but requires robust server infrastructure.

79. **Peer-to-Peer (P2P) Model:** In a P2P model, players connect directly to each other without a central server. This model can be suitable for small-scale games but may have limitations regarding security and scalability.

80. **Hybrid Model:** Some games use a combination of client-server and P2P models, where certain aspects of the game run on a central server (e.g., matchmaking and leaderboards), while actual gameplay occurs in P2P connections.

### Networking and Replication

Unreal Engine's networking framework allows you to replicate game state and events across clients and servers. Key networking concepts include:

- **Replication:** Use replication to synchronize critical game data, such as character positions, health, and interactions, across all connected players. Unreal Engine handles replication through properties and functions marked with "RepNotify" or "Replicated."

```
// Example Blueprint snippet for replicating a variable
Replicated
```

- **Remote Function Calls:** You can invoke remote function calls to execute functions on remote actors. These functions allow you to trigger actions on other players' machines, such as dealing damage or opening doors.

```
// Example Blueprint snippet for remote function calls
Server RPC
```

- **Ownership and Authority:** Unreal Engine distinguishes between server authority and client authority. The server typically has authority over critical game logic, while clients handle user input. Understanding this distinction is crucial for ensuring fair gameplay.

## Player Connectivity

To set up player connectivity in your multiplayer environment:

- **Matchmaking:** Implement a matchmaking system that pairs players based on skill levels, preferences, or other criteria. Unreal Engine provides tools and libraries to assist with matchmaking implementation.

- **Lobbies and Sessions:** Create lobbies or sessions to organize players before a match begins. These areas allow players to chat, customize their characters, and prepare for gameplay.

- **Session Management:** Manage game sessions, including starting, joining, and leaving sessions. Implement session host migration to handle situations where the host player disconnects.

- **Network Addressing:** Consider how players will connect to each other. You may need to implement features like NAT traversal or relay servers to ensure players can connect even in complex network environments.

## Player Authentication and Security

Online multiplayer games require robust player authentication and security measures to prevent cheating and protect player data. Key considerations include:

- **Player Accounts:** Implement player account systems for user authentication and authorization. This helps track player progress, achievements, and ensures secure login.

- **Data Encryption:** Encrypt network traffic to protect sensitive information, such as player credentials and in-game communication.

- **Anti-Cheat Measures:** Use anti-cheat solutions to detect and prevent cheating behaviors, such as aimbots, wallhacks, or speed hacks.

- **Server Security:** Ensure the security of your game servers to prevent unauthorized access and DDoS attacks.

## Testing and Optimization

Thorough testing is crucial for multiplayer games to identify and resolve issues related to networking, performance, and balance. Consider the following aspects:

- **Latency and Lag Compensation:** Implement lag compensation techniques to ensure fair gameplay, even for players with varying latency.

- **Load Testing:** Simulate heavy player loads to test your server's scalability and identify potential bottlenecks.

- **Balancing:** Continuously balance your game based on player feedback and performance data. Address overpowered abilities or strategies that may negatively affect gameplay.

- **Cross-Platform Play:** If you intend to support cross-platform play, thoroughly test and ensure that gameplay remains balanced and fair across different platforms.

In summary, setting up a multiplayer environment in Unreal Engine involves understanding the game's architecture, managing player connectivity, implementing security measures, and conducting thorough testing. Properly configured multiplayer functionality is crucial for delivering a seamless and enjoyable online gaming experience.

---

## Section 9.3: Networking and Player Connectivity

Networking and player connectivity are fundamental aspects of multiplayer game development in Unreal Engine. In this section, we'll delve into the essential components and considerations for managing networking and player connectivity in your multiplayer game.

### Replication in Unreal Engine

Replication is the process of synchronizing game state and events across multiple players in a multiplayer environment. Unreal Engine provides a robust replication framework that simplifies this complex task. Key concepts include:

- **Replicated Variables:** Use replicated variables to automatically synchronize important data between the server and clients. By marking a variable as "Replicated" in Blueprint or using "RepNotify" in C++, you ensure that changes to that variable are replicated to all relevant clients.

```
// Example Blueprint snippet for replicating a variable
Replicated
```

- **Remote Function Calls:** Unreal Engine allows you to invoke remote function calls to execute functions on remote actors. These functions enable interactions and actions that affect other players or objects on their machines.

```
// Example Blueprint snippet for remote function calls
Server RPC
```

- **Remote Procedure Calls (RPCs):** RPCs enable you to send custom messages between clients and the server. They are useful for handling complex interactions or triggering specific events across the network.

## Server-Client Architecture

Understanding the server-client architecture is crucial for effective networking in multiplayer games. Unreal Engine typically follows a client-server model, where one player (the server) hosts the game session, and others (clients) connect to it. Key considerations include:

- **Server Authority:** The server often has authority over critical game logic, ensuring fairness and security. Clients handle user input and send it to the server for validation.

- **Client Prediction:** Clients can implement prediction techniques to provide a smoother player experience. For example, clients may predict character movement locally while awaiting server confirmation.

- **Latency Compensation:** Implement lag compensation techniques to address issues related to latency. Techniques like client-side prediction and rollback netcode help ensure fair gameplay, even with varying player latencies.

## Player Connectivity

To manage player connectivity effectively, consider the following aspects:

- **Matchmaking:** Implement a matchmaking system that pairs players based on skill levels, preferences, or other criteria. Unreal Engine provides tools and libraries to assist with matchmaking implementation.

- **Lobbies and Sessions:** Create lobbies or sessions where players can congregate before a match begins. These areas allow players to chat, customize their characters, and prepare for gameplay.

- **Session Management:** Develop session management features that enable players to start, join, and leave sessions gracefully. Implement session host migration to handle scenarios where the host player disconnects.

- **Network Addressing:** Consider how players will connect to each other. You may need to implement features like NAT traversal or relay servers to ensure players can connect even in complex network environments.

## Player Interaction and Communication

Interactions and communication between players enhance the multiplayer experience. Unreal Engine provides tools for implementing player interaction, such as:

- **Voice Chat:** Integrate voice chat systems to enable players to communicate with each other during gameplay. Ensure that voice chat is secure and moderated to prevent abuse.

- **Text Chat:** Implement text chat features that allow players to send messages to each other. Implement chat filters and moderation tools to maintain a positive gaming environment.

- **Emotes and Gestures:** Add emotes and gesture systems that enable players to express themselves non-verbally. These can enhance social interactions and add a layer of fun to the game.

## Security and Anti-Cheat Measures

Maintaining a secure multiplayer environment is crucial to prevent cheating and protect player data. Key security measures include:

- **Player Authentication:** Implement player account systems for user authentication and authorization. This helps track player progress, achievements, and ensures secure login.

- **Data Encryption:** Encrypt network traffic to protect sensitive information, such as player credentials and in-game communication.

- **Anti-Cheat Solutions:** Use anti-cheat solutions to detect and prevent cheating behaviors, such as aimbots, wallhacks, or speed hacks. Regularly update and improve anti-cheat measures to stay ahead of cheaters.

- **Server Security:** Ensure the security of your game servers to prevent unauthorized access and DDoS attacks. Regularly update server software and implement security patches.

## Testing and Optimization

Thorough testing and optimization are critical for multiplayer games. Consider these aspects during development:

- **Load Testing:** Simulate heavy player loads to test your server's scalability and identify potential bottlenecks. Ensure that the game performs well under various player counts.

- **Latency Testing:** Test the game under different network conditions to identify latency issues. Implement measures to mitigate the impact of latency on gameplay.

- **Balancing:** Continuously balance your game based on player feedback and performance data. Address overpowered abilities or strategies that may negatively affect gameplay.

- **Cross-Platform Play:** If you intend to support cross-platform play, thoroughly test and ensure that gameplay remains balanced and fair across different platforms.

In conclusion, networking and player connectivity are foundational elements of multiplayer game development in Unreal Engine. Understanding replication

## Section 9.4: Designing for Multiplayer Gameplay

Designing multiplayer gameplay presents a unique set of challenges and opportunities in game development. This section will explore the considerations and best practices when designing gameplay experiences tailored for multiplayer in Unreal Engine.

### Player Roles and Dynamics

In multiplayer games, players often take on specific roles or classes that contribute to team dynamics and gameplay variety. When designing for multiplayer, consider:

- **Balanced Roles:** Ensure that each player role is balanced and contributes meaningfully to the team's success. Avoid situations where one role dominates the game excessively.

- **Synergy:** Encourage synergy between player roles. Players should benefit from working together, combining their abilities, and strategizing as a team.

- **Counterplay:** Create opportunities for counterplay, where one role's strengths can be countered by another role's weaknesses. This adds depth to the gameplay and promotes strategy.

### Map Design and Flow

Map design plays a crucial role in multiplayer gameplay. Consider the following when designing maps:

- **Balance:** Balance map layouts to provide fair opportunities for both teams or all players. Ensure that no side has an inherent advantage.

- **Variety:** Incorporate a variety of terrain, cover, and strategic points to keep gameplay engaging and dynamic. Avoid overly symmetrical maps that may become predictable.

- **Chokepoints:** Use chokepoints strategically to create tension and conflict zones. Chokepoints can lead to exciting battles but should be balanced to prevent bottlenecks.

- **Verticality:** Introduce vertical elements in maps to add depth and strategy. Multi-level structures and terrain can change the flow of the game.

### Player Progression and Rewards

Consider implementing progression systems that reward players for their performance and encourage continued play:

- **Experience Points (XP):** Award XP for in-game actions, such as kills, objectives completed, or team support. Allow players to level up and unlock new abilities or cosmetics.

- **Unlockables:** Provide unlockable content, such as character skins, weapons, or abilities, that players can earn as they progress. Unlockables add a sense of achievement and personalization.

- **Leaderboards:** Implement leaderboards to showcase the top-performing players or teams. Leaderboards encourage competition and recognition.

## Game Modes

Multiplayer games often feature various game modes to keep gameplay fresh and cater to different player preferences. Consider the following:

- **Team-Based Modes:** Create team-based game modes like Capture the Flag, Team Deathmatch, or Domination. These modes foster cooperation and competition.

- **Free-for-All:** Offer free-for-all modes for players who prefer solo competition. These modes can be intense and highly competitive.

- **Objective-Based Modes:** Design game modes with specific objectives, such as escorting a payload or capturing control points. Objectives add depth and strategy to matches.

## Balancing and Playtesting

Balancing multiplayer gameplay is an ongoing process that requires careful consideration and playtesting:

- **Regular Testing:** Conduct playtests with a diverse group of players to gather feedback on gameplay balance, map design, and overall fun factor.

- **Iteration:** Be prepared to iterate on game balance based on player feedback and data analysis. Balance adjustments can involve tweaking player abilities, map layouts, or scoring mechanics.

- **Matchmaking:** Implement a matchmaking system that pairs players with similar skill levels to ensure fair and enjoyable matches.

## Community Engagement

Building and engaging with your game's community is essential for the long-term success of your multiplayer game:

- **Feedback Channels:** Provide players with channels to give feedback and report issues. Actively listen to player feedback and communicate your development plans.

- **Events and Tournaments:** Host in-game events, tournaments, or challenges to keep the community engaged and foster a sense of competition.

- **Community Management:** Invest in community management to address concerns, moderate discussions, and maintain a positive and inclusive gaming environment.

## Cross-Platform Play

If your game supports cross-platform play, ensure that gameplay remains balanced and fair across different platforms. Address any potential advantages or disadvantages that specific platforms may have.

## Player Behavior and Toxicity

Toxic behavior can negatively impact the multiplayer experience. Implement measures to discourage toxicity, such as:

- **Reporting and Moderation:** Allow players to report toxic behavior, and implement moderation tools to handle reported cases.

- **Penalties:** Apply penalties, such as temporary suspensions or chat restrictions, to players who engage in toxic behavior.

- **Positive Reinforcement:** Promote positive player behavior through rewards or recognition systems for sportsmanship and teamwork.

In conclusion, designing for multiplayer gameplay in Unreal Engine involves considerations such as player roles, map design, progression systems, game modes, balancing, community engagement, and addressing toxic behavior. By carefully crafting multiplayer experiences that are engaging, balanced, and inclusive, you can create a thriving multiplayer community and deliver memorable gaming experiences for players.

---

## Section 9.5: Testing and Optimizing Multiplayer Features

Testing and optimizing multiplayer features are crucial steps in the development of a successful multiplayer game using Unreal Engine. In this section, we will explore the best practices and considerations for ensuring that your multiplayer features work smoothly, provide a great user experience, and are optimized for performance.

## Latency and Network Testing

Testing your game under various network conditions is essential to address issues related to latency and ensure a smooth multiplayer experience. Consider the following:

- **Ping Simulation:** Simulate different levels of latency, including high ping and packet loss scenarios, to identify potential problems and improve lag compensation mechanisms.

- **Real-World Testing:** Conduct real-world testing with players from different geographic locations to assess how the game performs across diverse network environments.

- **Stress Testing:** Simulate heavy player loads to test your server's scalability and identify potential bottlenecks. Ensure that your game can handle peak loads during peak hours or special events.

### Server Performance

Optimizing server performance is critical to ensure that your game runs smoothly and can accommodate the expected number of players. Here are some optimization strategies:

- **Server Profiling:** Use profiling tools to identify performance bottlenecks on the server. Optimize server-side code and minimize unnecessary calculations.

- **Concurrent Execution:** Implement concurrency and parallelism in your server architecture to handle multiple client connections efficiently.

- **Server Tick Rate:** Adjust the server tick rate based on your game's needs. Lower tick rates can reduce server load but may impact gameplay responsiveness.

- **Scalability:** Plan for server scalability to accommodate an increasing number of players. Implement load balancing and server clustering as needed.

### Client Performance

Optimizing client performance is equally important to provide a smooth and enjoyable experience for players. Consider the following:

- **Client-Side Prediction:** Implement client-side prediction to reduce the perceived impact of latency. Clients can predict character movement locally while awaiting server confirmation.

- **Client Profiling:** Use profiling tools to identify performance bottlenecks on the client side. Optimize rendering, physics, and other resource-intensive tasks.

- **Network Bandwidth:** Efficiently use network bandwidth by minimizing unnecessary data transfer. Use network compression and only replicate essential data.

- **Graphics Settings:** Allow players to adjust graphics settings to optimize performance based on their hardware capabilities. Implement scalable graphics options.

## Balancing and Fairness

Balancing multiplayer gameplay is an ongoing process that requires careful consideration and adjustments. Here are some best practices:

- **Data-Driven Balancing:** Use data analytics to monitor player performance and identify balance issues. Make data-driven decisions when adjusting character abilities, weapons, or game rules.

- **Frequent Updates:** Regularly update the game with balance adjustments based on player feedback and data analysis. Keep an eye on win rates, pick rates, and player complaints.

- **Matchmaking:** Implement a matchmaking system that pairs players with similar skill levels to ensure fair and enjoyable matches. Continuously improve matchmaking algorithms.

- **Community Feedback:** Actively engage with the player community and listen to their feedback regarding balance issues. Maintain open communication channels for player suggestions and concerns.

## Cross-Platform Play

If your game supports cross-platform play, thoroughly test and ensure that gameplay remains balanced and fair across different platforms. Address any potential advantages or disadvantages that specific platforms may have.

## Performance Monitoring and Analytics

Implement performance monitoring and analytics tools to gather data on player behavior, server performance, and gameplay balance. This data can be invaluable for making informed decisions and optimizations.

- **Player Metrics:** Monitor player engagement, retention, and churn rates to understand player behavior and preferences.

- **Server Metrics:** Gather server performance data, including CPU and memory usage, network latency, and error rates, to identify and address issues promptly.

- **Gameplay Metrics:** Collect data on player interactions, such as kills, deaths, and ability usage, to assess balance and identify areas for improvement.

- **Heatmaps:** Use heatmaps to visualize player movement and hotspots on maps, helping you adjust level design and balance.

## Player Feedback and Iteration

Encourage player feedback and iterate on your multiplayer features based on that feedback. Maintain open communication channels with your player community and actively address their concerns and suggestions.

- **Feedback Channels:** Provide players with convenient ways to submit feedback, report issues, and share suggestions. Actively listen to and acknowledge player feedback.

- **Regular Updates:** Keep the game fresh and engaging with regular updates and content additions based on player preferences and feedback.

- **Transparency:** Maintain transparency in your development process. Share development roadmaps, patch notes, and upcoming features with your community.

In conclusion, testing and optimizing multiplayer features in Unreal Engine are critical for delivering a smooth, fair, and engaging multiplayer experience. By addressing latency, server and client performance, balance issues, and player feedback, you can create a multiplayer game that captivates and retains players.

# Chapter 10: Using Physics and Simulations

## Section 10.1: Physics Engine Basics in Unreal

Unreal Engine includes a powerful and robust physics engine that allows developers to create realistic interactions and simulations within their games. Understanding the basics of the physics engine is essential for implementing dynamic and immersive experiences. In this section, we will explore the fundamental concepts and features of the physics engine in Unreal Engine.

### Introduction to the Physics Engine

Unreal Engine's physics engine is based on NVIDIA's PhysX technology, which provides advanced physics simulation capabilities. It allows you to simulate the behavior of objects, characters, vehicles, and more, making your game world feel dynamic and responsive.

The physics engine in Unreal Engine is responsible for handling various aspects of the virtual world, including:

- **Collision Detection:** Detecting when objects in the game world interact with each other, whether through collisions or overlaps.

- **Physics Simulation:** Simulating the movement and behavior of objects based on physical properties like mass, friction, and gravity.

- **Ragdoll Physics:** Simulating the realistic motion of characters or creatures when they are affected by external forces or animations.

- **Vehicles and Constraints:** Implementing complex interactions such as vehicle physics and physics-based constraints between objects.

### Physics Objects and Components

In Unreal Engine, you work with physics through various objects and components. Some of the essential elements include:

- **Static Meshes:** These are non-moving objects with physical representations. They are used for level geometry, props, and environmental objects.

- **Skeletal Meshes:** These are used for characters and creatures and can have physics-enabled bones for realistic animations and ragdoll effects.

- **Physics Assets:** Physics assets define the physical properties and constraints of skeletal meshes, allowing for precise control over how they react to forces.

- **Collision Components:** Actors in Unreal Engine often have collision components that define their physical boundaries. These components can be simple shapes like spheres, boxes, or complex concave shapes.

## Setting Up Physics

To enable physics in Unreal Engine, you need to follow these steps:

81. **Enable Physics Simulation:** For each object or actor that needs physics simulation, you enable physics simulation by toggling the "Simulate Physics" checkbox in the object's details panel.

82. **Configuring Mass and Physical Properties:** You can adjust the mass, friction, restitution (bounciness), and other physical properties to fine-tune how an object behaves.

83. **Collision Setup:** Configure collision settings for objects to determine how they interact with other objects, such as blocking, overlapping, or generating hit events.

84. **Constraints and Joints:** If your game requires complex interactions between objects, you can use constraints and joints to define how they connect and move together.

## Physics Debugging

Unreal Engine provides various tools for debugging and visualizing physics interactions. These tools help you identify issues and fine-tune physics simulations:

- **Collision Visibility:** You can toggle the visibility of collision shapes to visualize how objects collide and interact.

- **Physics Debug Views:** Unreal Engine offers debug views that show physics shapes, constraints, and collision channels, making it easier to diagnose physics-related problems.

- **Ragdoll Visualization:** When working with ragdolls, you can enable visualization modes to see how skeletal meshes react to forces and animations.

## Performance Considerations

While physics simulation can add realism to your game, it can also be resource-intensive. To optimize performance:

- **Use Simple Collision Shapes:** For objects that don't require precise collision detection, use simpler collision shapes like spheres or capsules to reduce computational overhead.

- **Adjust Physics Detail Levels:** Unreal Engine allows you to set different levels of detail for physics simulation, reducing complexity for distant objects.

- **Limit the Use of Physics Constraints:** Complex constraints can impact performance. Use them judiciously, and consider alternatives for simpler interactions.

- **Profiling:** Use profiling tools to identify performance bottlenecks related to physics simulation, and optimize accordingly.

In summary, Unreal Engine's physics engine offers powerful tools for creating realistic interactions and simulations in your games. Understanding the basics of physics objects, components, and simulation setup is crucial for implementing dynamic and immersive gameplay experiences. Properly configured physics can greatly enhance the realism and immersion of your game.

---

## Section 10.2: Implementing Realistic Physics Behaviors

Implementing realistic physics behaviors is a key aspect of creating immersive and dynamic experiences in Unreal Engine. In this section, we'll explore how to achieve realistic physics interactions for objects and characters in your game.

### Physics Materials

Physics materials allow you to define how objects interact with each other in terms of friction, restitution (bounciness), and other physical properties. Unreal Engine provides a system for creating and applying physics materials to objects and surfaces.

To create a physics material, follow these steps:

85. In the Content Browser, right-click and choose "Physics Material."
86. Configure the properties of the physics material, including friction and restitution.
87. Apply the physics material to a Static Mesh or other objects by setting its Physical Material property.

By adjusting the values of friction and restitution in your physics materials, you can control how objects slide, bounce, or react to forces, making interactions in your game more realistic.

### Ragdoll Physics

Ragdoll physics is commonly used for simulating the motion of characters and creatures when they are affected by external forces, such as collisions or explosions. Unreal Engine provides a robust system for setting up and controlling ragdoll physics for skeletal meshes.

To implement ragdoll physics for a character, follow these steps:

88. Create a physics asset for the character's skeletal mesh. This asset defines the physical properties of bones and how they are connected.

89. Enable ragdoll physics by setting the "Ragdoll" option to "Physics Asset" in the character's details panel.

90. Configure bone constraints and limits in the physics asset to control how the character's body reacts to external forces.

91. Define hit reactions and animations that transition smoothly between ragdoll and animated states.

Ragdoll physics can add realism to character animations, making them respond convincingly to in-game events.

## Vehicle Physics

If your game includes vehicles, Unreal Engine provides a comprehensive vehicle physics system that allows you to create realistic vehicle behaviors. You can simulate various types of vehicles, from cars to tanks, and adjust parameters like suspension, tire friction, and handling characteristics.

To implement vehicle physics:

92. Create a Vehicle Blueprint, specifying the vehicle's mesh, wheels, and other components.

93. Adjust vehicle settings, such as mass, suspension, and tire properties, to achieve the desired behavior.

94. Use the VehicleMovementComponent to handle vehicle physics and input controls.

95. Implement additional features like engine sounds, headlights, and vehicle animations to enhance the player's experience.

By fine-tuning the parameters and controls in the Vehicle Blueprint, you can create realistic and responsive vehicles in your game.

## Cloth Simulation

Unreal Engine supports cloth simulation, allowing you to create realistic cloth and fabric behavior for characters and objects. Cloth simulation is commonly used for clothing, flags, banners, and other flexible surfaces.

To implement cloth simulation:

96. Import a Skeletal Mesh or Static Mesh that requires cloth simulation.

97. Enable cloth simulation by adding a Cloth Component to the object.

98. Configure the cloth properties, including mass, damping, and stiffness, to control how the cloth responds to forces.

99. Use the Cloth Paint tool to define how the cloth is attached to the character or object.

Cloth simulation adds a level of realism to your game by making cloth and fabric move naturally in response to character movements and environmental forces.

### Fluid Simulation

Unreal Engine also supports fluid simulation through plugins and third-party solutions. While the engine itself does not provide built-in fluid simulation, you can integrate external plugins or tools to create realistic fluid behavior, such as water, smoke, or fire.

When implementing fluid simulation:

100. Choose a suitable fluid simulation solution or plugin that integrates with Unreal Engine.
101. Configure the parameters of the fluid simulation, including fluid density, viscosity, and initial conditions.
102. Integrate the fluid simulation into your game world and ensure it interacts realistically with other objects and characters.

Fluid simulation can enhance the visual quality and realism of your game's environments, especially for scenes involving liquids or gaseous effects.

In conclusion, Unreal Engine offers versatile tools and systems for implementing realistic physics behaviors in your game. Whether you're simulating object interactions, character movements, vehicle dynamics, cloth behavior, or fluid simulations, understanding these features and how to configure them is essential for creating engaging and immersive gameplay experiences.

---

## Section 10.3: Creating Environmental Effects

Creating environmental effects in Unreal Engine allows you to enhance the realism and immersion of your game world. These effects can include things like weather, destruction, and environmental interactions. In this section, we'll explore how to implement various environmental effects to make your game world more dynamic and engaging.

### Weather Systems

Weather systems can add depth and atmosphere to your game's environments. Unreal Engine provides tools and techniques to create realistic weather effects such as rain, snow, fog, and wind.

#### *Rain and Snow*

To implement rain or snow in your game, you can use particle systems to generate precipitation effects. These particle systems can simulate raindrops or snowflakes falling from the sky. You can control parameters like particle density, size, and movement to achieve the desired look and behavior.

You can also enhance the effect by adding sound effects, such as rain or snowfall sounds, to create a more immersive experience. Additionally, you may want to adjust the lighting and materials to reflect the wet or snowy environment accurately.

## Fog

Fog is an essential element for creating atmospheric scenes. Unreal Engine's fog settings allow you to control the density, color, and distance of the fog. You can use fog to obscure distant objects, create a sense of depth, and evoke different moods in your game.

Dynamic fog can be particularly useful for games that involve changing weather conditions. By adjusting fog settings over time, you can simulate transitions between clear skies and thick fog, enhancing gameplay variety.

## Wind

Implementing wind in your game can affect various elements, including foliage, particles, and cloth simulation. You can use the Wind Actor to define wind zones within your levels. Objects within these zones will react to the wind's direction and strength.

For example, trees and grass can sway in the wind, particles can follow wind patterns, and cloth materials can flutter realistically. This adds a dynamic element to your environments and makes them feel more alive.

## Destruction and Destructible Objects

Destructible objects allow players to interact with the game world in a tangible way. Unreal Engine provides a destructible mesh system that enables you to create objects that can break apart realistically when subjected to forces.

To implement destructible objects:

103. Create a Destructible Mesh by fracturing a static mesh into smaller pieces.

104. Set up collision properties for the destructible mesh to ensure that it reacts correctly to player interactions.

105. Apply damage to the destructible mesh, and it will break into pieces dynamically based on its fracture settings.

Destructible objects can be used for creating dynamic destruction sequences, destructible environments, or interactive puzzles within your game.

## Interactive Environmental Objects

Interactive environmental objects can add depth and interactivity to your game world. These objects can include things like switches, levers, doors, and movable props.

To implement interactive environmental objects:

106. Create a blueprint for the object and define its behavior and interactions.

107. Set up collision and physics properties to ensure that the object reacts correctly to player actions.

108. Implement logic to handle player interactions, such as triggering animations, moving objects, or changing the state of the environment.

By creating interactive environmental objects, you can design puzzles, challenges, or gameplay mechanics that engage players and encourage exploration.

## Dynamic Day-Night Cycles

Implementing a dynamic day-night cycle can have a profound impact on your game's atmosphere and visual appeal. Unreal Engine provides a Day/Night Cycle system that allows you to simulate the passage of time, changing lighting conditions, and dynamic skyboxes.

To create a dynamic day-night cycle:

109. Set up directional light and skylight components to mimic the sun's movement and changing angles.

110. Use Blueprint scripting to control the rotation of the directional light and adjust the sky and atmospheric settings.

111. Animate the cycle over time, simulating day and night transitions.

A dynamic day-night cycle can influence gameplay elements, such as visibility, enemy behavior, or mission objectives. It also adds variety to your game's environments and keeps players engaged.

In conclusion, implementing environmental effects in Unreal Engine allows you to create immersive and dynamic game worlds. By leveraging weather systems, destructible objects, interactive environmental elements, and dynamic day-night cycles, you can enhance the realism and player engagement in your game. These techniques add depth and atmosphere to your levels, making them more captivating and memorable for players.

## Section 10.4: Simulation Tools and Techniques

In Unreal Engine, simulation tools and techniques play a crucial role in creating immersive and dynamic experiences. These tools enable you to simulate various aspects of your game world, from complex physics interactions to realistic AI behaviors. In this section, we'll explore some of the simulation tools and techniques available in Unreal Engine.

Blueprint Visual Scripting is Unreal Engine's node-based scripting system that allows designers and developers to create gameplay logic without writing code. It's a powerful tool for simulating game behaviors, interactions, and events.

With Blueprint Visual Scripting, you can:

- **Create Custom Gameplay:** Develop custom game mechanics, player abilities, and interactive objects by connecting nodes and defining logic.

- **Simulate AI Behaviors:** Design AI behaviors and decision-making processes for NPCs and enemies, including pathfinding, combat tactics, and more.

- **Implement Triggers and Events:** Set up triggers, events, and conditions that drive the progression of your game, such as quest objectives, cutscenes, and scripted sequences.

- **Prototype Quickly:** Rapidly prototype and iterate on game features and mechanics to test gameplay concepts and ideas.

Blueprint Visual Scripting provides a visual and intuitive way to simulate game logic and interactions, making it accessible to a wide range of developers and designers.

## Behavior Trees and AI

Unreal Engine offers a Behavior Tree system for creating complex AI behaviors. Behavior Trees allow you to simulate decision-making processes for NPCs and control their actions based on various factors and conditions.

Key components of Behavior Trees include:

- **Blackboard:** A data storage system that stores variables and information used by the Behavior Tree to make decisions.

- **Tasks:** Individual actions that AI characters can perform, such as moving, attacking, or interacting with objects.

- **Decorators:** Conditions that determine whether a task should execute or abort based on specific criteria.

- **Composite Nodes:** Organizational nodes that define the structure and flow of the tree, including sequences, selectors, and parallel nodes.

By designing Behavior Trees, you can simulate realistic AI behaviors, such as enemy patrols, squad coordination, and decision-making based on sensory input.

## Chaos Physics

Chaos Physics is a physics simulation system within Unreal Engine that allows for highly realistic and dynamic physics interactions. It can be used to simulate the destruction of environments, realistic vehicle physics, and complex object interactions.

Chaos Physics includes features such as:

- **Fracturing:** Creating detailed fractures and destruction effects for objects.

- **Advanced Vehicles:** Simulating complex vehicle dynamics, including suspension, tire physics, and soft-body simulation.

- **Cloth Simulation:** Generating realistic cloth and fabric behavior.

Chaos Physics offers a high level of fidelity for simulating physical interactions in your game world, making it suitable for applications that require advanced physics simulation.

## Level Sequencer

Level Sequencer is a cinematic tool in Unreal Engine that allows you to create and simulate complex cinematic sequences, cutscenes, and animations. It's particularly useful for storytelling and narrative-driven games.

With Level Sequencer, you can:

- **Animate Actors:** Animate characters, objects, and cameras within your scenes to create cinematic sequences.

- **Control Timings:** Set up precise timings for animations, camera movements, and events to synchronize with your game's narrative.

- **Trigger Events:** Trigger in-game events, such as dialogue, scripted actions, and particle effects, as part of your cinematic sequences.

Level Sequencer provides a visual interface for simulating and controlling cinematic experiences, allowing you to craft compelling narratives in your game.

## Gameplay Debugger

The Gameplay Debugger is a tool that helps developers simulate and diagnose gameplay issues during development. It provides real-time insights into the state of your game, including AI behavior, variables, and events.

With the Gameplay Debugger, you can:

- **Simulate AI Behaviors:** Debug and simulate AI decisions, paths, and actions to identify issues or fine-tune AI behavior.

- **Inspect Variables:** View and modify variables and properties of in-game objects, allowing you to simulate different game states.

- **Record and Playback:** Record gameplay sessions and play them back for debugging and analysis.

The Gameplay Debugger is a valuable tool for simulating and troubleshooting gameplay scenarios, ensuring that your game behaves as intended.

In conclusion, Unreal Engine offers a wide range of simulation tools and techniques that empower developers to create immersive and dynamic experiences. Whether you're using Blueprint Visual Scripting, Behavior Trees, Chaos Physics, Level Sequencer, or the Gameplay Debugger, these tools allow you to simulate and control various aspects of your game world, from gameplay logic to AI behaviors and cinematic sequences.

---

## Section 10.5: Balancing Realism and Performance

Balancing realism and performance is a critical consideration when developing games in Unreal Engine. While you may want to create realistic and immersive experiences, you also need to ensure that your game runs smoothly on a variety of hardware configurations. In this section, we'll explore techniques for achieving this balance.

### Level of Detail (LOD)

Level of Detail (LOD) is a technique used to optimize the rendering of objects in the game world based on their distance from the camera. Unreal Engine allows you to create multiple versions of an object with decreasing detail levels.

For example, a complex 3D model may have several LODs:

- **High Detail:** Used when the object is close to the camera, providing a highly detailed representation.

- **Medium Detail:** Used as the object moves farther away, reducing polygon count and texture resolution.

- **Low Detail:** Used for distant objects, with further reduced detail to improve performance.

Implementing LODs helps balance realism and performance by ensuring that only the necessary level of detail is rendered, reducing the computational load on the GPU and CPU.

### Occlusion Culling

Occlusion culling is a technique that prevents rendering objects that are not visible to the camera. Unreal Engine employs an automatic occlusion culling system that identifies and hides objects that are obstructed by others or located outside the camera's view frustum.

This technique improves performance by reducing the number of objects rendered, especially in complex scenes with many objects. It allows you to maintain realism in your game world while optimizing rendering performance.

Optimizing materials and textures is crucial for balancing realism and performance. High-resolution textures and complex materials can consume significant GPU memory and impact rendering performance.

To optimize materials and textures:

- Use texture streaming to load high-resolution textures only when they are close to the camera.

- Compress textures to reduce memory usage without sacrificing visual quality.

- Use material instances to create variations of materials with different properties, allowing you to reuse shaders and reduce GPU overhead.

- Simplify or combine materials where possible to reduce draw calls and rendering complexity.

Balancing the visual fidelity of materials and textures with their impact on performance is essential for achieving a smooth gameplay experience.

## Lightmap Resolution

Lightmaps are essential for realistic lighting and shadows in your game. However, high-resolution lightmaps can increase memory usage and loading times. Balancing lightmap resolution is crucial.

To optimize lightmaps:

- Adjust the lightmap resolution for objects based on their importance and visibility in the scene.

- Use Lightmass Importance Volumes to specify areas that require higher-quality lighting.

- Bake lighting selectively for specific objects or areas to control the quality of indirect lighting.

By carefully managing lightmap resolution, you can maintain realism in lighting and shadows while optimizing performance.

## LODs for Skeletal Meshes

In addition to static objects, LODs are also applicable to skeletal meshes used for characters and creatures. Implementing LODs for skeletal meshes involves creating simplified versions of character models for use at different distances from the camera.

This technique reduces the polygon count and animation complexity of characters when they are far from the camera, improving CPU and GPU performance. It allows you to balance realism and performance for character rendering.

## Particle System Optimization

Particle systems are commonly used for various visual effects in games. However, poorly optimized particle systems can impact performance significantly.

To optimize particle systems:

- Limit the number of active particles and particle emitters in complex scenes.

- Use GPU particle simulation for improved performance on compatible hardware.

- Adjust particle LOD settings to reduce the particle count as objects move farther from the camera.

Balancing the visual impact of particle effects with their performance impact is essential for maintaining a smooth frame rate.

## Performance Testing and Profiling

To find the right balance between realism and performance, it's crucial to conduct performance testing and profiling throughout development. Unreal Engine provides built-in profiling tools that help identify performance bottlenecks and areas that require optimization.

Use tools like the Unreal Insights profiler, GPU Visualizer, and CPU Profiler to monitor and analyze performance metrics. Regular testing on different hardware configurations can also help ensure that your game runs smoothly for a wide audience.

In conclusion, achieving a balance between realism and performance is a fundamental aspect of game development in Unreal Engine. By implementing LODs, occlusion culling, optimizing materials and textures, managing lightmap resolution, using LODs for skeletal meshes, optimizing particle systems, and conducting performance testing, you can create games that offer immersive experiences while running smoothly on various hardware platforms. Balancing these aspects is crucial for delivering a compelling and accessible gaming experience to players.

# Chapter 11: Advanced Lighting and Rendering

## 11.1 Lighting Techniques in Unreal Engine

In this section, we will delve into the various advanced lighting techniques available in Unreal Engine. Proper lighting is crucial for creating visually stunning and immersive game environments. Unreal Engine provides a wide range of tools and features to achieve realistic and captivating lighting effects.

### 11.1.1 Dynamic and Static Lighting

Unreal Engine distinguishes between two main types of lighting: dynamic and static. Dynamic lighting is calculated in real-time and is suitable for moving objects and changing environments. It includes features like dynamic shadows and light shafts, which contribute to the realism of your game. However, dynamic lighting can be resource-intensive, so it's essential to use it judiciously to maintain performance.

Static lighting, on the other hand, is precomputed and baked into the environment. It's suitable for static objects and environments where lighting doesn't change frequently. Unreal Engine's Lightmass system is used for baking static lighting, and it can produce highly realistic results. Baked lighting is efficient in terms of performance but lacks the flexibility of dynamic lighting.

### 11.1.2 Special Effects and Post-Processing

Unreal Engine offers a variety of special effects and post-processing features to enhance the visual quality of your game. These effects can simulate various phenomena such as lens flares, bloom, motion blur, and depth of field. Post-processing can be customized and applied to different parts of the game world, allowing you to achieve specific artistic styles and atmospheres.

To implement post-processing effects, you can use Unreal's Material Editor to create custom post-process materials. These materials can be applied to cameras or specific objects, giving you fine-grained control over the visual effects.

### 11.1.3 Rendering Optimization Techniques

Optimizing rendering performance is crucial to ensure your game runs smoothly on a variety of hardware configurations. Unreal Engine provides several techniques for rendering optimization:

#### 11.1.3.1 Level of Detail (LOD)

Level of Detail (LOD) is a technique that involves using different versions of a 3D model at varying levels of detail. When an object is far away from the camera, a simplified version of the model is used, reducing the number of polygons rendered. As the object gets closer, higher-detail models are gradually swapped in. Implementing LOD can significantly improve performance by reducing the GPU workload.

Here's an example of how to set up LODs for a static mesh in Unreal Engine:

```
// Unreal Engine LOD setup example
StaticMeshComponent->SetForcedLod(1); // Use LOD 1 when the object is at a distance
StaticMeshComponent->SetLODDistanceFactor(1, 0.5); // Adjust LOD transition distance
```

### 11.1.3.2 Culling Techniques

Culling involves determining which objects should be rendered and which can be culled (skipped) to save rendering resources. Unreal Engine employs various culling techniques, including frustum culling (removing objects outside the camera's view frustum), occlusion culling (hiding objects blocked by others), and distance-based culling.

```
// Example of enabling occlusion culling in Unreal Engine
Engine->GetView()->Family->EngineShowFlags.Occlusion = true;
```

### 11.1.3.3 Lightmap Resolution Optimization

Baked lighting in Unreal Engine relies on lightmaps, which are textures used to store lighting information. You can optimize rendering performance by adjusting the resolution of lightmaps. Higher resolution lightmaps result in more detailed lighting but require more memory and GPU power. You can balance visual quality and performance by carefully choosing lightmap resolutions for different objects in your level.

```
// Adjusting lightmap resolution for a static mesh
StaticMeshComponent->OverrideLightMapRes(512);
```

### 11.1.4 Achieving Photorealism

Photorealism is the ultimate goal for many game developers, aiming to create environments and assets that closely resemble real-world counterparts. Unreal Engine offers tools like ray tracing, global illumination, and high-fidelity materials to achieve photorealistic visuals. These advanced features can simulate real-world lighting behaviors, resulting in stunning graphics.

In the next subsections, we will explore these advanced lighting techniques and how to implement them effectively in Unreal Engine.

---

## 11.2 Working with Dynamic and Static Lighting

In this section, we will delve deeper into the concepts of dynamic and static lighting in Unreal Engine, exploring their advantages, use cases, and how to effectively work with them in your game development projects.

Dynamic lighting in Unreal Engine refers to lighting that is calculated and updated in real-time as the game runs. This type of lighting is well-suited for objects, characters, and environments where lighting conditions change frequently. Here are some key points to consider when working with dynamic lighting:

112. **Realism and Flexibility**: Dynamic lighting can provide a high level of realism as it accurately simulates real-world lighting conditions. This includes dynamic shadows, specular reflections, and light attenuation. It allows for dynamic day-night cycles and interactive lighting elements.

113. **Performance Considerations**: While dynamic lighting offers realism and flexibility, it can also be resource-intensive. Real-time calculations of lighting and shadows can put a significant load on the GPU and CPU. It's essential to optimize and balance dynamic lighting to ensure smooth gameplay.

114. **Dynamic Shadows**: Unreal Engine supports dynamic shadows, allowing objects to cast and receive real-time shadows. This enhances the visual quality of your game but comes at a cost in terms of performance. You can adjust the shadow quality and distance to optimize performance.

Here's an example of enabling dynamic shadows for a directional light in Unreal Engine:

```
// Enabling dynamic shadows for a directional light
DirectionalLightComponent->SetCastDynamicShadows(true);
```

5. **Light Mobility**: In Unreal Engine, lights can have different mobility settings, such as Static, Stationary, and Movable. Dynamic lights are typically set to Movable, which means they can change position and properties in real-time. However, keep in mind that Movable lights are more performance-intensive than Stationary or Static lights.

Static Lighting

Static lighting, as the name suggests, is precomputed and baked into the game's environment. It's suitable for objects, levels, and environments where lighting conditions do not change during gameplay. Static lighting provides several advantages:

115. **Performance Optimization**: Baked lighting is highly optimized for performance since the calculations are done in advance and stored in lightmaps. This results in faster rendering times and better frame rates.

116. **Lightmap Resolution**: When working with static lighting, you can control the resolution of lightmaps for individual objects. Higher resolution lightmaps provide more detailed lighting but require more memory. You can adjust lightmap resolutions to balance quality and performance.

```
// Adjusting lightmap resolution for a static mesh
StaticMeshComponent->OverrideLightMapRes(512);
```

4. **Lightmass**: Unreal Engine uses a tool called Lightmass to generate high-quality baked lighting. Lightmass takes into account various factors such as indirect lighting, bounce, and occlusion to create realistic lighting results. You can fine-tune Lightmass settings to achieve the desired lighting quality.

5. **Stability**: Since static lighting is precomputed, it offers stable and consistent lighting throughout the game. This can be advantageous for architectural visualization, interior design, and other applications where lighting accuracy is crucial.

In Unreal Engine, you can set the mobility of lights to Static for objects that do not need real-time lighting updates. This is typically done for static meshes that are part of the game's architecture or environment.

```
// Setting the mobility of a light to Static
PointLightComponent->SetMobility(EComponentMobility::Static);
```

6. **Reflections**: Baked lighting also affects reflections in your game. Unreal Engine uses reflection captures to capture and precompute reflections based on the static lighting information. These reflection captures enhance the visual quality of reflective surfaces in your game.

In conclusion, understanding the differences between dynamic and static lighting in Unreal Engine is crucial for creating visually appealing and well-performing game environments. Your choice between dynamic and static lighting should be based on the specific requirements of your game, balancing realism with performance considerations. Unreal Engine provides a versatile set of tools and settings to help you achieve the desired lighting effects for your project.

## 11.3 Special Effects and Post-Processing

In this section, we will explore the world of special effects and post-processing in Unreal Engine. These elements play a crucial role in enhancing the visual quality and realism of your game by simulating various optical phenomena and applying adjustments to the final rendered image.

### Special Effects

Special effects in Unreal Engine encompass a wide range of visual enhancements that can be applied to create specific atmospheric and artistic styles. These effects are often used to mimic real-world optical phenomena or to achieve a particular mood or tone in the game. Let's delve into some common special effects and how to implement them:

117. **Bloom**: Bloom is an effect that simulates the way light scatters and creates a halo or "glow" around bright objects. It adds a soft, dreamy quality to the scene. To enable

bloom in Unreal Engine, you can use post-process volume settings or adjust the bloom intensity in the camera settings.

```
// Enabling bloom in a post-process volume
PostProcessVolume->Settings.bOverride_BloomIntensity = true;
PostProcessVolume->Settings.BloomIntensity = 1.5f; // Adjust intensity as nee
ded
```

3. **Lens Flares**: Lens flares are artifacts caused by the scattering of light within camera lenses. They are often used to create dramatic or cinematic visual effects. Unreal Engine provides lens flare components that you can attach to lights in your scene.

```
// Adding a lens flare component to a light source
LightComponent->LensFlareSettings->bEnableLensFlare = true;
LightComponent->LensFlareSettings->LensFlareIntensity = 0.8f;
```

6. **Motion Blur**: Motion blur simulates the blurring of fast-moving objects in a scene, adding a sense of motion and realism. Unreal Engine allows you to enable motion blur in the camera settings or post-process volume settings.

```
// Enabling motion blur in a post-process volume
PostProcessVolume->Settings.bOverride_MotionBlurAmount = true;
PostProcessVolume->Settings.MotionBlurAmount = 0.5f; // Adjust the amount of
motion blur
```

6. **Depth of Field**: Depth of field is an effect that simulates the way camera lenses focus on specific objects, while blurring objects in the foreground and background. This effect can be used for cinematic shots or to draw the player's attention to a particular subject.

```
// Enabling depth of field in a post-process volume
PostProcessVolume->Settings.bOverride_DepthOfFieldFocalDistance = true;
PostProcessVolume->Settings.DepthOfFieldFocalDistance = 500.0f; // Adjust foc
al distance
```

5. **Chromatic Aberration**: Chromatic aberration simulates the dispersion of light into its constituent colors at the edges of objects in a scene. It can create a subtle but immersive effect when used sparingly.

```
// Enabling chromatic aberration in a post-process volume
PostProcessVolume->Settings.bOverride_ChromaticAberrationIntensity = true;
PostProcessVolume->Settings.ChromaticAberrationIntensity = 0.1f; // Adjust in
tensity
```

Post-Processing

Post-processing involves applying adjustments and filters to the final rendered image. Unreal Engine offers a comprehensive set of post-processing features that can be customized to achieve the desired visual style. Here are some key aspects of post-processing:

118. **Post-Process Volume**: Unreal Engine allows you to define post-process settings using volumes placed in your level. These volumes can have different settings and

can be used to transition between different visual styles as the player progresses through the game.

119. **Global Settings**: You can set global post-processing settings that apply to the entire game or specific levels. These settings can include color grading, contrast, saturation, and more.

```
// Adjusting global post-processing settings
GEngine->DefaultPostProcessSettings.ColorSaturation = 1.2f; // Increase satur
ation
GEngine->DefaultPostProcessSettings.AutoExposureBias = 0.5f; // Adjust exposu
re
```

7. **Material-Based Effects**: Unreal Engine allows you to create custom post-process materials to apply specific effects to the scene. These materials can be used for effects like vignetting, color correction, or custom shaders.

```
// Applying a custom post-process material to a camera
PostProcessComponent->AddOrUpdateBlendable(MyCustomPostProcessMaterial);
```

7. **Blendable Effects**: You can combine multiple post-process settings and materials by stacking them as blendable effects. This allows for complex and layered post-processing setups.

```
// Adding multiple blendable effects to a camera
PostProcessComponent->AddOrUpdateBlendable(BloomEffect);
PostProcessComponent->AddOrUpdateBlendable(LensFlareEffect);
```

5. **Optimization**: While post-processing adds visual quality, it can also be performance-intensive. It's essential to strike a balance between visual effects and performance, especially on lower-end hardware. Unreal Engine provides tools to optimize post-processing for different platforms and configurations.

In conclusion, special effects and post-processing are powerful tools in Unreal Engine for enhancing the visual quality and cinematic appeal of your game. Whether you aim to create a realistic and immersive experience or an artistic and stylized world, understanding and mastering these techniques will allow you to achieve your desired visual goals. Experimentation and fine-tuning are key to finding the perfect balance of effects for your game's unique aesthetic.

---

## 11.4 Rendering Optimization Techniques

In this section, we will explore various rendering optimization techniques in Unreal Engine. Optimizing rendering performance is crucial to ensure that your game runs smoothly on a wide range of hardware configurations, delivering a satisfying gaming experience to players.

## 11.4.1 Level of Detail (LOD)

Level of Detail (LOD) is a technique used to manage the complexity of 3D models as they appear at different distances from the camera. The idea is to use simplified versions of models when they are far away to reduce the number of polygons rendered, thus improving performance. As objects get closer to the camera, higher-detail versions of the models are progressively swapped in.

In Unreal Engine, you can create LODs for static meshes and skeletal meshes to control their visual fidelity at different distances. Here's an example of setting up LODs for a static mesh:

```
// Unreal Engine LOD setup example
StaticMeshComponent->SetForcedLod(1); // Use LOD 1 when the object is at a distance
StaticMeshComponent->SetLODDistanceFactor(1, 0.5); // Adjust LOD transition distance
```

It's essential to find the right balance between visual quality and performance by tweaking LOD settings for your assets.

## 11.4.2 Culling Techniques

Culling techniques are used to determine which objects should be rendered and which can be culled (skipped) to save rendering resources. Unreal Engine employs various culling methods to improve performance:

- **Frustum Culling**: This technique involves removing objects that are outside the camera's view frustum. Objects that are not visible to the player are automatically culled, reducing unnecessary rendering work.

  ```
  // Example of enabling frustum culling in Unreal Engine
  Object->SetIsTemporarilyHiddenInEditor(true);
  ```

- **Occlusion Culling**: Occlusion culling is used to hide objects that are entirely or partially obscured by other objects. It prevents rendering objects that are not visible due to occlusion, further improving performance.

  ```
  // Example of enabling occlusion culling in Unreal Engine
  Engine->GetView()->Family->EngineShowFlags.Occlusion = true;
  ```

- **Distance-Based Culling**: Objects that are far away from the camera can be culled if they are beyond a certain distance threshold. Unreal Engine allows you to define custom distance-based culling rules for optimization.

  ```
  // Example of enabling distance-based culling in Unreal Engine
  Object->SetIsDistanceCulled(true);
  ```

### 11.4.3 Lightmap Resolution Optimization

Lightmaps play a significant role in static lighting within Unreal Engine. They are used to store lighting information for objects and environments. Adjusting the resolution of lightmaps can have a substantial impact on both visual quality and performance.

Higher-resolution lightmaps result in more detailed lighting but also require more memory and GPU power. You can balance visual quality and performance by carefully choosing lightmap resolutions for different objects in your level. Unreal Engine provides settings to override lightmap resolutions on a per-object basis.

```
// Adjusting lightmap resolution for a static mesh
StaticMeshComponent->OverrideLightMapRes(512);
```

### 11.4.4 Material Optimization

Materials in Unreal Engine can have a significant impact on rendering performance. Complex and computationally expensive materials can strain the GPU and affect frame rates negatively. Here are some material optimization techniques:

- **Material Complexity**: Use the Material Complexity view mode to identify materials that are particularly complex and may impact performance. Simplify or optimize these materials where possible.

- **Material Instances**: Use material instances to create variations of a base material. Material instances are more efficient and allow you to tweak material parameters at runtime without incurring the cost of recreating the material from scratch.

- **Texture Compression**: Compress textures where appropriate to reduce memory usage and improve rendering performance. Unreal Engine provides various texture compression settings, including options for normal maps, roughness maps, and more.

- **Shader Complexity**: Monitor shader complexity using the Shader Complexity view mode. High shader complexity can lead to performance bottlenecks. Simplify shaders and reduce the number of shader instructions if necessary.

### 11.4.5 GPU Profiling and Optimization Tools

Unreal Engine offers GPU profiling and optimization tools to help you identify performance bottlenecks and optimize rendering. These tools provide insights into GPU usage, draw calls, and other performance-related metrics.

- **GPU Visualizer**: The GPU Visualizer tool in Unreal Engine's viewport provides a visual representation of GPU usage and can help you identify areas of optimization.

- **Stat Commands**: Unreal Engine provides a range of stat commands that allow you to gather performance statistics during gameplay. Use these commands to track GPU usage and identify areas that need optimization.

- **GPU Profiler**: Unreal Engine's GPU profiler allows you to analyze GPU performance in detail, helping you pinpoint specific rendering issues and bottlenecks.

Optimizing rendering performance in Unreal Engine requires a combination of techniques and tools. By carefully managing LODs, implementing culling techniques, optimizing materials, and using GPU profiling tools, you can ensure that your game delivers a smooth and enjoyable experience on a variety of hardware configurations. Regular testing and iteration are key to achieving optimal rendering performance in your Unreal Engine projects.

## 11.5 Achieving Photorealism

In this section, we will explore the quest for achieving photorealism in your Unreal Engine projects. Photorealism is the goal of creating game environments and assets that closely resemble their real-world counterparts, delivering an immersive and visually stunning experience to players.

### 11.5.1 Ray Tracing

One of the most significant advancements in Unreal Engine for achieving photorealism is the introduction of ray tracing. Ray tracing is a rendering technique that simulates the way light interacts with objects in the real world. It models the behavior of light rays as they bounce off surfaces, refract through materials, and create shadows and reflections.

Unreal Engine's ray tracing features include:

- **Global Illumination**: Ray tracing enables accurate global illumination, which means that indirect lighting from surfaces is realistically simulated. This results in more natural and convincing lighting in your scenes.

```
// Enabling ray traced global illumination in Unreal Engine
WorldSettings->bUseRayTracingGlobalIllumination = true;
```

- **Realistic Shadows**: Ray tracing produces highly detailed and soft shadows that closely mimic the behavior of light in the real world. This results in soft shadows with accurate penumbra (the transition between light and shadow).

```
// Enabling ray traced shadows in Unreal Engine
DirectionalLightComponent->RayTracingDistanceFieldShadows = true;
```

- **Reflections**: Ray tracing allows for accurate reflections, including reflections of dynamic objects. This feature is especially useful for achieving realistic materials and surfaces.

```
// Enabling ray traced reflections in Unreal Engine
ReflectionCaptureComponent->ReflectionSourceType = EReflectionSourceType::Ray
Tracing;
```

- **Translucency and Refraction**: Ray tracing can also handle complex materials with transparency and refraction. This is essential for realistic glass, water, and other transparent materials.

```
// Enabling ray traced translucency in Unreal Engine
Material->TranslucencyType = ETranslucencyType::RayTracing;
```

It's important to note that ray tracing is computationally intensive and may require powerful hardware to achieve real-time performance. However, it can significantly enhance the visual fidelity of your scenes and contribute to photorealism.

### 11.5.2 High-Fidelity Materials

Materials are a crucial component of achieving photorealism in Unreal Engine. Realistic materials are achieved by accurately simulating the physical properties of surfaces, including how they interact with light. Unreal Engine offers a wide range of material features to create high-fidelity materials:

- **Physically Based Rendering (PBR)**: PBR materials are designed to mimic the behavior of real-world materials. They take into account properties like albedo, specular reflection, roughness, and normal maps to achieve accurate surface appearances.

```
// Creating a PBR material in Unreal Engine
Material->SetMaterialDomain(EMaterialDomain::Surface);
Material->SetShadingModel(MSM_DefaultLit);
```

- **Subsurface Scattering**: Subsurface scattering is crucial for materials like skin, wax, and leaves. Unreal Engine allows you to simulate the scattering of light beneath the surface, adding realism to these materials.

```
// Enabling subsurface scattering in a material
Material->MaterialDomain = MD_Surface;
Material->ShadingModel = MSM_Subsurface;
```

- **Anisotropic Shading**: Anisotropic materials exhibit different shading patterns based on the direction of surface microfacets. Unreal Engine supports anisotropic shading for materials like brushed metal or hair.

```
// Enabling anisotropic shading in a material
Material->SetShadingModel(MSM_Anisotropic);
```

- **Material Layering**: Material layering allows you to combine multiple materials and textures to create complex surfaces. This is particularly useful for adding realism to terrain and organic objects.

```
// Creating a material layer blend in Unreal Engine
MaterialLayerBlend->BlendType = MCT_LayerBlend_Standard;
```

### 11.5.3 High-Quality Textures

High-quality textures are essential for achieving photorealism. Unreal Engine supports a variety of texture types, including:

- **High-Resolution Textures**: Use high-resolution texture maps to capture fine details in your assets. These maps include diffuse (albedo), normal, specular, roughness, and displacement maps.

- **Texture Streaming**: Unreal Engine's texture streaming system allows for efficient loading and unloading of textures based on the player's location in the game world. This ensures that high-resolution textures are used where needed, without consuming unnecessary memory.

```
// Adjusting texture streaming settings in Unreal Engine
Engine->TextureStreamingSettings.bTextureStreaming = true;
```

- **Texture Compression**: Optimize texture memory usage by using texture compression formats like BC7 or BC5. Unreal Engine provides options to control texture compression settings for different platforms.

```
// Adjusting texture compression settings in Unreal Engine
Texture->CompressionSettings = TC_BC7;
```

### 11.5.4 Post-Processing and Cinematics

In addition to rendering techniques, post-processing and cinematics play a vital role in achieving photorealism. Post-processing effects like color grading, depth of field, and motion blur can add a cinematic touch to your scenes.

```
// Enabling depth of field and motion blur in Unreal Engine
PostProcessVolume->Settings.bOverride_DepthOfFieldFocalDistance = true;
PostProcessVolume->Settings.DepthOfFieldFocalDistance = 500.0f;
PostProcessVolume->Settings.bOverride_MotionBlurAmount = true;
PostProcessVolume->Settings.MotionBlurAmount = 0.5f;
```

Cinematic tools in Unreal Engine, such as Sequencer, allow you to create highly detailed and realistic cutscenes and animations, further contributing to photorealism.

### 11.5.5 Realistic Sound and Physics

Photorealism isn't limited to visuals alone; it extends to audio and physics. Unreal Engine provides tools for realistic audio spatialization and physics simulations. Using these features, you can enhance the overall immersive experience of your game.

- **Audio Spatialization**: Unreal Engine's audio system supports spatial audio, allowing sounds to be perceived as coming from specific directions and locations within the game world. This enhances the realism of soundscapes.

- **Physics Simulation**: Unreal Engine's physics engine enables realistic object interactions, including collisions, rigid body dynamics, and soft body simulations. Realistic physics contribute to the overall authenticity of your game.

Achieving photorealism in Unreal Engine is a complex and iterative process that requires attention to detail and a deep understanding of the tools and techniques at your disposal. It often involves a combination of advanced rendering, materials, textures, audio, and physics to create a truly immersive and visually stunning experience for players. Regular testing, feedback, and fine-tuning are essential to achieving the desired level of photorealism in your projects.

---

# Chapter 12: Optimizing Game Performance

## 12.1 Understanding Performance Metrics

In this section, we will delve into the world of performance metrics in game development. Understanding performance metrics is essential for identifying and addressing performance bottlenecks, ensuring that your game runs smoothly and provides an enjoyable experience to players.

### 12.1.1 Frame Rate (FPS)

Frame rate, measured in frames per second (FPS), is one of the most critical performance metrics in gaming. It represents how many frames are rendered and displayed on the screen in one second. Higher frame rates generally result in smoother and more responsive gameplay.

- **Monitoring Frame Rate**: Unreal Engine provides built-in tools to monitor and display the frame rate during gameplay. You can enable on-screen frame rate counters to keep track of performance.

```
// Enabling on-screen frame rate counter in Unreal Engine
Engine->bSmoothFrameRate = false;
Engine->bUseFixedFrameRate = false;
Engine->bEnableOnScreenDebugMessages = true;
Engine->OnScreenDebugMessagesClass = UMyGameDebugHUD::StaticClass(); // Use y
our HUD class
```

- **Frame Rate Targets**: It's essential to set a target frame rate that your game aims to achieve. Common targets include 30 FPS, 60 FPS, and 120 FPS, depending on the platform and game type. Unreal Engine allows you to set frame rate targets in project settings.

```
// Setting a frame rate target in Unreal Engine
ProjectSettings->bUseVSync = true;
ProjectSettings->MaxSmoothedFrameRate = 60; // Set your target frame rate
```

### 12.1.2 Frame Time

Frame time is the time taken to render a single frame. It is inversely related to frame rate, meaning that lower frame times correspond to higher frame rates. Analyzing frame times can help identify specific performance issues within a frame.

- **Frame Time Profiling**: Unreal Engine provides tools for profiling frame times. You can use the built-in profiler to identify which parts of the frame are consuming the most time.

```
// Using the Unreal Engine profiler to analyze frame times
Profiler->EnableStatGroup(FGameThreadStats::GetGroupName());
```

- **Optimizing Frame Time**: To optimize frame times, you may need to focus on specific aspects of your game, such as rendering, physics, or AI. Profiling tools can help pinpoint areas that require optimization.

## 12.1.3 GPU and CPU Usage

Monitoring GPU and CPU usage is crucial for understanding the performance impact of various game systems and assets. High GPU or CPU usage can indicate performance bottlenecks.

- **GPU Profiling**: Unreal Engine provides GPU profiling tools to measure GPU usage. You can use these tools to identify which rendering tasks are most demanding on the GPU.

```
// Using GPU profiling in Unreal Engine
Engine->EnableGPUBatchTime(true);
```

- **CPU Profiling**: Profiling the CPU is essential to identify bottlenecks in game logic, physics calculations, and other CPU-bound tasks. Unreal Engine's CPU profiler allows you to analyze CPU usage.

```
// Using CPU profiling in Unreal Engine
Engine->EnableCPUProfiler(true);
```

- **Multi-threading**: Unreal Engine supports multi-threading, allowing you to distribute tasks across multiple CPU cores. Efficient multi-threading can significantly improve CPU performance.

```
// Enabling multi-threading in Unreal Engine
Engine->bUseBackgroundLevelStreaming = true;
Engine->SetMaxFrameTimeAgnosticAsyncTickRate(60);
```

## 12.1.4 Memory Usage

Memory usage is another critical performance metric. Games that consume excessive memory can lead to slowdowns, crashes, or poor performance on systems with limited RAM.

- **Memory Profiling**: Unreal Engine provides memory profiling tools to track memory usage. You can identify memory leaks, unnecessary allocations, and high memory-consuming assets.

```
// Using memory profiling in Unreal Engine
Engine->EnableMemoryProfiler(true);
```

- **Asset Optimization**: Reducing the memory footprint of assets, such as textures, models, and audio files, is essential for optimizing memory usage. Unreal Engine allows you to set asset-specific compression and streaming settings.

```
// Adjusting texture compression settings in Unreal Engine
Texture->CompressionSettings = TC_BC7;
```

### 12.1.5 Network Performance

For multiplayer or online games, network performance is critical. Monitoring metrics like latency, packet loss, and bandwidth usage is essential for delivering a smooth online experience.

- **Network Profiling**: Unreal Engine provides network profiling tools to monitor and analyze network performance. You can use these tools to identify latency issues and packet loss.

```
// Using network profiling in Unreal Engine
Engine->EnableNetworkProfiler(true);
```

- **Optimizing Networking**: Optimizing network performance involves reducing the amount of data sent over the network, implementing client-side prediction, and minimizing the impact of latency.

```
// Implementing client-side prediction in Unreal Engine
PlayerController->SetClientNetSendDeltaTime(0.03f);
```

Understanding and monitoring these performance metrics are fundamental to optimizing your game for a wide range of hardware and ensuring a smooth player experience. Regular profiling, testing, and iteration are essential for identifying and addressing performance bottlenecks in Unreal Engine projects.

---

## 12.2 Profiling and Identifying Bottlenecks

Profiling is a critical process in optimizing game performance in Unreal Engine. It involves gathering data on various aspects of your game's execution to identify performance bottlenecks and areas that require optimization. In this section, we'll explore the importance of profiling and some essential profiling tools and techniques.

### 12.2.1 Importance of Profiling

Profiling allows you to:

- **Identify Performance Bottlenecks**: Profiling helps pinpoint which parts of your game are causing performance issues, such as low frame rates or high CPU usage.

- **Optimize Efficiently**: By identifying specific bottlenecks, you can focus your optimization efforts where they will have the most significant impact, saving time and resources.

- **Measure Progress**: Profiling provides a way to measure the impact of your optimization efforts, ensuring that changes result in improved performance.

- **Maintain Consistency**: Profiling helps ensure that your game maintains consistent performance across different hardware configurations and under various conditions.

## 12.2.2 Profiling Tools

Unreal Engine provides a range of built-in profiling tools and third-party tools that can help you analyze and optimize your game's performance.

### Unreal Insights

Unreal Insights is a built-in profiling tool that provides detailed insights into various aspects of your game's performance, including CPU, GPU, memory, and rendering. It allows you to record and analyze performance data during gameplay.

```
// Enabling Unreal Insights
Edit -> Editor Preferences -> Enable "Unreal Insights" Plugin
```

### Stat Commands

Unreal Engine offers a set of stat commands that allow you to gather performance statistics during gameplay. These commands provide real-time information on aspects like frame rate, CPU usage, GPU usage, and memory usage.

```
// Example of using stat commands in Unreal Engine
stat FPS // Display frame rate statistics
stat Unit // Display CPU and GPU timings
```

### CPU and GPU Profilers

Unreal Engine includes CPU and GPU profilers that allow you to analyze the performance of your game's code and rendering. These profilers can help identify bottlenecks in specific functions or GPU tasks.

```
// Enabling CPU and GPU profilers
Edit -> Editor Preferences -> Enable "Enable advanced GPU profiling" and "Ena
ble advanced CPU profiling"
```

### Third-Party Profiling Tools

In addition to built-in tools, you can use third-party profiling tools like NVIDIA Nsight, Intel Graphics Performance Analyzers, and Visual Studio's built-in profiling tools to gain more in-depth insights into your game's performance.

## 12.2.3 Profiling Workflow

Profiling is an iterative process that involves the following steps:

120. **Set Performance Goals**: Define your performance goals, such as target frame rate, memory usage, and network latency. These goals serve as benchmarks for optimization.

121. **Profile Baseline**: Start by profiling your game without any optimizations to establish a baseline. Record data on frame rate, CPU usage, GPU usage, memory usage, and other relevant metrics.

122. **Identify Bottlenecks**: Analyze the profiling data to identify performance bottlenecks. Look for functions, systems, or assets that consume a disproportionate amount of resources.

123. **Optimize**: Once bottlenecks are identified, focus on optimizing the areas that have the most significant impact on performance. This may involve code optimization, asset optimization, or changes to game logic.

124. **Profile Again**: After making optimizations, profile your game again to measure the impact of your changes. Ensure that your optimizations have improved performance and that new bottlenecks haven't emerged.

125. **Iterate**: Continue the profiling and optimization process iteratively until you achieve your performance goals. Be prepared to revisit and reoptimize as needed.

### 12.2.4 Common Bottlenecks

Profiling can reveal various common bottlenecks in games, including:

- **CPU Bound**: This occurs when the CPU is the limiting factor for performance. It can be caused by complex game logic, physics calculations, or AI processing.

- **GPU Bound**: GPU-bound scenarios happen when the GPU is the performance bottleneck. This can be due to rendering complexity, shader computations, or inefficient GPU utilization.

- **Memory Bound**: Memory bottlenecks result from excessive memory usage, leading to slowdowns or crashes. Profiling can help identify memory leaks and high memory-consuming assets.

- **Network Latency**: In multiplayer or online games, network latency can be a significant bottleneck. Profiling network performance can help identify latency issues and packet loss.

- **Asset Loading**: Loading and unloading assets during gameplay can cause hitches and frame drops. Profiling can help optimize asset streaming and loading processes.

### 12.2.5 Real-Time Profiling

In addition to post-mortem profiling, Unreal Engine allows real-time profiling during gameplay. This means you can analyze performance data while the game is running, making it easier to identify issues as they occur.

Real-time profiling tools, such as Unreal Insights and stat commands, provide immediate feedback on performance, making them invaluable during development and testing phases.

In conclusion, profiling is a crucial aspect of optimizing game performance in Unreal Engine. By using the built-in profiling tools and third-party options, you can identify bottlenecks, measure progress, and ensure that your game delivers a smooth and enjoyable experience to players. Profiling should be an integral part of your game development workflow, helping you achieve your performance goals efficiently and effectively.

---

## 12.3 Techniques for Optimizing Performance

Optimizing performance in Unreal Engine is a crucial aspect of game development, ensuring that your game runs smoothly on a wide range of hardware configurations. In this section, we'll explore various techniques and best practices to help you achieve optimal performance.

### 12.3.1 Level of Detail (LOD)

Level of Detail (LOD) is a fundamental technique for optimizing performance in 3D environments. It involves using simplified versions of models when they are far away from the camera, reducing the number of polygons rendered.

In Unreal Engine, you can set up LODs for static and skeletal meshes. Here are some LOD optimization tips:

- **Use Automatic LOD Generation**: Unreal Engine provides tools for automatically generating LODs for your 3D models. Start with automatic generation and refine them manually if necessary.

- **Consider LOD Transition Distances**: Adjust the distances at which LODs switch to balance visual quality and performance. Closer transitions can be smoother but may impact performance.

- **Optimize LOD Models**: When creating manual LODs, focus on reducing the polygon count while preserving essential details. Remove unnecessary geometry and simplify complex areas.

```
// Setting LOD distances in Unreal Engine
StaticMeshComponent->SetForcedLod(1); // Use LOD 1 when the object is at a di
stance
StaticMeshComponent->SetLODDistanceFactor(1, 0.5); // Adjust LOD transition d
istance
```

### 12.3.2 Occlusion Culling

Occlusion culling is a technique used to hide objects that are entirely or partially obscured by other objects. Unreal Engine employs occlusion culling to improve performance by not rendering objects that are not visible to the player.

Here's how you can optimize occlusion culling:

- **Use Occlusion Volumes**: Place occlusion volumes in your level to define areas where occlusion culling should be active. This helps Unreal Engine determine which objects to cull.

- **Optimize Occluder Meshes**: If you have complex objects that act as occluders, simplify their geometry to reduce the rendering cost when used for occlusion culling.

```
// Enabling occlusion culling in Unreal Engine
Engine->GetView()->Family->EngineShowFlags.Occlusion = true;
```

### 12.3.3 Texture and Material Optimization

Textures and materials can have a significant impact on performance. To optimize them:

- **Texture Compression**: Use appropriate texture compression settings to reduce memory usage and improve rendering performance. Unreal Engine provides various compression options.

- **Texture Streaming**: Implement texture streaming to load high-resolution textures only where they are needed, reducing memory overhead.

- **Material Instances**: Use material instances to create variations of materials without duplicating shader code. This reduces the CPU and GPU workload.

- **Shader Complexity**: Monitor shader complexity using the Shader Complexity view mode. Simplify shaders and reduce the number of shader instructions if they are overly complex.

```
// Adjusting texture compression settings in Unreal Engine
Texture->CompressionSettings = TC_BC7;
```

### 12.3.4 Lighting Optimization

Realistic lighting can be computationally expensive. To optimize lighting:

- **Use Static Lighting**: Whenever possible, use static lighting instead of fully dynamic lighting. Static lighting is precomputed and can significantly improve performance.

- **Optimize Shadow Settings**: Adjust shadow settings to balance quality and performance. Reducing shadow resolution and distance can have a positive impact.

- **Lightmap Resolution**: Carefully set lightmap resolutions for objects in your scene. Lower resolutions can save memory but may reduce visual quality.

```
// Adjusting lightmap resolution for a static mesh
StaticMeshComponent->OverrideLightMapRes(512);
```

### 12.3.5 Script and Blueprint Optimization

Script and Blueprint execution can impact CPU performance. To optimize scripts:

- **Reduce Tick Frequency**: Limit the frequency of script execution by increasing the tick interval for less critical objects. This reduces the CPU load.

- **Multithreading**: Take advantage of Unreal Engine's multithreading capabilities to distribute script execution across CPU cores efficiently.

- **Avoid Costly Operations**: Minimize expensive operations within scripts, such as complex loops or frequent data manipulation.

### 12.3.6 Asset and Resource Management

Effective asset and resource management is vital for performance:

- **Asset Streaming**: Implement asset streaming to load assets on-demand. This prevents unnecessary memory consumption and reduces loading times.

- **Memory Cleanup**: Properly manage memory by unloading assets that are no longer needed. Avoid memory leaks by tracking object lifetimes.

- **Asset Bundles**: Organize assets into bundles or packages to reduce the overhead of managing individual assets.

Optimizing performance in Unreal Engine is an ongoing process that requires careful consideration of various factors, including rendering, scripting, and asset management. Regular profiling and testing are essential to identify and address performance bottlenecks, ensuring that your game delivers a smooth and enjoyable experience to players across different hardware configurations.

---

## 12.4 Balancing Visual Quality and Performance

Balancing visual quality and performance is a critical aspect of game development in Unreal Engine. While achieving stunning visuals is desirable, it's equally important to ensure that your game runs smoothly on a variety of hardware configurations. In this section, we'll explore techniques and best practices for finding the right balance between visual fidelity and performance.

### 12.4.1 Graphics Settings

Unreal Engine provides a range of graphics settings that allow players to adjust visual quality to suit their hardware capabilities. Implementing these settings can enhance player experience and performance optimization:

- **Graphics Presets**: Offer predefined graphics presets (e.g., low, medium, high, ultra) that adjust various graphical settings, including resolution, texture quality, shadow quality, and more.

- **Customizable Options**: Allow players to customize individual graphics settings, such as texture resolution, shadow quality, anti-aliasing, and post-processing effects. Provide sliders or dropdown menus for adjustment.

```
// Implementing graphics settings customization in Unreal Engine
PlayerSettings->GraphicsQuality = EGraphicsQuality::High;
PlayerSettings->TextureQuality = ETextureQuality::High;
PlayerSettings->ShadowQuality = EShadowQuality::High;
```

- **Performance Warning**: Display a warning or notification if the selected graphics settings are likely to result in poor performance on the player's hardware. Suggest adjusting settings for smoother gameplay.

### 12.4.2 Scalability Settings

Unreal Engine includes scalability settings that allow you to define multiple levels of detail (LOD) for assets and effects. These settings dynamically adapt to the player's hardware without requiring manual adjustments:

- **Scalability Groups**: Assign assets and effects to scalability groups based on their importance and performance impact. For example, critical assets can belong to a "high" group, while less crucial ones are in a "low" group.

```
// Assigning assets to scalability groups in Unreal Engine
StaticMeshComponent->SetScalabilityGroup(EScalabilityGroup::High);
ParticleSystemComponent->SetScalabilityGroup(EScalabilityGroup::Low);
```

- **Automatic LOD**: Utilize automatic LOD generation for assets. Unreal Engine can generate multiple LODs for static and skeletal meshes, automatically selecting the appropriate LOD based on the player's hardware.

- **Quality Levels**: Define quality levels that correspond to different combinations of scalability settings. Allow players to choose a quality level that balances visual quality and performance.

### 12.4.3 Dynamic Resolution

Dynamic resolution is a technique that adjusts the rendering resolution in real-time based on the player's hardware capabilities and the complexity of the scene. This can significantly improve performance while maintaining acceptable visual quality:

- **Dynamic Resolution Scaling**: Implement dynamic resolution scaling to lower the rendering resolution when performance drops below a specified threshold. This ensures a smoother frame rate during demanding scenes.

```
// Enabling dynamic resolution scaling in Unreal Engine
Engine->bUseDynamicResolution = true;
```

```
Engine->DynamicResolutionMinPercentage = 50;
Engine->DynamicResolutionMaxPercentage = 100;
```

- **Performance Metrics**: Use performance metrics to dynamically adjust the resolution scaling factor. Monitor frame rate, CPU, and GPU usage to determine when to apply dynamic resolution changes.

### 12.4.4 Loading Screen Optimization

Loading screens are an opportunity to optimize performance without compromising player experience:

- **Asynchronous Loading**: Implement asynchronous loading to load assets in the background while displaying a loading screen. This reduces loading times and prevents frame rate drops during level transitions.

```
// Implementing asynchronous loading in Unreal Engine
UGameplayStatics::LoadStreamLevel(this, "LevelName", true, true, FLatentActio
nInfo());
```

- **Progress Indicators**: Display loading progress indicators to keep players informed about the loading process. This can reduce perceived loading times.

- **Asset Streaming**: Utilize asset streaming to load assets progressively as the player explores the level. This minimizes the initial loading impact.

### 12.4.5 Cross-Platform Optimization

Consider the diversity of hardware across different platforms. Balancing visual quality and performance becomes even more critical when targeting multiple platforms:

- **Platform-Specific Settings**: Adjust graphics settings, scalability settings, and resolution scaling factors for each target platform to optimize performance without sacrificing visual quality.

- **Testing and Profiling**: Test your game on various platforms and use platform-specific profiling tools to identify and address performance issues unique to each platform.

- **Fallback Assets**: Provide platform-specific asset packages that include lower-resolution textures or simplified models to ensure optimal performance on less powerful platforms.

Balancing visual quality and performance is an ongoing process that requires constant testing and iteration. It's crucial to gather player feedback, monitor performance metrics, and make adjustments as needed to create a satisfying gaming experience across a wide range of hardware configurations.

## 12.5 Preparing for Different Hardware Configurations

One of the key challenges in game development is ensuring that your game performs well on a variety of hardware configurations. Players may have different graphics cards, CPUs, and amounts of RAM, and it's essential to prepare your game to accommodate these differences. In this section, we'll explore strategies for preparing your game for different hardware configurations.

### 12.5.1 Hardware Profiling

Before optimizing your game for different hardware configurations, it's essential to have a clear understanding of the hardware landscape. Profiling tools and hardware surveys can help you gather data on the most common hardware configurations among your player base.

- **Hardware Surveys**: Conduct surveys or collect data from existing players to determine the most prevalent hardware setups. This information can guide your optimization efforts.

- **Profiling Tools**: Use profiling tools, such as Unreal Engine's built-in profiling features and third-party tools, to analyze the performance of your game on various hardware configurations.

```
// Using Unreal Engine's built-in hardware profiling tools
Engine->EnableGPUProfiling(true);
Engine->EnableCPUProfiling(true);
```

### 12.5.2 Scalability Options

Scalability options allow you to adjust the visual fidelity and performance of your game dynamically. Implementing scalability settings is an effective way to accommodate different hardware configurations:

- **Scalability Groups**: Organize assets, effects, and settings into scalability groups based on their performance impact. Assign different assets to different groups to control how they adapt to hardware variations.

```
// Setting scalability groups in Unreal Engine
StaticMeshComponent->SetScalabilityGroup(EScalabilityGroup::High);
ParticleSystemComponent->SetScalabilityGroup(EScalabilityGroup::Low);
```

- **Quality Levels**: Define quality levels that represent different combinations of scalability settings. Allow players to select a quality level that matches their hardware capabilities.

- **Auto-Adjustment**: Implement auto-adjustment mechanisms that dynamically adapt scalability settings based on the detected hardware configuration. This ensures that the game runs optimally without manual intervention.

### 12.5.3 Minimum System Requirements

Clearly define and communicate the minimum system requirements for your game. These requirements should specify the minimum hardware specifications needed to run the game at an acceptable level of performance.

- **Hardware Guidelines**: Provide specific guidelines for CPU, GPU, RAM, and storage requirements. Include information about supported DirectX or OpenGL versions.

- **Operating System**: Specify the supported operating systems, including version numbers and architecture (32-bit or 64-bit).

- **Driver Requirements**: Indicate any necessary graphics driver versions or updates for optimal performance.

### 12.5.4 Testing and Quality Assurance

Extensive testing across different hardware configurations is crucial to ensure your game's compatibility and performance. Quality assurance (QA) teams can play a significant role in identifying issues and verifying that the game performs well on various systems.

- **Diverse Test Environments**: Test the game on a wide range of hardware configurations, including both high-end and low-end systems. This includes testing on different graphics cards, CPUs, and memory capacities.

- **Performance Benchmarks**: Establish performance benchmarks on representative hardware configurations. Use these benchmarks as reference points to assess performance on other systems.

- **Issue Reporting**: Encourage players to report performance issues and hardware-specific problems. Gather feedback and prioritize fixes based on player reports.

### 12.5.5 Regular Updates and Optimization

Game development doesn't end with the initial release. To maintain compatibility with evolving hardware and software, it's essential to plan for regular updates and ongoing optimization:

- **Post-Launch Updates**: Commit to post-launch updates that address performance issues and compatibility with new hardware.

- **Driver Updates**: Stay informed about graphics driver updates and ensure that your game remains compatible with the latest drivers.

- **Community Feedback**: Engage with your player community and listen to their hardware-related concerns. Address these concerns through updates and patches.

- **Performance Metrics**: Continue to monitor performance metrics and hardware usage, even after launch. Use this data to identify and address emerging performance bottlenecks.

Preparing for different hardware configurations is a fundamental aspect of game development, ensuring that your game reaches the widest possible audience and provides a satisfying experience for all players, regardless of their hardware capabilities. By implementing scalability options, defining minimum system requirements, conducting thorough testing, and committing to ongoing updates, you can optimize your game's performance across a diverse range of hardware setups.

---

# Chapter 13: Testing and Debugging

## 13.1 Developing a Testing Strategy

Testing and debugging are integral parts of the game development process, ensuring that your game is free of critical issues and functions as intended. In this section, we'll delve into the importance of developing a comprehensive testing strategy.

### 13.1.1 The Importance of Testing

Testing is essential for several reasons:

- **Bug Detection**: Testing helps identify and eliminate bugs, glitches, and other issues that could negatively impact gameplay and user experience.

- **Quality Assurance**: Rigorous testing ensures that your game meets quality standards, enhancing player satisfaction and reducing the likelihood of negative reviews.

- **Feature Validation**: It verifies that all game features, mechanics, and systems work as intended, preventing incomplete or broken elements from reaching players.

- **Stability and Performance**: Testing helps ensure the game's stability, performance, and optimization on various hardware configurations.

### 13.1.2 Types of Testing

A robust testing strategy incorporates various types of testing, each serving a specific purpose:

- **Functional Testing**: Focuses on verifying that individual features and gameplay mechanics work correctly. This includes testing player movements, interactions, and game rules.

- **Integration Testing**: Ensures that different components, such as scripts, assets, and systems, integrate seamlessly without conflicts or errors.

- **Regression Testing**: Checks for unintended side effects when new changes are introduced. It helps prevent the reintroduction of previously fixed bugs.

- **User Interface (UI) Testing**: Evaluates the usability, functionality, and visual appeal of the game's user interface elements, including menus, HUDs, and UI animations.

- **Performance Testing**: Analyzes the game's performance under various conditions, including stress testing to determine how the game handles extreme loads.

- **Compatibility Testing**: Ensures that the game runs smoothly on different platforms, operating systems, and hardware configurations.

### 13.1.3 Creating a Testing Plan

Developing a structured testing plan is crucial for effective testing. Here's how to create one:

- **Identify Test Scenarios**: List all possible scenarios and interactions within the game, including edge cases and uncommon player choices.

- **Prioritize Test Cases**: Assign priorities to test cases based on their impact on gameplay and potential severity of issues.

- **Set Clear Objectives**: Define clear objectives and expected outcomes for each test case.

- **Choose Testing Tools**: Select appropriate testing tools, such as automation frameworks and bug tracking systems, to streamline the testing process.

```
// Example of using automation frameworks in Unreal Engine
UATests->RunFunctionalTests();
```

- **Allocate Resources**: Allocate sufficient time, personnel, and hardware resources for testing. Consider using both in-house testers and external playtesters.

- **Create Test Scripts**: Develop detailed test scripts and procedures that testers can follow to execute test cases accurately.

### 13.1.4 Automated Testing

Automated testing involves using scripts and tools to conduct repetitive and systematic tests. This approach can significantly speed up testing processes, especially for regression testing and repetitive tasks.

- **Unit Tests**: Create unit tests for individual code modules and functions to verify their correctness in isolation.

- **Integration Tests**: Develop integration tests to validate the interactions between various components and systems within the game.

- **Continuous Integration (CI)**: Implement CI pipelines that automatically run tests whenever code changes are committed. This helps catch issues early in development.

### 13.1.5 User Testing and Feedback

While automated testing is valuable, user testing remains essential. Real players can provide valuable feedback and uncover issues that automated tests might miss.

- **Beta Testing**: Conduct beta tests with a group of external players to gather feedback, identify gameplay issues, and assess the overall player experience.

- **Feedback Integration**: Implement a system for collecting and managing player feedback. Actively address reported issues and consider player suggestions for improvements.

- **Usability Testing**: Evaluate the game's user interface and overall usability by observing how players interact with the game and gather their feedback on the user experience.

### 13.1.6 Localization Testing

If your game targets a global audience, consider localization testing to ensure that the game is culturally and linguistically appropriate for different regions.

- **Language Testing**: Verify that all in-game text, subtitles, and audio translations are accurate and culturally sensitive.

- **Cultural Considerations**: Assess whether game content, imagery, and themes are respectful and appropriate for the target audience.

- **Region-Specific Issues**: Address region-specific issues, such as date formats, currencies, and legal requirements.

Developing a comprehensive testing strategy is a fundamental step in delivering a high-quality game. It involves a combination of manual testing, automated testing, user feedback, and localization testing. A well-executed testing plan not only helps eliminate bugs and issues but also enhances player satisfaction and ensures the overall success of your game.

## 13.2 Implementing Automated Tests

Automated testing is a crucial component of a robust testing and debugging strategy in game development. It involves the use of scripts and testing frameworks to automatically verify that different aspects of your game work correctly and consistently. In this section, we'll explore the implementation of automated tests in Unreal Engine and why they are valuable.

### 13.2.1 Benefits of Automated Tests

Automated tests offer several benefits in game development:

- **Consistency**: Automated tests provide consistent and repeatable results, ensuring that the same tests can be run multiple times without variation.

- **Regression Testing**: They are particularly useful for regression testing, where you can quickly verify that recent code changes have not introduced new bugs or broken existing functionality.

- **Time Efficiency**: Automated tests can run quickly, allowing you to catch issues early in the development process, saving time and resources.

- **Coverage**: You can create a wide range of test cases to cover different aspects of your game, including gameplay mechanics, UI interactions, and performance benchmarks.

### 13.2.2 Types of Automated Tests

There are various types of automated tests you can implement in Unreal Engine:

- **Unit Tests**: These tests focus on verifying the correctness of individual code modules, classes, or functions in isolation. Unit tests are typically small in scope and ensure that specific pieces of code behave as expected.

- **Integration Tests**: Integration tests check how different components and systems work together. They validate that interactions between various parts of the game function correctly.

- **Functional Tests**: Functional tests focus on verifying that specific game features and mechanics work as intended. These tests simulate user interactions and test the game's functionality from a user's perspective.

### 13.2.3 Automation Frameworks

Unreal Engine provides automation frameworks that make it easier to implement automated tests:

- **Automation System**: Unreal Engine's Automation System allows you to write and execute automated tests within the editor. It supports various test types, including unit, integration, and functional tests.

- **Gameplay Testing Framework**: This framework is specifically designed for testing gameplay mechanics and interactions. It includes features for simulating player input and validating game behavior.

### 13.2.4 Writing Automated Tests

Here's an overview of how to write automated tests in Unreal Engine:

- **Test Case Creation**: Begin by creating test cases for specific aspects of your game. Define what you want to test and what constitutes a successful outcome.

- **Write Test Code**: Write test code that simulates the desired interactions or actions within the game. For example, if you're testing a player's ability to jump, you would write code that simulates a jump action and then checks if the character correctly jumps.

```
// Example of a simple Unreal Engine automated test
UFUNCTION()
```

```
void TestJump()
{
    // Simulate a jump action
    AMyCharacter* MyCharacter = SpawnCharacter();
    MyCharacter->Jump();

    // Check if the character is in the air
    TestTrue("Character should be in the air after jumping", MyCharacter->IsF
alling());
}
```

- **Run Tests**: Execute your automated tests using the automation framework. You can run tests within the Unreal Editor or through command-line tools.

- **Review Results**: Review the test results to identify any failures or issues. Failed tests indicate areas of the game that require attention or debugging.

### 13.2.5 Continuous Integration (CI)

Incorporating automated tests into your CI pipeline is essential for ongoing testing and early bug detection. CI tools can automatically trigger test runs whenever code changes are pushed to the repository.

- **Jenkins, Travis CI, and Others**: CI platforms like Jenkins, Travis CI, or Azure DevOps can be configured to run your automated tests after every code commit.

- **Automated Build and Test**: Set up a workflow that not only builds your game but also runs automated tests to catch regressions and issues as soon as they are introduced.

Automated tests are a valuable addition to your game development process. They provide a safety net that helps you catch and address issues early, ensuring that your game is more stable, reliable, and bug-free. By implementing different types of automated tests and incorporating them into your CI pipeline, you can streamline your testing efforts and improve the overall quality of your game.

## 13.3 Bug Tracking and Management

Effective bug tracking and management are essential for maintaining a stable and polished game throughout its development cycle. In this section, we'll explore the importance of a structured approach to tracking and managing bugs in Unreal Engine.

### 13.3.1 The Significance of Bug Tracking

Bug tracking serves several critical purposes:

- **Issue Documentation**: It provides a centralized repository for documenting and tracking all issues, including bugs, glitches, feature requests, and improvements.

- **Prioritization**: Bugs are categorized and prioritized based on their impact on gameplay, severity, and other factors. This helps development teams focus on critical issues first.

- **Communication**: Bug tracking facilitates communication among team members, ensuring that everyone is aware of the current state of the game and the tasks that need attention.

- **Historical Records**: It creates a historical record of the development process, allowing teams to learn from past mistakes and improvements.

### 13.3.2 Bug Tracking Tools

Unreal Engine supports integration with various bug tracking and project management tools, making it easier to manage issues:

- **Jira**: Jira is a popular project management tool that offers issue tracking, project planning, and agile development capabilities. You can integrate Unreal Engine with Jira to sync tasks and issues seamlessly.

- **Trello**: Trello is a visual project management tool that uses boards and cards to organize tasks. You can use Trello in combination with Unreal Engine to manage tasks and issues.

- **GitHub Issues**: If you are using GitHub for version control, you can utilize GitHub Issues for bug tracking and task management. Unreal Engine has integration options with GitHub.

### 13.3.3 Bug Reporting Workflow

Establishing a clear bug reporting workflow ensures that all team members can report, track, and resolve issues effectively:

126. **Bug Identification**: Anyone on the development team can identify a bug or issue during testing, development, or gameplay.

127. **Bug Reporting**: The person who identifies the bug reports it in the bug tracking system. They provide detailed information about the issue, including steps to reproduce it, screenshots, and any relevant logs.

128. **Issue Assignment**: A team member, typically a lead or project manager, reviews the reported issue and assigns it to the appropriate team member for resolution.

129. **Bug Resolution**: The assigned team member investigates and resolves the bug. This may involve coding fixes, adjustments to assets, or changes to game settings.

130. **Verification**: After the bug is fixed, it goes through a verification process. Another team member, often a tester or QA specialist, verifies that the bug is indeed resolved.

```
// Example of setting bug status in Unreal Engine's Jira integration
JiraIntegration->SetIssueStatus("BUG-123", EIssueStatus::Resolved);
```

8. **Closure**: If the bug is verified as resolved, it is marked as closed or completed in the bug tracking system.

### 13.3.4 Bug Categories and Prioritization

To manage bugs effectively, categorize and prioritize them based on their impact and severity:

- **Critical Bugs**: These are showstopper issues that prevent gameplay or cause crashes. They should be addressed immediately.

- **Major Bugs**: Major bugs affect gameplay significantly but may not be showstoppers. They should be resolved promptly.

- **Minor Bugs**: Minor bugs are non-critical issues that do not significantly affect gameplay but should still be fixed to improve the overall experience.

- **Cosmetic Bugs**: Cosmetic bugs are visual or audio issues that do not impact gameplay. They are often lower in priority but should be addressed for polish.

- **Enhancements**: Enhancements are feature requests or improvements that are not bugs but can enhance the game. They are typically tracked separately.

### 13.3.5 Bug Tracking Best Practices

Consider the following best practices when implementing bug tracking in Unreal Engine:

- **Consistent Naming Conventions**: Use consistent naming conventions for bug reports to make them easy to search and organize.

- **Detailed Descriptions**: Encourage team members to provide detailed bug descriptions, including steps to reproduce, platform information, and any relevant assets.

- **Attachments and Screenshots**: Allow users to attach screenshots, videos, logs, or other relevant files to bug reports.

- **Regular Review Meetings**: Conduct regular bug review meetings to prioritize and assign bugs, ensuring that they are addressed in a timely manner.

- **Integration with Version Control**: Ensure that your bug tracking system integrates seamlessly with your version control system to link issues with code changes.

Effective bug tracking and management are essential for delivering a high-quality game. By implementing a structured workflow, using bug tracking tools, and adhering to best practices, you can efficiently identify, resolve, and prioritize issues throughout the development process, ultimately leading to a more polished and bug-free game.

## 13.4 User Testing and Feedback Integration

User testing and feedback integration are integral components of the game development process that allow you to gather valuable insights, identify issues, and enhance the overall player experience. In this section, we'll explore the importance of involving real players in testing and how to effectively integrate their feedback into your Unreal Engine project.

### 13.4.1 The Value of User Testing

User testing provides several key benefits:

- **Real-World Feedback**: It allows you to gather feedback from real players who experience your game as intended. This feedback is invaluable for understanding how players perceive and interact with your game.

- **Identifying Issues**: User testing helps identify issues that might not be apparent to the development team. Players can uncover gameplay problems, usability issues, and bugs that need attention.

- **Usability Insights**: It provides insights into the game's usability, user interface (UI) design, and overall user experience. Understanding how players navigate menus and interact with the UI can lead to improvements.

- **Validation of Features**: User testing validates whether your game's features and mechanics resonate with players and meet their expectations.

### 13.4.2 Conducting User Testing

Here's a step-by-step guide to conducting effective user testing in your Unreal Engine project:

131. **Define Test Objectives**: Clearly define the objectives of the user testing session. What specific aspects of the game do you want to test, and what questions do you want to answer?

132. **Select Test Participants**: Identify a diverse group of participants who represent your target audience. Ensure that the test group includes both experienced and novice players.

133. **Prepare Test Scenarios**: Create test scenarios or tasks for participants to complete during the testing session. These scenarios should align with your objectives.

134. **Facilitate Testing**: Conduct the testing session, either in person or remotely, while recording the participants' interactions, feedback, and observations.

135. **Gather Feedback**: After the testing session, collect feedback from participants through interviews, surveys, or questionnaires. Ask open-ended questions to encourage detailed responses.

136. **Analyze Data**: Analyze the data collected during the testing session to identify patterns, common issues, and areas of improvement. Look for recurring themes in participant feedback.

```
// Example of analyzing user testing feedback in Unreal Engine
void AnalyzeUserTestingFeedback()
{
    // Process feedback data and identify common issues
    // Categorize feedback into usability, gameplay, and technical issues
}
```

10. **Prioritize Changes**: Based on the feedback and data analysis, prioritize changes and improvements to address critical issues first.

### 13.4.3 Feedback Integration Workflow

Integrating user feedback into your Unreal Engine project involves a structured workflow:

137. **Feedback Collection**: Collect feedback from user testing sessions, online forums, social media, and other sources. Use tools like surveys or dedicated feedback forms within the game.

138. **Categorization**: Categorize feedback into different types, such as usability issues, gameplay suggestions, and technical problems.

139. **Issue Creation**: For actionable feedback, create corresponding issues or tasks in your bug tracking system. Include relevant details and attach feedback documentation.

140. **Prioritization**: Prioritize feedback based on its impact, frequency, and alignment with project goals. Critical issues should be addressed first.

141. **Assignment**: Assign issues to relevant team members responsible for addressing them. Provide context and additional information as needed.

142. **Resolution**: Team members work on resolving the identified issues, whether they involve code changes, asset adjustments, or design revisions.

143. **Verification**: After implementing changes, verify that the issues have been resolved successfully. User testing can be conducted again to validate improvements.

144. **Feedback Loop**: Maintain an ongoing feedback loop with users and playtesters. Continue to gather feedback at various stages of development to ensure that issues are addressed.

To facilitate feedback collection from players within your game, consider implementing in-game feedback mechanisms:

- **Feedback Forms**: Create in-game forms or pop-ups that allow players to provide feedback directly. Include fields for describing issues, suggestions, or praise.

```
// Example of creating an in-game feedback form in Unreal Engine
UUserWidget* FeedbackForm = CreateWidget(this, UFeedbackFormWidget::StaticCla
ss());
FeedbackForm->AddToViewport();
```

- **Bug Reporting Button**: Include a dedicated "Report a Bug" button in the game's UI, which opens a form for reporting issues.

- **Player Surveys**: Periodically present players with surveys that gather feedback on specific aspects of the game, such as gameplay mechanics or level design.

- **Telemetry and Analytics**: Use telemetry and analytics tools to track player behavior and performance metrics. This data can help identify trends and issues.

Effective integration of user testing and feedback mechanisms into your Unreal Engine project ensures that player perspectives are considered throughout development. It allows you to create a more player-centric and polished game, improving its chances of success and positive reception upon release.

---

## 13.5 Preparing for Launch: Final Checks

As you approach the final stages of game development, it's crucial to perform a series of checks and preparations to ensure a successful launch. In this section, we'll explore the key tasks and considerations when preparing your Unreal Engine game for release.

### 13.5.1 Quality Assurance

Quality assurance (QA) plays a pivotal role in the final checks before launch:

- **Testing**: Continue to conduct thorough testing to identify and resolve any remaining bugs, glitches, or gameplay issues. Pay special attention to issues that could negatively impact the player's experience.

- **Performance Optimization**: Optimize the game's performance for various hardware configurations to ensure a smooth and enjoyable experience for players with different systems.

- **Compatibility Testing**: Test the game on different platforms, including consoles, PC, and mobile devices, to ensure it runs correctly and is compatible with all intended platforms.

### 13.5.2 Finalizing Assets and Content

Ensure that all in-game assets and content are finalized and ready for release:

- **Art and Animation**: Review all character models, textures, animations, and environmental assets to ensure they meet quality standards and are error-free.

- **Sound and Music**: Verify that all audio assets, including music, sound effects, and voiceovers, are correctly implemented and enhance the overall game experience.

- **Localization**: Double-check all localized content, translations, and cultural adaptations to ensure accuracy and appropriateness for target regions.

### 13.5.3 Compliance and Certification

If you plan to release your game on specific platforms or marketplaces, you'll need to adhere to their compliance and certification requirements:

- **Platform-Specific Guidelines**: Familiarize yourself with the guidelines and requirements of platforms such as Steam, PlayStation, Xbox, or the App Store. Ensure that your game complies with their standards.

- **Age Ratings**: Obtain age ratings or content classifications as required by regulatory bodies in different regions. This is important for compliance and accessibility.

- **Legal Compliance**: Review and update legal documentation, including privacy policies, terms of service, and end-user license agreements (EULAs), to ensure compliance with relevant laws and regulations.

### 13.5.4 Marketing and Promotion

Effective marketing and promotion are essential for a successful game launch:

- **Marketing Materials**: Prepare marketing materials, including trailers, gameplay videos, screenshots, and promotional images. These assets are crucial for marketing campaigns.

- **Social Media and Online Presence**: Maintain an active online presence through social media, forums, and your game's website to engage with your audience and build anticipation.

- **Press and Influencers**: Reach out to gaming press and influencers to generate interest and coverage for your game. Provide them with early access if possible.

Plan the logistics of your game's release:

- **Release Date**: Choose a release date that considers market trends, holidays, and potential competition. Announce the release date to build anticipation.

- **Pre-Orders**: If applicable, set up pre-order options on platforms that support them. Pre-orders can help generate early sales and excitement.

- **Patch and Update Strategy**: Develop a strategy for post-launch patches and updates to address any issues that may arise after release and to provide ongoing support and content.

### 13.5.6 Distribution and Storefronts

Determine where and how you'll distribute your game:

- **Storefronts**: Ensure that your game is correctly listed on digital storefronts and marketplaces. Follow their submission processes and guidelines.

- **Pricing**: Set appropriate pricing for your game, considering factors like game content, market competition, and player expectations.

- **Distribution Channels**: Decide whether you'll offer your game through multiple distribution channels, such as your website, Steam, Epic Games Store, or other platforms.

### 13.5.7 Player Support

Prepare for player support and inquiries:

- **Customer Support**: Set up a system for addressing player inquiries, bug reports, and technical issues promptly. Provide clear contact information for support.

- **FAQ and Knowledge Base**: Create a frequently asked questions (FAQ) section and knowledge base on your website to help players find solutions to common issues.

- **Community Management**: Assign community managers to engage with players on social media, forums, and community platforms to address concerns and foster a positive community.

### 13.5.8 Backup and Recovery

Take precautions to protect your game and data:

- **Backups**: Regularly back up all game assets, code, and data to prevent data loss due to unexpected issues or hardware failures.

- **Disaster Recovery**: Develop a disaster recovery plan in case of catastrophic events that could disrupt the game's availability.

### 13.5.9 Monitoring and Analytics

Implement monitoring and analytics tools to gather data and insights:

- **Player Behavior**: Use analytics tools to monitor player behavior, track metrics, and gather insights into how players interact with your game.

- **Performance Metrics**: Monitor server performance and player data to identify and address any performance or connectivity issues.

### 13.5.10 Launch Readiness Checklist

Create a launch readiness checklist that includes all the tasks and considerations mentioned above. Ensure that each item is completed and verified before proceeding with the game's release.

The final checks and preparations before launching your Unreal Engine game are critical for a smooth and successful release. By addressing quality assurance, finalizing assets, complying with platform requirements, planning marketing efforts, and preparing for player support, you can increase the likelihood of a positive reception and a successful launch.

## 14.1 Preparing Your Game for Packaging

Before your Unreal Engine game can be distributed to players, it needs to go through a packaging process. Packaging is the step where all the necessary files and assets are compiled and bundled into a format that can be distributed to various platforms and operating systems. In this section, we'll explore the essential considerations and steps for preparing your game for packaging.

### 14.1.1 Packaging Platforms

Unreal Engine supports packaging your game for various platforms, including:

- **Windows**: Packaging for Windows allows you to create executable files (.exe) for PCs running Windows. You can also target different Windows versions, such as Windows 7, Windows 10, and beyond.

- **Linux**: Linux packaging enables you to create builds for Linux distributions. You can choose between different distribution options and architectures, such as Ubuntu or CentOS.

- **Mac**: If you want to release your game on macOS, Unreal Engine supports packaging for Mac, creating .app bundles that can run on Apple's operating system.

- **Android**: For mobile gaming, you can package your game for Android devices. This involves creating .apk files that can be installed on Android smartphones and tablets.

- **iOS**: To target Apple devices like iPhones and iPads, you can package your game for iOS. This process creates .ipa files that can be distributed through the App Store.

- **Consoles**: Unreal Engine supports packaging for various game consoles, including PlayStation, Xbox, and Nintendo platforms. Each platform has its specific requirements and procedures.

### 14.1.2 Pre-Packaging Checklist

Before initiating the packaging process, ensure that you've completed the following tasks:

- **Final Testing**: Perform thorough testing and quality assurance to identify and resolve any critical issues, bugs, or performance problems.

- **Content Optimization**: Optimize in-game assets, including textures, models, and audio files, to reduce the game's size and improve performance.

- **Code Optimization**: Review and optimize your game's code to enhance performance and stability. Remove any unused or unnecessary assets and code.

- **Platform Requirements**: Familiarize yourself with the specific requirements and guidelines for the platform you're targeting. Different platforms may have unique packaging requirements.

### 14.1.3 Packaging Settings

Unreal Engine provides a range of settings and configurations to customize the packaging process for your game. Here are some key settings to consider:

- **Build Configuration**: Choose the appropriate build configuration, such as Debug, Development, or Shipping. The Shipping configuration is optimized for performance and should be used for the final release.

- **Target Platform**: Select the platform you want to package your game for, such as Windows, Linux, Android, iOS, or a specific console.

- **Cooking**: Cooking refers to the process of preparing assets and data for packaging. Configure cooking settings, including which maps, assets, and content should be included in the packaged build.

- **Package Options**: Customize package settings, such as whether to create a single executable file, package additional content, or create a dedicated server build.

- **Distribution Method**: Decide how you plan to distribute your game, whether through digital storefronts like Steam or Epic Games Store, mobile app stores, or other distribution channels.

### 14.1.4 Packaging Process

The packaging process typically involves the following steps:

145. **Cooking**: Unreal Engine cooks the game's assets, ensuring they are optimized and prepared for packaging.

146. **Compiling**: The game's code is compiled for the target platform, creating executable files and binaries.

147. **Bundling**: All the necessary files, including assets, code, and engine components, are bundled together into a distribution package.

148. **Signing and Certificates**: For some platforms, such as iOS and Android, you'll need to sign your game with the appropriate certificates to ensure it can run on the platform.

149. **Testing**: Perform final testing on the packaged build to ensure it works correctly and doesn't have any packaging-related issues.

150. **Distribution**: Once the build passes testing, you can distribute it through the chosen distribution channels.

### 14.1.5 Automation and Batch Processing

For large projects or multiple platform targets, consider setting up automation and batch processing for packaging. Unreal Engine provides command-line tools and scripting capabilities that allow you to automate the packaging process for different platforms and configurations. This can significantly streamline the packaging workflow and ensure consistency.

```
# Example of using Unreal Automation Tool (UAT) to automate packaging
./Engine/Build/BatchFiles/RunUAT.sh BuildCookRun -project="PathToYourProject.
uproject" -platform=Windows -clientconfig=Shipping -cook -allmaps -build -sta
ge -pak -archive
```

### 14.1.6 Packaging for Different Operating Systems

When packaging for different operating systems (e.g., Windows, Linux, macOS), consider the platform-specific requirements and guidelines. Ensure that your game's user interface, controls, and performance are optimized for each platform.

### 14.1.7 Version Control and Backup

Before packaging, make sure your project is under version control, and you have a backup of your project files. This ensures that you can easily revert to a previous state if issues arise during packaging.

### 14.1.8 Post-Packaging Testing

After packaging your game, conduct additional testing on the packaged build to confirm that it functions correctly on the target platform. Address any issues that may have arisen during the packaging process.

By following these guidelines and considering the platform-specific requirements, you can effectively prepare your Unreal Engine game for packaging and ensure a smooth and successful distribution to players on various platforms and operating systems.

---

## 14.2 Understanding Distribution Platforms

Distribution platforms play a vital role in getting your Unreal Engine game into the hands of players. These platforms provide a marketplace where you can publish and sell your game. In this section, we'll explore the importance of distribution platforms and considerations when choosing the right ones for your game.

### 14.2.1 Benefits of Distribution Platforms

Distribution platforms offer several advantages for game developers:

- **Access to a Wide Audience**: Platforms like Steam, Epic Games Store, and app stores for mobile devices have millions of active users. Publishing on these platforms gives your game access to a broad audience.

- **Marketing and Promotion**: Many distribution platforms offer marketing and promotional opportunities, such as featured spots, discounts, and events, which can help increase the visibility of your game.

- **Payment Processing**: Distribution platforms handle payment processing, making it easier to sell your game and collect revenue from players.

- **User Reviews and Ratings**: Platforms often have user review systems that allow players to provide feedback and ratings. Positive reviews can boost your game's reputation.

- **Updates and Patches**: Distribution platforms provide mechanisms for delivering updates and patches to your game, ensuring that players receive the latest improvements and bug fixes.

### 14.2.2 Types of Distribution Platforms

There are several types of distribution platforms you can consider for your Unreal Engine game:

- **PC Gaming Platforms**: These platforms cater to PC gamers and include:
    - **Steam**: Steam is one of the largest and most popular PC gaming platforms, known for its extensive library and community features. It offers both traditional games and VR experiences.
    - **Epic Games Store**: Developed by Epic Games, this store focuses on offering a curated selection of games and often features exclusive titles.
    - **GOG (Good Old Games)**: GOG specializes in DRM-free games, and it appeals to players who prefer to own their games outright.

- **Console Platforms**: If you're developing for consoles like PlayStation, Xbox, or Nintendo, you'll need to publish your game through the respective console manufacturer's platform.

- **Mobile App Stores**: For mobile game developers targeting iOS and Android, the Apple App Store and Google Play Store are the primary distribution platforms.

- **Web and Browser Games**: Web platforms like itch.io and Kongregate allow you to publish browser-based games that players can access without downloading.

- **VR Platforms**: If your game is designed for virtual reality, platforms like Oculus Store and SteamVR offer distribution for VR experiences.

- **Alternative Platforms**: There are various other distribution platforms that cater to niche audiences or specific types of games. These platforms may be worth considering depending on your game's target market.

### 14.2.3 Platform Selection Criteria

When choosing distribution platforms for your game, consider the following criteria:

- **Target Audience**: Identify your game's target audience and choose platforms that align with your demographic. Different platforms may cater to different player bases.

- **Revenue Sharing**: Review the revenue-sharing model of each platform. Some platforms take a percentage of your game's sales, while others may have flat fees or different arrangements.

- **Publishing Costs**: Consider any upfront costs associated with publishing on a platform, such as registration fees or certification expenses for console platforms.

- **Marketing Opportunities**: Assess the marketing and promotional opportunities each platform offers. Look for platforms that can help you market your game effectively.

- **Distribution Regions**: Determine the regions or countries where you want to distribute your game. Ensure that the selected platforms support your desired regions.

- **Platform Restrictions**: Be aware of any platform-specific restrictions, guidelines, or content policies that may affect your game's eligibility or content.

- **Community and Reviews**: Research the community and review systems on each platform. Consider how user reviews and community engagement can impact your game's success.

### 14.2.4 Platform-Specific Requirements

Each distribution platform may have its own set of requirements for submitting and publishing games. These requirements often include:

- **Technical Requirements**: Ensure that your game meets the platform's technical specifications, including performance, resolution, and compatibility.

- **Legal and Licensing**: Comply with platform-specific legal agreements, licensing, and content policies. This includes obtaining necessary age ratings or certifications.

- **Marketing Assets**: Prepare marketing materials such as game trailers, screenshots, and promotional images that meet the platform's guidelines.

- **Payment and Revenue Sharing**: Understand the platform's payment methods and revenue-sharing models. Set up the necessary payment accounts.

- **Localization**: If your game targets international audiences, provide localized content, translations, and support for multiple languages.

Once you've selected the distribution platforms and prepared your game, you'll need to go through the submission and approval process. This typically involves:

151. **Platform Registration**: Create developer accounts on the chosen platforms if you haven't already.

152. **Submission**: Submit your game build and all required documentation to the platform. This includes technical files, marketing assets, and legal agreements.

153. **Review and Testing**: The platform's review team will test your game to ensure it meets their requirements, is free of critical issues, and complies with their policies.

154. **Approval**: If your game passes the review process, it will be approved for publication on the platform. You'll receive instructions on setting up store listings and release details.

155. **Launch**: Once your game is approved, you can set a release date and make your game available for pre-orders or preloads, depending on the platform's features.

## 14.2.6 Post-Launch Maintenance

After launching your game on distribution platforms, it's important to continue monitoring and maintaining your presence:

- **Customer Support**: Provide customer support for players who encounter issues or have questions about your game.

- **Updates and Patches**: Regularly release updates, patches, and new content to keep your game fresh and address player feedback.

- **Marketing and Promotion**: Maintain marketing efforts to keep players engaged and attract new ones. Consider running promotions or participating in platform-specific events.

- **Community Engagement**: Engage with your game's community on platform forums, social media, and in-game to foster

---

## 14.3 Packaging for Different Operating Systems

Packaging your Unreal Engine game for different operating systems requires careful consideration of each platform's unique requirements and configurations. In this section, we'll delve into the specifics of packaging for various operating systems, including Windows, Linux, and macOS.

### 14.3.1 Packaging for Windows

Packaging your game for Windows is a common choice due to the wide availability of Windows-based PCs. Here are the key steps to package your Unreal Engine game for Windows:

*Step 1: Configure Project Settings*
- Open your Unreal Engine project and navigate to the "Edit" menu.
- Select "Project Settings."
- In the "Platforms" section, choose "Windows" as your target platform.
- Adjust other settings as needed, such as graphics quality and input configurations, to suit Windows systems.

*Step 2: Build Configuration*
- Set your build configuration to "Shipping" for the final release build. This ensures optimal performance and removes debug information.

*Step 3: Cook Your Project*
- Use the Unreal Engine "Cook" process to prepare your game's assets and content for packaging.
- Open the Unreal Engine Editor and select "File" > "Package Project" > "Windows."
- Follow the on-screen instructions to cook and package your game for Windows.

*Step 4: Create an Installer (Optional)*
- Consider creating an installer for your game using third-party software like Inno Setup or NSIS (Nullsoft Scriptable Install System). This simplifies the installation process for players.

*Step 5: Testing*
- Test your packaged game on Windows systems to ensure it runs correctly, has no compatibility issues, and performs well.

*Step 6: Distribution*
- Choose your distribution platform(s) for Windows, such as Steam, Epic Games Store, or your own website.
- Follow the platform-specific guidelines for submitting and publishing your game.

### 14.3.2 Packaging for Linux

Packaging your game for Linux allows you to reach a different audience of Linux users. Here's how to package your Unreal Engine game for Linux:

*Step 1: Configure Project Settings*
- Open your Unreal Engine project and navigate to the "Edit" menu.

- Select "Project Settings."
- In the "Platforms" section, choose "Linux" as your target platform.
- Configure other settings, including distribution method and compatibility.

*Step 2: Build Configuration*
- Set your build configuration to "Shipping" for the final release build.

*Step 3: Cook Your Project*
- Use the Unreal Engine "Cook" process to prepare your game's assets and content for packaging.
- Open the Unreal Engine Editor and select "File" > "Package Project" > "Linux."
- Follow the on-screen instructions to cook and package your game for Linux.

*Step 4: Distribution Methods*
- Consider the various methods of distribution for Linux, including:

    - **Steam**: Publish your game on Steam for Linux if it meets their requirements.
    - **Direct Download**: Offer your game for direct download from your website or trusted platforms.
    - **Linux Package Managers**: Explore packaging your game as a Linux package (e.g., .deb for Debian-based systems) for distribution through package managers.

*Step 5: Testing*
- Test your packaged game on Linux distributions to ensure it runs smoothly, adheres to Linux standards, and doesn't have compatibility issues.

*Step 6: Distribution*
- Follow the guidelines of your chosen distribution method to publish your game for Linux.

### 14.3.3 Packaging for macOS

For macOS, packaging your Unreal Engine game involves specific steps to ensure compatibility with Apple's operating system. Here's a guide to packaging for macOS:

*Step 1: Configure Project Settings*
- Open your Unreal Engine project and navigate to the "Edit" menu.
- Select "Project Settings."
- In the "Platforms" section, choose "Mac" as your target platform.
- Configure settings like macOS version compatibility and graphics quality.

*Step 2: Build Configuration*
- Set your build configuration to "Shipping" for the final release build.

*Step 3: Cook Your Project*
- Use the Unreal Engine "Cook" process to prepare your game's assets and content for packaging.
- Open the Unreal Engine Editor and select "File" > "Package Project" > "Mac."
- Follow the on-screen instructions to cook and package your game for macOS.

*Step 4: Code Signing*
- To distribute your game on macOS, you must code-sign your application using an Apple Developer ID certificate.

*Step 5: Distribution*
- Distribute your game on the Apple App Store, or consider offering direct downloads from your website.

*Step 6: Testing*
- Thoroughly test your packaged game on macOS systems to ensure it functions correctly and adheres to macOS guidelines.

### 14.3.4 Platform-Specific Considerations

When packaging for different operating systems, keep these platform-specific considerations in mind:

- **File Paths**: Be mindful of file path differences between operating systems, particularly when referencing assets and external files.

- **System Libraries**: Ensure compatibility with required system libraries and dependencies for each platform.

- **Permissions**: Understand how each operating system handles file permissions and ensure your game's installer or packaging process addresses this.

- **User Interface**: Adapt your game's user interface and controls to match the conventions of the target operating system.

- **Performance**: Optimize your game's performance for each platform, considering hardware variations and capabilities.

By carefully addressing the requirements and considerations of each operating system, you can successfully package your Unreal Engine game for Windows, Linux, macOS, and other platforms, reaching a diverse player base.

## 14.4 Security and Anti-Cheat Measures

Ensuring the security of your Unreal Engine game and implementing anti-cheat measures is essential to maintain fair gameplay, protect player data, and prevent unauthorized access. In this section, we'll explore various security strategies and anti-cheat techniques to safeguard your game.

### 14.4.1 Game Data Encryption

Encrypting sensitive game data is a fundamental security practice. By encrypting data like player profiles, in-game transactions, and communication between the client and server, you can protect it from unauthorized access. Unreal Engine provides encryption libraries and tools to help implement data encryption effectively.

Here's a basic example of encrypting and decrypting a string using Unreal Engine's encryption functions:

```
FString OriginalData = "SensitiveDataToEncrypt";
FString EncryptedData = FPlatformCrypto::EncryptAES(OriginalData, EncryptionK
ey);
FString DecryptedData = FPlatformCrypto::DecryptAES(EncryptedData, Encryption
Key);
```

In this code snippet, EncryptionKey should be securely managed to prevent exposure.

### 14.4.2 User Authentication

Implementing robust user authentication mechanisms is crucial to ensure that only authorized players can access your game's online features. Use techniques like OAuth, OpenID, or third-party authentication providers to authenticate users securely. Unreal Engine offers plugins and integrations for various authentication services, simplifying the implementation process.

### 14.4.3 Server-Side Logic

Move critical game logic and data processing to the server to prevent client-side manipulation. By enforcing server-side authority for important actions like scoring, item acquisition, and game progression, you can mitigate cheating attempts. Unreal Engine's dedicated server support facilitates this approach.

### 14.4.4 Code Obfuscation

Obfuscating your game's code makes it harder for cheaters to reverse engineer or tamper with it. Code obfuscation tools can rename variables, functions, and classes, making the code less readable and more challenging to exploit. While this won't provide complete security, it adds an additional layer of defense.

### 14.4.5 Anti-Cheat Systems

Dedicated anti-cheat systems are crucial for maintaining a fair gaming environment. Popular anti-cheat solutions like Easy Anti-Cheat (EAC) and BattleEye provide Unreal Engine integration options. These systems detect and prevent various cheating methods, including aimbots, wallhacks, and speed hacks.

To integrate an anti-cheat system into your game, follow the provided documentation and SDKs. Typically, it involves server-side components for cheat detection and client-side components for cheat prevention.

### 14.4.6 Fair Play Monitoring

Implement mechanisms to monitor and report player behavior for fair play. This includes detecting suspicious activities like abnormal game progress, high scores, or unusual player interactions. Analyze game logs and statistics to identify potential cheaters and take appropriate actions.

### 14.4.7 Regular Updates and Patching

Continuously update and patch your game to address security vulnerabilities and cheating exploits. Cheaters often look for weaknesses in older game versions, so keeping your game up-to-date is essential.

### 14.4.8 Reporting and Community Involvement

Encourage your player community to report cheaters and suspicious activities. Create reporting tools and channels where players can submit evidence of cheating. Engage with your community to maintain a healthy gaming environment and address concerns promptly.

### 14.4.9 Legal Measures

Consider legal actions against cheaters who engage in activities like distributing cheats, hacks, or engaging in cyberattacks. Consult legal experts and familiarize yourself with relevant laws and regulations in your jurisdiction.

### 14.4.10 Privacy and Data Protection

Protecting player privacy and data is as crucial as preventing cheating. Ensure compliance with data protection laws like GDPR (General Data Protection Regulation) and CCPA (California Consumer Privacy Act). Collect and store only necessary player data and implement secure data storage practices.

### 14.4.11 Regular Security Audits

Perform regular security audits and penetration testing to identify vulnerabilities in your game's infrastructure, server systems, and network configurations. Address any vulnerabilities promptly to prevent security breaches.

By implementing a comprehensive security strategy that includes encryption, user authentication, server-side logic, code obfuscation, anti-cheat systems, and fair play monitoring, you can enhance the security of your Unreal Engine game and provide players with a fair and enjoyable gaming experience while protecting their data and the integrity of your game.

---

## 14.5 Post-Deployment Support and Updates

The journey of game development doesn't end with the launch of your Unreal Engine game. In fact, post-deployment support and updates are critical aspects of maintaining a successful game. This section discusses the importance of ongoing support, bug fixes, content updates, and player engagement strategies.

### 14.5.1 Player Feedback and Bug Reporting

After releasing your game, players will provide feedback, report bugs, and share their experiences. Actively listen to your player community through forums, social media, and support channels. Collect bug reports and feedback systematically, categorize them, and prioritize fixes and improvements based on their impact on gameplay and player satisfaction.

### 14.5.2 Patching and Bug Fixes

Regularly release patches and bug fixes to address reported issues and improve game stability. Develop a patching and update system that allows players to download and apply updates seamlessly. Ensure that critical issues, such as game-breaking bugs or security vulnerabilities, are addressed promptly.

```cpp
// Sample Unreal Engine C++ code for applying a patch
void ApplyPatch()
{
    // Code for applying the patch and updating game files
}
```

### 14.5.3 Content Updates

Keep players engaged by delivering new content updates. This can include additional levels, characters, weapons, skins, and features. Content updates breathe new life into your game, attract returning players, and entice new ones. Regularly communicate your content roadmap to players to maintain excitement.

### 14.5.4 Community Engagement

Engage with your player community through social media, forums, and in-game events. Run contests, surveys, and community-driven initiatives to foster a sense of belonging.

Listen to player suggestions and involve them in shaping the future of your game. Show appreciation for dedicated players with in-game rewards or recognition.

### 14.5.5 Balancing and Gameplay Tweaks

Monitor game balance and player feedback to identify areas that require adjustment. Tweaking gameplay elements, such as character abilities, weapon stats, or difficulty levels, can enhance the overall player experience. Be transparent about balance changes and explain the reasoning behind them.

```
// Unreal Engine blueprint example for adjusting character abilities
if (playerFeedback.ImproveCharacterBalance)
{
    AdjustCharacterAbilities();
}
```

### 14.5.6 Performance Optimization

Continue optimizing your game's performance, especially for lower-end hardware configurations. Regularly profile and identify performance bottlenecks. Implement optimizations to improve frame rates, reduce load times, and enhance overall gameplay fluidity.

### 14.5.7 Events and Seasons

Host in-game events and seasonal content to celebrate holidays or special occasions. These limited-time events can introduce unique challenges, rewards, and themes. Events create a sense of urgency and encourage player participation.

### 14.5.8 Monetization Strategies

Evaluate and refine your game's monetization strategies based on player behavior and feedback. Consider offering cosmetic items, battle passes, or in-game purchases that enhance the player's experience without compromising game balance. Ensure that monetization remains fair and transparent.

```
// Unreal Engine blueprint example for implementing in-game purchases
if (playerWantsCosmeticItem)
{
    OfferCosmeticItemForPurchase();
}
```

### 14.5.9 Analyzing Player Data

Leverage player data and analytics to make informed decisions. Track player retention, engagement, and monetization metrics. Analyze which features are popular and where players tend to drop off. Use data to inform your development and marketing strategies.

### 14.5.10 Roadmap and Planning

Maintain a clear roadmap for post-launch support and updates. Outline your goals, timelines, and key milestones for upcoming patches and content releases. Share the roadmap with your player community to manage their expectations and build anticipation.

### 14.5.11 Player Support

Continue providing player support through customer service channels. Respond to player inquiries, resolve issues, and offer assistance. Good customer support can lead to positive reviews and player loyalty.

### 14.5.12 Celebrate Milestones

Celebrate game milestones, anniversaries, and achievements with your player community. Host special in-game events or giveaways to mark these occasions and show appreciation for player support.

Post-deployment support and updates are integral to building a thriving player base and maintaining a successful Unreal Engine game. By actively engaging with players, addressing their feedback, delivering quality updates, and continuously improving the gaming experience, you can ensure the longevity and success of your game in a competitive market.

# 15. Marketing Your Game

## 15.1 Developing a Marketing Strategy

Marketing is a crucial component of a successful Unreal Engine game launch. Without effective marketing, even the most exceptional games can go unnoticed. In this section, we'll explore how to develop a marketing strategy that can help you reach your target audience and maximize your game's visibility.

### 15.1.1 Define Your Target Audience

Before diving into marketing tactics, it's essential to define your target audience. Understanding your ideal players' demographics, preferences, and behaviors allows you to tailor your marketing efforts effectively. Consider factors like age, gender, interests, and gaming platforms.

### 15.1.2 Unique Selling Proposition (USP)

Identify what makes your game unique and compelling. Your Unique Selling Proposition (USP) is the key feature or aspect of your game that sets it apart from the competition. Whether it's innovative gameplay mechanics, stunning graphics, or a captivating storyline, your USP is your primary marketing hook.

**USP Example**: Our game offers a groundbreaking physics-based sandbox world where players can create and destroy environments in real-time.

### 15.1.3 Market Research

Conduct thorough market research to gain insights into your industry, competitors, and player trends. Analyze successful games in your genre and identify strategies that worked for them. Tools like Steam Spy, Google Trends, and social media analytics can provide valuable data.

### 15.1.4 Budget and Resources

Determine your marketing budget and allocate resources effectively. Marketing expenses may include advertising costs, promotional materials, and hiring marketing professionals or agencies. Ensure that your budget aligns with your game's revenue potential.

### 15.1.5 Marketing Channels

Explore various marketing channels to reach your target audience:

- **Social Media**: Establish a strong presence on platforms like Facebook, Twitter, Instagram, and TikTok. Share engaging content, teasers, and behind-the-scenes glimpses of your game's development.

- **Email Marketing**: Build an email list of interested players and send newsletters with updates, special offers, and game-related content.

- **Content Creation**: Partner with content creators (YouTubers, streamers, bloggers) who cater to your game's audience. They can create gameplay videos, reviews, and tutorials that showcase your game.

- **Press Releases**: Distribute press releases to gaming news websites, blogs, and magazines. Highlight your game's unique features and significant milestones.

- **Community Forums**: Participate in gaming forums and communities related to your genre. Engage in discussions, share your game's progress, and build relationships with potential players.

- **Influencer Marketing**: Collaborate with influencers who can promote your game to their followers. Ensure that their audience aligns with your target demographic.

### 15.1.6 Marketing Materials

Create compelling marketing materials, including:

- **Game Trailers**: Produce high-quality trailers that showcase gameplay, story, and visuals. A captivating trailer can generate excitement and anticipation.

- **Screenshots and Artwork**: Share stunning screenshots and concept art that highlight your game's aesthetics.

- **Website**: Develop a professional website with information about your game, press kit, and contact details. Your website serves as a central hub for potential players and press.

- **Press Kit**: Create a press kit with game assets, such as high-resolution images, videos, logos, and a press release. Make it easily accessible on your website.

### 15.1.7 Pre-launch Hype

Build anticipation for your game before its launch:

- **Teasers**: Release teaser trailers, posters, or concept art to tease your game's theme and features.

- **Demo or Beta**: Offer a playable demo or beta version to gather feedback and generate excitement.

- **Countdowns**: Create countdowns to your game's launch on your website and social media profiles.

- **Contests and Giveaways**: Organize contests or giveaways with in-game rewards to engage your audience.

### 15.1.8 Launch Day Strategy

Plan your launch day meticulously:

- **Release Timing**: Choose a release time that maximizes visibility, considering time zones and peak gaming hours.

- **Promotion**: Coordinate marketing efforts, including social media announcements, press releases, and influencer partnerships, to coincide with the launch.

- **Community Engagement**: Be available to engage with players on launch day, addressing questions, issues, and feedback promptly.

### 15.1.9 Post-launch Marketing

Marketing doesn't stop after launch:

- **Regular Updates**: Continue promoting your game with regular updates, new content, and feature additions.

- **Player Feedback**: Listen to player feedback and incorporate player suggestions when feasible.

- **Events and Sales**: Host in-game events, sales, or special offers to maintain player engagement.

- **Expand to New Platforms**: Consider porting your game to other platforms to reach a broader audience.

### 15.1.10 Metrics and Analysis

Monitor the effectiveness of your marketing efforts:

- **Analytics Tools**: Use analytics tools to track website traffic, social media engagement, conversion rates, and player demographics.

- **KPIs**: Define key performance indicators (KPIs) and measure them regularly to assess your marketing's impact.

- **Adjust Strategies**: Based on data and performance metrics, refine your marketing strategies for better results.

Developing a robust marketing strategy for your Unreal Engine game is essential for its success. By understanding your target audience, highlighting your USP, conducting market research, allocating resources wisely, and utilizing various marketing channels, you can maximize your game's visibility and create a strong player community. Marketing is an ongoing effort that continues even after launch to maintain player engagement and drive long-term success.

## 15.2 Building an Online Presence and Community

Building an online presence and fostering a strong community around your Unreal Engine game is a crucial aspect of successful game marketing. An engaged community can help generate buzz, provide valuable feedback, and ensure the long-term success of your game. In this section, we'll explore how to establish and nurture an online presence and community.

### 15.2.1 Create a Dedicated Website

Start by creating a dedicated website for your game. A professional website serves as a central hub for information about your game, including trailers, screenshots, development updates, and press materials. Ensure that your website is user-friendly, mobile-responsive, and easy to navigate.

### 15.2.2 Engage on Social Media

Utilize social media platforms to connect with potential players and fans. Establish profiles on platforms like Facebook, Twitter, Instagram, and TikTok. Regularly share updates, teasers, concept art, and behind-the-scenes content related to your game's development.

**Social Media Tip**: Use relevant hashtags and engage with trending topics to expand your reach.

### 15.2.3 Developer Blogs and Dev Diaries

Maintain a developer blog or dev diary where you document your game's development journey. Share insights, challenges, and progress updates. Engage with readers by responding to comments and questions. Developer blogs humanize your development team and create a sense of transparency.

### 15.2.4 Community Forums and Discord

Participate in gaming community forums and create a dedicated Discord server for your game. These platforms provide spaces for players to discuss your game, share experiences, and interact with your team. Encourage open discussions and address player questions and concerns.

### 15.2.5 Content Creation

Leverage content creators in the gaming community to showcase your game. Collaborate with YouTubers, Twitch streamers, bloggers, and podcasters who cater to your game's target audience. Provide them with early access to your game or exclusive content to generate excitement.

### 15.2.6 Regular Updates

Consistently share development updates to keep your community informed and engaged. Post about new features, improvements, and milestones. Regular updates demonstrate your commitment to the game and maintain player interest.

### 15.2.7 Player Feedback Integration

Encourage players to provide feedback and suggestions. Actively listen to your community's input and consider implementing player-driven ideas when appropriate. Players appreciate when they see their feedback leading to positive changes in the game.

**Feedback Example**: "We heard your feedback, and we're adding a new map based on your suggestions in the next update!"

### 15.2.8 Exclusive Content for Supporters

Reward your most dedicated supporters and early adopters with exclusive in-game content. This can include unique skins, badges, or early access to upcoming features. Recognizing and appreciating your community's loyalty fosters goodwill.

### 15.2.9 Community Events

Organize community events and challenges within your game. Events can range from in-game tournaments to themed contests. Offer attractive rewards to participants to incentivize engagement. Community events build a sense of camaraderie among players.

### 15.2.10 Transparency and Communication

Maintain transparent communication with your community. Address issues, challenges, and delays openly and honestly. Building trust with your community is essential for long-term support.

**Transparency Example**: "We encountered a technical issue that's causing a slight delay in the next update. We apologize for the inconvenience and are working diligently to resolve it."

### 15.2.11 Beta Testing and Early Access

Consider offering beta testing or early access to your game. This allows dedicated players to experience the game before the official launch and provide valuable feedback. Their involvement can help identify and address issues.

### 15.2.12 Encourage User-Generated Content

If feasible, encourage players to create user-generated content (UGC) for your game. UGC can include custom levels, mods, skins, and more. Showcase outstanding UGC within the game or on your website to acknowledge player creativity.

Building an online presence and community around your Unreal Engine game requires dedication and consistent engagement. By creating a welcoming and interactive space for your players, actively communicating updates, and valuing player feedback, you can cultivate a passionate community that supports your game's success throughout its lifecycle.

## 15.3 Utilizing Social Media and Influencers

Social media and influencers play a significant role in promoting your Unreal Engine game. Leveraging these platforms effectively can help you reach a wider audience and build a dedicated fan base. In this section, we'll explore strategies for utilizing social media and collaborating with influencers to enhance your game's visibility.

### 15.3.1 Choosing the Right Social Media Platforms

Selecting the appropriate social media platforms for your game is crucial. Different platforms cater to diverse audiences and content types. Consider the following when choosing where to establish your presence:

- **Facebook**: Ideal for sharing game updates, trailers, and community engagement. It offers advertising tools for targeted promotion.

- **Twitter**: Great for quick updates, announcements, and engaging with your community through tweets and hashtags.

- **Instagram**: Suitable for visually appealing content, such as screenshots, concept art, and behind-the-scenes photos.

- **YouTube**: Essential for uploading trailers, developer diaries, and gameplay videos. Create a channel to showcase your game's features.

- **Twitch**: Connect with live-streaming gamers and consider live-streaming your game's development or hosting game-related events.

- **TikTok**: Utilize short, attention-grabbing videos to create viral marketing moments and challenges related to your game.

### 15.3.2 Consistent Posting Schedule

Maintain a consistent posting schedule across your chosen social media platforms. Regular updates keep your audience engaged and informed. Use social media management tools to schedule posts in advance and maintain a steady flow of content.

### 15.3.3 Engaging Content

Create engaging and shareable content that resonates with your target audience. Consider the following content ideas:

- **Game Teasers**: Share teasers and snippets of gameplay to generate excitement.

- **Behind-the-Scenes**: Offer glimpses of your development process, including concept art, design discussions, and developer interviews.

- **Player Spotlights**: Highlight exceptional players, fan art, or user-generated content related to your game.

- **Polls and Q&A**: Interact with your audience by conducting polls, asking questions, or hosting Q&A sessions.

- **Challenges and Contests**: Launch social media challenges or contests that encourage user participation and creativity.

### 15.3.4 Hashtags and Trends

Utilize relevant hashtags and trends to increase the discoverability of your posts. Research popular gaming and industry-specific hashtags and incorporate them into your content. Join trending conversations when applicable to expand your reach.

### 15.3.5 Influencer Partnerships

Collaborating with influencers can significantly impact your game's visibility. Identify influencers whose audience aligns with your target demographic. Reach out to them with collaboration proposals, offering early access to your game or exclusive content.

`**Influencer Collaboration**`: "We're excited to partner with `[Influencer Name]` to bring you an exclusive sneak peek of our upcoming content!"

### 15.3.6 Sponsored Posts

Consider investing in sponsored posts or advertisements on social media platforms. Sponsored content can reach a broader audience and target users based on their interests and demographics. Set a budget and create compelling ad creatives.

### 15.3.7 Community Engagement

Engage with your social media community by responding to comments, questions, and feedback promptly. Show appreciation for fan art, fan theories, and user-generated content. Building a positive online community fosters loyalty and enthusiasm.

### 15.3.8 Analytics and Insights

Use built-in analytics tools on social media platforms to track the performance of your posts and campaigns. Monitor engagement, reach, click-through rates, and audience demographics. Analyze data to refine your social media strategy.

### 15.3.9 Trendjacking and Timely Posts

Stay informed about gaming industry trends, events, and relevant news. Capitalize on trending topics by creating timely content or participating in conversations. Trendjacking can boost your visibility and relevance.

### 15.3.10 Cross-Promotion

Collaborate with other developers or game-related businesses for cross-promotion. Promote each other's games or products to tap into each other's audiences. Cross-promotion can expand your reach beyond your immediate fan base.

Evaluate the return on investment (ROI) of your social media and influencer marketing efforts. Calculate the impact of each campaign on game downloads, sales, or player engagement. Adjust your strategies based on the performance data.

Effectively utilizing social media and influencer partnerships can significantly boost your Unreal Engine game's visibility and player engagement. By consistently posting engaging content, collaborating with influencers, utilizing hashtags, and staying attuned to industry trends, you can create a strong online presence that resonates with your target audience and drives success for your game.

---

## 15.4 Creating Promotional Materials

Promotional materials play a pivotal role in marketing your Unreal Engine game. These materials serve as visual and informational assets that help generate interest, excitement, and engagement among your target audience. In this section, we'll explore key promotional materials and how to create them effectively.

### 15.4.1 Key Promotional Materials

156. **Game Trailers**: Game trailers are among the most critical promotional materials. They provide a visual overview of your game's features, gameplay, and storyline. A well-crafted trailer can captivate potential players and drive anticipation.

157. **Screenshots and Artwork**: High-quality screenshots and concept art showcase the aesthetics and visual appeal of your game. These visuals can be shared on social media, your website, and in marketing campaigns.

158. **Logo and Branding**: Establish a memorable logo and consistent branding elements for your game. These elements should be present in all promotional materials, creating a cohesive identity.

159. **Press Kit**: Create a press kit that includes assets for journalists, content creators, and influencers. This kit typically contains high-resolution images, videos, logos, and a press release.

160. **Website**: Develop a professional website that serves as a central hub for promotional materials, game information, press coverage, and contact details. Your website should be easy to navigate and mobile-responsive.

161. **Game Description**: Craft a compelling game description that succinctly conveys your game's unique selling points, story, and features. This description is often used in app stores and marketing materials.

162. **Posters and Banners**: Design promotional posters and banners that can be used in physical or digital marketing campaigns. These materials should feature captivating visuals and key information.

163. **Teasers**: Short teaser videos or animations can be used to generate excitement and curiosity. Teasers offer a sneak peek into your game's world or story without revealing too much.

### 15.4.2 Design Principles

When creating promotional materials, adhere to design principles that make your assets visually appealing and effective:

- **Consistency**: Maintain consistent branding elements, colors, and typography across all materials. Consistency reinforces your game's identity.

- **Clarity**: Ensure that your materials convey information clearly and concisely. Avoid clutter and prioritize key messages.

- **Visual Hierarchy**: Arrange content in a way that guides the viewer's attention. Important information should stand out.

- **Quality Imagery**: Use high-resolution images and graphics to maintain visual quality, even when assets are enlarged or viewed on high-resolution screens.

- **Engaging Visuals**: Choose visuals that evoke emotions and curiosity. Engaging visuals can pique interest and encourage further exploration.

### 15.4.3 Tailored Messaging

Customize promotional materials for different target audiences. Tailor your messaging and visuals to resonate with specific demographics, interests, and platforms. For example, materials for gamers might focus on gameplay and mechanics, while materials for investors emphasize market potential and ROI.

### 15.4.4 Storytelling

Craft a compelling narrative for your promotional materials. Storytelling can engage viewers on an emotional level and leave a lasting impression. Highlight the game's unique features and the player's role within the story.

**Storytelling Example**: "Embark on an epic adventure as you explore a mysterious world filled with hidden secrets and formidable challenges."

### 15.4.5 Call to Action (CTA)

Include a clear and compelling call to action in your promotional materials. A CTA encourages viewers to take a specific action, such as visiting your website, joining a mailing list, or pre-ordering the game. Use action-oriented language.

**CTA Example**: "Join the adventure today and be the first to experience our game. Pre-order now!"

### 15.4.6 Localization

If you plan to target international markets, consider localizing your promotional materials. Translate text, voiceovers, and subtitles to cater to non-English-speaking audiences. Localization can significantly broaden your game's reach.

### 15.4.7 Testing and Feedback

Before finalizing promotional materials, gather feedback from your team, playtesters, and trusted peers. Testing helps identify areas for improvement and ensures that the materials effectively convey your game's appeal.

Creating effective promotional materials is a critical step in marketing your Unreal Engine game. By understanding the key materials, adhering to design principles, tailoring messaging, storytelling, incorporating CTAs, considering localization, and seeking feedback, you can develop compelling assets that capture the essence of your game and resonate with your target audience. These materials are essential tools in generating interest and driving success for your game.

---

## 15.5 Launching and Post-Launch Marketing

The launch of your Unreal Engine game is a crucial milestone, but it's just the beginning of your marketing journey. Post-launch marketing is essential for sustaining player engagement, expanding your player base, and achieving long-term success. In this section, we'll delve into strategies for both launching your game and maintaining momentum in the post-launch phase.

### 15.5.1 Pre-Launch Marketing

Before your game's launch, execute a well-planned pre-launch marketing campaign to build anticipation. Here are key pre-launch strategies:

164. **Teasers and Trailers**: Continue releasing teasers and trailers, gradually revealing more about the game's story and features. Create a countdown to generate excitement.

165. **Press Coverage**: Reach out to gaming journalists and influencers for reviews and coverage. Provide them with early access to your game.

166. **Demo or Beta**: Offer a demo or beta version of your game to allow players to experience it before the official launch. Collect feedback and generate interest.

167. **Email Subscribers**: Utilize your email subscriber list to provide exclusive updates and offers to dedicated followers.

168. **Social Media**: Maintain an active presence on social media platforms, posting regularly and engaging with your audience. Host giveaways and contests to encourage sharing.

169. **Community Events**: Organize in-game events, challenges, or competitions to engage players and build a sense of community.

170. **Collaborations**: Partner with other developers, brands, or influencers for cross-promotion. Leverage their audience to expand your reach.

### 15.5.2 Launch Day Strategies

On launch day, maximize visibility and impact with the following strategies:

171. **Press Releases**: Distribute press releases to announce your game's availability. Share them with gaming news outlets and influencers.

172. **Live Streams**: Host live streaming events on platforms like Twitch or YouTube to showcase gameplay and interact with viewers.

173. **Launch Party**: Organize a virtual or physical launch party to celebrate the release. Invite fans, influencers, and press.

174. **Digital Storefronts**: Ensure your game is prominently featured on digital storefronts like Steam, Epic Games Store, or app stores. Optimize your store page with compelling visuals and descriptions.

175. **Reviews and Ratings**: Encourage players to leave reviews and ratings on platforms like Steam. Positive reviews boost visibility.

176. **Support Channels**: Prepare support channels for addressing player inquiries and issues promptly.

### 15.5.3 Post-Launch Marketing

Post-launch marketing is essential for maintaining player interest and growing your player base over time. Here's how to keep the momentum going:

177. **Content Updates**: Plan and release regular content updates, including new levels, features, characters, or cosmetics. Keep players engaged with fresh experiences.

178. **Player Feedback**: Continuously gather and analyze player feedback. Address issues, implement suggestions, and communicate updates transparently.

179. **Community Engagement**: Stay active in your game's community forums, Discord server, and social media. Engage with players, host Q&A sessions, and encourage user-generated content.

180. **Events and Challenges**: Organize seasonal events, challenges, or tournaments to maintain player engagement and provide rewards.

181. **Cross-Promotion**: Collaborate with other developers or brands for cross-promotion to reach new audiences.

182. **DLC and Monetization**: Consider offering downloadable content (DLC) or additional monetization options, such as cosmetics or in-game items.

183. **Analytics and Optimization**: Continuously analyze player data, conversion rates, and user acquisition channels. Adjust your marketing strategies based on insights.

184. **Player Loyalty Programs**: Reward loyal players with exclusive content or discounts. Recognizing and appreciating dedicated fans fosters loyalty.

185. **Email Marketing**: Continue using email marketing to communicate updates, events, and offers to your subscriber list.

186. **User-Generated Content**: Encourage and feature user-generated content, such as fan art, mods, or community-created levels.

### 15.5.4 Marketing Metrics

Monitor the following marketing metrics to assess the effectiveness of your post-launch strategies:

- **Player Retention**: Measure how many players continue to engage with your game over time.

- **User Acquisition Cost (UA Cost)**: Calculate the cost of acquiring new players through marketing campaigns.

- **Churn Rate**: Determine the rate at which players stop playing your game.

- **Conversion Rate**: Evaluate how effectively your marketing efforts convert potential players into actual players.

- **Lifetime Value (LTV)**: Estimate the total revenue a player generates during their engagement with your game.

- **Return on Investment (ROI)**: Assess the overall effectiveness of your marketing campaigns by comparing costs to revenue generated.

- **Player Feedback**: Monitor player sentiment through reviews, social media comments, and community interactions.

- **Active Player Metrics**: Track the number of daily, weekly, and monthly active players.

Launching and maintaining a successful Unreal Engine game requires a strategic approach to marketing. By implementing pre-launch, launch day, and post-launch strategies, analyzing marketing metrics, and remaining actively engaged with your community, you can build and sustain a thriving player base and achieve long-term success in the competitive gaming industry.

# Chapter 16: Legal and Ethical Considerations

## 16.1 Understanding Copyright and Intellectual Property

In the world of game development, understanding copyright and intellectual property (IP) is crucial. This section will delve into the key concepts and considerations surrounding these topics.

### Copyright Basics

Copyright is a legal protection granted to the creators of original works, including video games. It gives creators exclusive rights to reproduce, distribute, and display their work. In the context of game development, this means that the game's code, artwork, music, and other creative assets are automatically protected by copyright as soon as they are created.

### Licensing and Legal Agreements

When using third-party assets or collaborating with others, it's important to understand licensing agreements. Many game development assets, such as sound effects, music, and 3D models, are available under various licenses. Common types of licenses include:

- **Public Domain:** Assets in the public domain are not protected by copyright and can be used freely.
- **Creative Commons:** Creative Commons licenses come in different flavors, allowing various levels of use and modification, as long as the terms are followed.
- **Commercial Licenses:** Some assets may require a purchase or licensing fee for commercial use.
- **Open Source:** Open-source licenses allow you to use and modify the source code of certain software components, but they may come with specific requirements, such as sharing your modifications.

It's crucial to read and adhere to the terms of these licenses to avoid legal issues.

### Ethical Considerations in Game Development

Ethics play a significant role in game development. Developers should consider the potential impact of their games on players and society as a whole. Some ethical considerations include:

- **Representation:** Ensure diverse and respectful representation of different cultures, genders, and backgrounds in your game's characters and storylines.
- **Microtransactions:** Be transparent about in-game purchases and avoid predatory monetization practices that target vulnerable players.
- **Mature Content:** Clearly label and restrict access to mature or sensitive content, and provide tools for parents to control what their children can access.

- **Accessibility:** Make efforts to make your game accessible to players with disabilities by including features like subtitles, adjustable text size, and controller remapping.

### Privacy and Data Protection

With the collection of user data becoming increasingly common in games, it's essential to prioritize user privacy and data protection. Implement proper consent mechanisms and inform players about the data you collect, how it's used, and who it's shared with. Comply with relevant data protection laws, such as the General Data Protection Regulation (GDPR) in Europe.

### Community Management and Fair Play

Creating a positive and inclusive gaming community is vital. Establish clear rules for player behavior and enforce them consistently. Combat toxic behavior, such as harassment and cheating, to maintain a healthy gaming environment. Engage with your community, listen to feedback, and take appropriate actions to address concerns.

In conclusion, legal and ethical considerations are integral to responsible game development. Understanding copyright, licensing, ethical principles, privacy, and community management will help you navigate the complex landscape of game development while upholding ethical standards and legal obligations.

---

## 16.2 Licensing and Legal Agreements

In the world of game development, navigating licensing and legal agreements is crucial for protecting your intellectual property, collaborating with others, and ensuring your game's compliance with legal standards. This section explores the various aspects of licensing and legal agreements in game development.

## Types of Licensing

**1. End-User License Agreement (EULA):** *EULAs are contracts between game developers and players. They outline the terms and conditions under which players can use the game. EULAs typically cover aspects like licensing terms, limitations of liability, intellectual property rights, and code of conduct. It's essential to draft a clear and user-friendly EULA to establish legal boundaries for players.*

**2. Software Licenses:** *When using third-party software libraries, engines, or tools, developers must understand and adhere to their respective software licenses. Common licenses include MIT, GPL, Apache, and proprietary licenses. Developers should carefully review these licenses to ensure compliance with their terms, especially if they plan to distribute their game.*

**3. Asset Licensing:** *Game development often involves using assets such as music, 3D models, textures, and sound effects created by others. Asset licensing agreements specify how these assets can be used, whether they require attribution, and any royalties or fees involved. Make sure to read and comply with the terms of asset licenses to avoid legal disputes.*

**4. Collaboration Agreements:** *When working with a team or collaborators, it's essential to establish clear agreements that define each party's roles, responsibilities, ownership of assets, revenue sharing, and dispute resolution mechanisms. Collaboration agreements help prevent conflicts and ensure everyone's contributions are properly acknowledged.*

## Intellectual Property (IP) Protection

**5. Trademark:** *Registering trademarks for your game's name, logo, and branding can protect your brand identity from infringement. Trademarks help establish a unique presence in the market and prevent others from using similar names or logos.*

**6. Copyright:** *As mentioned in the previous section, copyright automatically protects your game's creative assets. Registering your copyright can provide additional legal benefits and strengthen your position in case of infringement.*

**7. Patents:** *In some cases, game developers may seek patents for unique game mechanics, technologies, or innovations. While patenting can be a complex and costly process, it offers exclusive rights to the patented invention for a limited time.*

## Legal Compliance

**8. Age Ratings and Content Guidelines:** *Different countries have specific age rating systems and content guidelines for games. Ensure your game complies with these regulations, especially if you plan to distribute it internationally. Age-appropriate labeling and content warnings are essential.*

*9. **Data Protection and Privacy Laws:** If your game collects and stores user data, such as personal information or gameplay statistics, you must comply with data protection and privacy laws. Implement clear privacy policies, secure data storage, and obtain informed consent from players.*

*10. **Consumer Protection Laws:** Consumer protection laws vary by region and can affect refund policies, in-game purchases, and advertising practices. Familiarize yourself with these laws to avoid legal issues related to consumer rights.*

In conclusion, understanding and properly managing licensing and legal agreements is a fundamental aspect of game development. It helps protect your intellectual property, maintain legal compliance, and establish clear rules for collaboration and player engagement. Developers should seek legal counsel when drafting complex agreements and ensure that their games adhere to relevant laws and regulations.

---

## 16.3 Ethical Considerations in Game Development

Ethics in game development are essential for creating games that not only entertain but also respect the well-being and values of players and society as a whole. In this section, we explore various ethical considerations that game developers should keep in mind during the development process.

### Representation and Diversity

Developers have a responsibility to represent diverse perspectives and demographics in their games. This includes portraying characters of different genders, ethnicities, sexual orientations, and backgrounds in a respectful and non-stereotypical manner. Diverse representation fosters inclusivity and ensures that players from various backgrounds can see themselves in the game world.

### Microtransactions and Monetization

Ethical concerns often arise in the realm of microtransactions and monetization. Developers should be transparent about in-game purchases and avoid manipulative tactics that encourage excessive spending, especially by vulnerable players. Implementing fair pricing and providing value for purchases is crucial to building trust with players.

### Mature Content and Age Ratings

Games with mature or sensitive content should clearly label their content and enforce age restrictions to prevent underage players from accessing inappropriate material. Providing parental controls and guidance on the game's content can help parents make informed decisions about their children's gaming experiences.

## Accessibility

Developers should prioritize making their games accessible to players with disabilities. This includes providing options for customizable controls, subtitles, screen readers, and other features that enhance the gaming experience for those with disabilities. Accessibility features promote inclusivity and ensure that everyone can enjoy the game.

## Online Safety and Moderation

Online gaming communities can sometimes become toxic environments, plagued by harassment, hate speech, and other harmful behaviors. Game developers should implement robust moderation tools, reporting mechanisms, and consequences for abusive behavior to create safe and enjoyable online spaces for players.

## User Data and Privacy

Respecting player privacy is crucial in the age of data collection. Developers should be transparent about the data they collect, how it's used, and who it's shared with. Obtaining informed consent for data collection and adhering to data protection laws, such as GDPR, is essential to protect players' privacy.

## Social Impact and Responsibility

Game developers should consider the potential social impact of their games. Games have the power to shape opinions and influence behavior. Ethical considerations include avoiding the glorification of violence, promoting positive values, and addressing social issues responsibly and sensitively in storytelling.

## Fairness and Balance

Game developers must strive for fairness and balance in gameplay. Avoiding pay-to-win mechanics, ensuring balanced multiplayer experiences, and preventing cheating are ethical priorities. Players should feel that their achievements are earned through skill and effort, not purchased advantages.

## Continuous Improvement

Ethical game development is an ongoing process. Developers should actively seek feedback from players and the community, listen to concerns, and be willing to make changes to address ethical issues. Acknowledging mistakes and demonstrating a commitment to improvement fosters trust among players.

## Conclusion

Ethical considerations in game development go beyond merely complying with laws and regulations. They involve a commitment to creating games that contribute positively to society, respect players' rights and values, and provide enjoyable and inclusive experiences. Game developers should actively engage with the broader ethical discourse in the industry and stay vigilant in upholding ethical standards throughout the development and post-launch phases.

## 16.4 Privacy and Data Protection

Privacy and data protection are paramount concerns in modern game development, especially with the prevalence of online multiplayer and data-driven experiences. In this section, we'll delve into the key aspects of privacy and data protection that game developers should consider throughout the development process.

### Data Collection and Consent

When collecting player data, developers must be transparent about what data is being collected, why it's necessary, and how it will be used. Players should give informed consent for data collection. Providing a clear and concise privacy policy that explains these details is crucial. Ensure that players have the option to opt out of data collection if they choose.

### Compliance with Data Protection Laws

Game developers should be aware of and comply with data protection laws applicable to their target regions. For example, the General Data Protection Regulation (GDPR) in Europe imposes strict rules on data handling and requires consent, data access, and the right to be forgotten. Non-compliance can result in hefty fines.

### Secure Data Storage and Handling

Protecting player data from unauthorized access and breaches is a primary responsibility. Implement robust security measures to safeguard sensitive information. Use encryption for data in transit and at rest, and regularly audit and update security protocols to stay ahead of potential threats.

### Minimization of Data

Collect only the data necessary for your game's functionality and player experience. Avoid collecting excessive or unrelated information. This not only respects player privacy but also simplifies data management and reduces security risks.

### Third-Party Services and Data Sharing

If your game uses third-party services, such as cloud storage or analytics platforms, ensure that these services also adhere to data protection regulations. Clearly communicate to players if their data will be shared with third parties and for what purposes. Obtain explicit consent when necessary.

### Data Retention Policies

Establish clear data retention policies. Determine how long you will retain player data and the reasons for doing so. Once data is no longer needed, it should be securely deleted. Inform players about your data retention practices in your privacy policy.

### Children's Data

If your game is targeted at or likely to attract children, you must comply with additional regulations, such as the Children's Online Privacy Protection Act (COPPA) in the United States. Obtain parental consent for data collection from children under a certain age and take extra precautions to protect their privacy.

### Data Breach Response Plan

Develop a data breach response plan in case of a security incident. This plan should outline the steps to take if player data is compromised, including notifying affected players and regulatory authorities as required by law.

### Player Access and Control

Allow players to access and modify their personal data. This includes providing mechanisms for players to delete their accounts and associated data if they choose to stop using the game.

### Regular Audits and Updates

Privacy and data protection practices should be subject to regular audits and updates. Stay informed about evolving data protection laws and best practices in the industry and adapt your policies and procedures accordingly.

In conclusion, prioritizing privacy and data protection is not only a legal obligation but also a matter of trust and player confidence. Players are more likely to engage with a game that respects their privacy rights and provides clear information about data handling practices. Game developers should integrate these principles into their development processes from the outset and remain vigilant in upholding them throughout the game's lifecycle.

---

## 16.5 Community Management and Fair Play

Community management and ensuring fair play are essential aspects of game development, especially for online multiplayer games. This section explores the key considerations and practices for maintaining a positive and enjoyable gaming community.

### Establishing Community Guidelines

Game developers should create clear and comprehensive community guidelines that outline expected player behavior, rules, and consequences for violations. These guidelines should address issues like harassment, hate speech, cheating, and unsportsmanlike conduct. By setting expectations from the beginning, developers can foster a respectful gaming environment.

## Active Moderation

Implementing effective moderation tools and having a team of moderators or community managers is crucial for enforcing community guidelines. Moderators should be trained to handle various situations, be responsive to player reports, and apply consequences fairly and consistently. Timely intervention can prevent conflicts from escalating.

## Reporting Mechanisms

Provide players with user-friendly reporting mechanisms to report abusive behavior, cheating, or other violations. Ensure that these reports are reviewed promptly, and appropriate actions are taken. Transparency in the reporting process helps build trust among players.

## Preventing Toxicity

Toxic behavior can harm the overall gaming experience and drive players away. Developers should actively combat toxicity by monitoring in-game chats, forums, and social media channels associated with the game. Encourage positive interactions and discourage negative behavior through various means, such as warnings, temporary suspensions, or permanent bans.

## Fairness and Anti-Cheat Measures

Maintaining a level playing field is essential for competitive games. Implement anti-cheat measures to detect and prevent cheating, hacking, and unfair advantages. Regularly update and improve these measures to stay ahead of cheaters' tactics.

```python
# Example of a simple anti-cheat check in Python
def check_for_cheating(player_data):
    if player_data["kills"] > player_data["deaths"]:
        return "Cheater detected: excessive kills"
    return "No cheating detected"
```

## Transparency and Communication

Transparent communication with the player community is vital. Developers should be open about game changes, updates, and the reasons behind them. Address player concerns and feedback constructively, and involve the community in discussions about the game's future direction.

## Inclusivity and Diversity

Create an inclusive environment that welcomes players from diverse backgrounds. Avoid promoting stereotypes or discriminatory content. Embrace opportunities for cultural representation and celebrate the richness of player diversity.

### Player Feedback

Listen to player feedback and actively incorporate it into game development when feasible. Players appreciate when their opinions are valued and see the game evolve based on their input. This can lead to a more loyal and engaged player base.

### Events and Community Building

Organize in-game events, tournaments, and activities to foster a sense of community among players. Encourage collaboration and friendly competition. Recognize and reward positive contributions to the community.

### Data Protection and Privacy

Respect player privacy by adhering to data protection regulations when managing community data, such as user profiles and communication logs. Ensure that player data is handled securely and in compliance with applicable laws.

In conclusion, community management and fair play are integral to creating a positive and thriving gaming community. Developers should proactively address issues related to player behavior, cheating, and toxicity to maintain a welcoming environment where players can enjoy their gaming experience. A well-managed community not only benefits players but also contributes to the long-term success of the game.

# Chapter 17: Expanding Game Features

## 17.1 Planning for Expansion and DLC

Expanding a game's features and content after its initial release can be a strategic move for developers. It allows you to keep players engaged, attract new ones, and generate additional revenue. In this section, we'll explore the importance of planning for expansion and downloadable content (DLC) in your game development journey.

### Setting Clear Goals

Before diving into expansion and DLC planning, define clear goals for what you want to achieve. Are you aiming to extend the game's storyline, introduce new gameplay mechanics, or provide cosmetic customization options? Understanding your objectives will guide your decisions throughout the expansion process.

### Player Feedback and Community Input

Listening to player feedback and considering community input can help you identify areas for improvement and expansion. Analyze player reviews, forums, and social media discussions to gain insights into what players want and expect from your game. Engage with your community to understand their desires and pain points.

### Monetization Strategies

Decide on a monetization strategy for your expansion content. This can include options like paid DLC, free updates, or a combination of both. Consider the impact on your player base and revenue goals. Be transparent about your pricing and what players can expect to receive in return.

### Expansion Planning

When planning an expansion, create a roadmap that outlines the development timeline, key features, and content additions. Ensure that the expansion aligns with your game's core identity and provides meaningful value to players. Factor in testing and quality assurance to maintain a high-quality experience.

**Expansion Roadmap**

- Month 1: Concept and Design Phase
- Month 2-4: Development and Testing
- Month 5: Marketing and Teasers
- Month 6: Release and Post-Launch Support

### Compatibility and Updates

Consider how the expansion will integrate with the existing game. Ensure that it is compatible with different platforms and configurations. Prepare a plan for patching and updates to address any issues or bugs that may arise post-launch.

### Community Engagement

Involve your community in the expansion process. Share teasers, development updates, and sneak peeks to build anticipation. Encourage players to provide feedback during beta testing or early access phases. Engaging the community can create a sense of ownership and excitement around the expansion.

### Marketing and Promotion

Develop a marketing strategy specifically tailored to promote the expansion. Utilize social media, email newsletters, and press releases to reach your audience. Highlight the expansion's unique features and benefits to entice both existing players and potential new customers.

### Post-Launch Support

Once the expansion is released, continue to support it with regular updates, bug fixes, and community engagement. Address player feedback promptly to ensure a positive experience. Consider adding additional content or features based on ongoing player input.

### Analyzing Performance

After the expansion's release, closely monitor its performance. Track metrics such as player engagement, revenue generated, and player feedback. Use this data to inform future expansion plans and to refine your approach for ongoing content updates.

### Conclusion

Planning for expansion and DLC is a strategic endeavor that can breathe new life into your game and keep players engaged over time. By setting clear goals, listening to your community, and executing a well-thought-out plan, you can create successful and enjoyable expansion content that enhances your game's longevity and player experience.

---

## 17.2 Integrating New Game Modes

Introducing new game modes is a common way to expand a game's features and provide fresh experiences for players. In this section, we'll explore the process of integrating new game modes into your game and discuss key considerations for success.

## Understanding Player Preferences

Before creating new game modes, it's essential to understand your player base's preferences. Analyze player feedback, conduct surveys, and review gameplay data to identify which types of game modes are likely to resonate with your audience. This research will help you prioritize the development of modes that players will enjoy.

## Balancing and Testing

Balancing is crucial when introducing new game modes. Ensure that the new mode provides a fair and enjoyable experience for all players. Test extensively to identify any issues with game mechanics, player progression, or power dynamics. Adjust and refine the mode based on player feedback and testing results.

```python
# Example of a simple game mode balancing algorithm in Python
def balance_game_mode(players):
    if len(players) < 2:
        return "Not enough players for this mode"
    elif len(players) > 10:
        return "Too many players for this mode"
    else:
        return "Game mode is balanced"
```

## Integration with Core Gameplay

New game modes should seamlessly integrate with the core gameplay of your game. Maintain consistency in terms of controls, UI design, and overall game mechanics. Avoid creating modes that feel disconnected or jarring when players transition between them.

## User Interface and Accessibility

Update the user interface (UI) to accommodate new game modes. Ensure that players can easily select and understand the rules of each mode. Implement accessibility features to make the modes accessible to all players, including those with disabilities.

**New Game Mode UI**

```
- Main Menu
  - Play
    - Quick Match
    - Custom Game
  - New Game Modes
    - Mode 1
    - Mode 2
    - ...
```

### Tutorial and Onboarding

If the new game modes introduce unique mechanics or rules, provide tutorials or onboarding experiences to help players understand how to play. Clear instructions and guidance can enhance the player experience and reduce frustration.

### Player Progression and Rewards

Consider how the new game modes will impact player progression and rewards. Ensure that players can earn experience, achievements, or in-game currency through the new modes. This incentivizes participation and encourages players to explore the additional content.

### Community Engagement

Engage with your community to build excitement around the new game modes. Share teasers, development updates, and sneak peeks to create anticipation. Consider involving the community in beta testing or early access to gather feedback and make improvements.

### Post-Launch Support

After the new game modes are released, continue to support them with updates and balance adjustments. Address any issues or bugs promptly, and remain open to player feedback for ongoing improvement. Regularly rotate or introduce new modes to keep the gameplay experience fresh.

### Marketing and Promotion

Promote the new game modes effectively through marketing channels. Utilize social media, website updates, and in-game announcements to inform players about the additions. Highlight the unique features and benefits of each mode to attract both current and potential players.

### Analyzing Performance

Monitor the performance of the new game modes closely. Track metrics such as player engagement, mode popularity, and player feedback. Use this data to make informed decisions about further updates and to plan for future game mode additions.

### Conclusion

Integrating new game modes into your game can breathe new life into the player experience and extend the game's longevity. By understanding player preferences, maintaining balance, and ensuring a seamless integration process, you can successfully introduce exciting new gameplay options that enhance your game and keep players engaged.

## 17.3 Adding Additional Levels and Content

Expanding a game's content by adding new levels, challenges, and experiences is a common way to keep players engaged and excited. In this section, we'll explore the process of adding additional levels and content to your game and discuss key considerations for success.

### Content Planning

Before creating new levels and content, it's crucial to plan your additions carefully. Consider the overall game narrative, progression, and pacing. Define the goals and objectives of each new level and how they contribute to the player's overall experience. Create a content roadmap to guide your development process.

**Content Roadmap**

- New Levels
    - Level 1: Forest Adventure
    - Level 2: Underwater Challenge
- Additional Challenges
    - Time Trials
    - Puzzles

### Level Design

Maintain consistency in level design while introducing new elements and challenges. Ensure that new levels align with the game's art style, theme, and gameplay mechanics. Create levels that offer a mix of familiar and fresh experiences to keep players engaged.

### Progression and Difficulty

Consider the progression curve and difficulty level of new content. Ensure that it aligns with the player's skill development throughout the game. Gradually introduce new challenges and mechanics to avoid overwhelming players.

```python
# Example of a level progression algorithm in Python
def adjust_difficulty(player_level):
    if player_level < 10:
        return "Easy levels"
    elif 10 <= player_level < 20:
        return "Moderate levels"
    else:
        return "Challenging levels"
```

### Player Rewards

Incorporate rewards for completing new levels or challenges. These rewards can include in-game currency, cosmetic items, experience points, or access to additional content. Rewards incentivize player engagement and provide a sense of accomplishment.

### Accessibility

Ensure that new content is accessible to all players, including those with disabilities. Implement features like adjustable difficulty settings, subtitles, and alternative control schemes to accommodate a diverse player base.

### Playtesting and Feedback

Conduct thorough playtesting of new levels and content. Gather feedback from playtesters to identify any issues, bugs, or areas for improvement. Iterate on the design based on feedback to create a polished and enjoyable experience.

### Integration with Core Gameplay

New levels and content should seamlessly integrate with the core gameplay of your game. Maintain consistency in terms of controls, UI design, and overall game mechanics. Avoid creating content that feels disconnected from the rest of the game.

### Content Promotion

Effectively promote new content to inform and engage your player community. Utilize in-game announcements, social media, email newsletters, and website updates to spread the word. Tease the content with trailers, screenshots, and sneak peeks to generate excitement.

### Post-Launch Support

After releasing new levels and content, continue to support it with updates and improvements. Address any issues or bugs promptly, and remain open to player feedback for ongoing refinement. Regularly release fresh content to maintain player interest.

### Analyzing Performance

Monitor the performance of new levels and content closely. Track metrics such as player engagement, completion rates, and player feedback. Use this data to make informed decisions about further updates and to plan for future content additions.

### Conclusion

Adding additional levels and content to your game is a valuable strategy for enhancing player engagement and extending the game's lifespan. By carefully planning your content, maintaining consistency, and considering player progression and accessibility, you can create a compelling and enjoyable experience that keeps players excited about your game.

---

## 17.4 Community-Driven Content and Modding

Empowering your game's community to create and contribute content can significantly enhance the longevity and appeal of your game. In this section, we'll explore the concept of community-driven content and modding, along with the benefits and considerations associated with it.

## What is Community-Driven Content?

Community-driven content refers to game content and modifications created by the player community rather than the game's developers. It can include user-generated levels, custom character skins, gameplay modifications, and more. Modding, short for modification, is a common practice in which players modify or extend a game's original content.

## Benefits of Community-Driven Content

187. **Extended Lifespan:** Community-created content can breathe new life into older games, keeping them relevant and playable for years.

188. **Player Engagement:** Modding and community-driven content encourage players to stay engaged with your game, as they become content creators themselves.

189. **Diversity of Content:** The community can introduce a wide range of content and gameplay experiences that cater to different player preferences.

190. **Free Marketing:** Player-generated content can attract new players to your game, acting as a form of free marketing.

191. **Learning Opportunity:** Modding and content creation provide a learning platform for aspiring game developers and designers.

## Supporting Modding and Community-Driven Content

To enable modding and community-driven content, consider these steps:

1. *Modding Tools: Provide modding tools and documentation that empower the community to create content. Tools like level editors, scripting languages, and asset creation guides are essential.*

2. *Modding Community Hub: Establish a dedicated online hub or forum where modders can share their work, seek help, and collaborate. Encourage discussions and showcase notable creations.*

3. *Compatibility and Integration: Ensure that mods are easy to install and compatible with the base game. Consider integrating a mod manager or workshop feature to streamline the process.*

```python
# Example of a simple mod integration function in Python
def integrate_mod(mod_data, game_data):
    if is_compatible(mod_data, game_data):
        return "Mod successfully integrated"
    else:
        return "Mod is not compatible with the current game version"
```

**4. Moderation and Quality Control:** *Implement moderation to prevent malicious or inappropriate content from circulating within the community. Encourage quality control and peer reviews to maintain a high standard of content.*

**5. Licensing and Ownership:** *Clearly define ownership and licensing terms for community-created content. Ensure that modders understand their rights and responsibilities when using your game's assets.*

## Challenges and Considerations

While community-driven content offers numerous benefits, it also comes with challenges:

**1. Quality Control:** *Maintaining quality and ensuring that mods do not negatively impact the player experience can be challenging.*

**2. Legal Issues:** *Addressing potential copyright violations or disputes over ownership of user-generated content requires careful consideration.*

**3. Technical Compatibility:** *Keeping mods compatible with game updates and patches can be a technical challenge.*

**4. Community Management:** *Moderating community interactions and addressing conflicts or disputes can be time-consuming.*

## Conclusion

Community-driven content and modding can be powerful tools for extending the life and appeal of your game. By providing the right tools, fostering a supportive community, and addressing challenges thoughtfully, you can create an environment where players actively contribute to the game's content and enjoy a richer, more engaging gaming experience.

---

## 17.5 Keeping Your Game Relevant Post-Launch

Ensuring that your game remains relevant and appealing to players after its initial launch is essential for long-term success. In this section, we'll explore strategies and practices for keeping your game fresh and engaging in the months and years following its release.

### Ongoing Updates and Patches

Regularly releasing updates and patches is a fundamental practice for maintaining a healthy player base. These updates can include bug fixes, performance improvements, and quality-of-life enhancements. Listening to player feedback and addressing their concerns demonstrates your commitment to the game's ongoing improvement.

```python
# Example of releasing a patch in Python
def release_patch(patch_number):
```

```
if patch_number > current_game_version:
    update_game(patch_number)
    return "Patch successfully released"
else:
    return "Patch version is not higher than the current game version"
```

## Seasonal Events and Content

Introducing seasonal events and themed content can keep players engaged throughout the year. Events like holiday celebrations, special challenges, and limited-time rewards create a sense of anticipation and encourage players to return to the game regularly.

## Expansion Packs and DLC

Continuously expanding your game with new content through expansion packs or downloadable content (DLC) provides players with fresh experiences. Plan and release expansions strategically to maintain interest and revenue streams.

## Community Engagement

Staying actively engaged with your game's community is vital. Interact with players on forums, social media, and in-game chats. Listen to their feedback, respond to their questions, and involve them in discussions about the game's future direction. Players who feel heard and valued are more likely to remain loyal.

## Player-Generated Content

If your game supports modding and user-generated content, encourage the community to create and share new content regularly. Host contests or events that spotlight outstanding player creations. Continuously update modding tools and documentation to support content creators.

## Competitive Play and eSports

Develop a competitive scene or support eSports tournaments if your game is suitable. Organize regular competitions with prizes to maintain a competitive player base. eSports events can attract a dedicated following and enhance your game's visibility.

## Cross-Platform Play

Consider implementing cross-platform play to expand your game's player base. Allowing players on different platforms to compete or cooperate can increase the game's longevity and social aspects.

## Data-Driven Decision Making

Analyze player data and in-game metrics to make informed decisions about updates and improvements. Identify popular features and areas that may need adjustment. Data-driven insights help you prioritize development efforts effectively.

### Marketing and Promotion

Continue marketing your game post-launch. Announce major updates, expansions, or events to attract new players and re-engage lapsed ones. Utilize social media, email newsletters, and partnerships to reach a wider audience.

### Player Retention Strategies

Implement player retention strategies, such as loyalty programs, daily rewards, and progression systems. Reward players for their commitment to the game, encouraging them to continue playing.

### Conclusion

Keeping your game relevant post-launch requires a combination of ongoing updates, community engagement, player-generated content, and strategic marketing. By continuously evolving your game based on player feedback and data analysis, you can create a vibrant and long-lasting gaming experience that retains its appeal over time.

# Chapter 18: Virtual Reality and Unreal

## 18.1 Basics of VR Development in Unreal

Virtual Reality (VR) is a rapidly evolving technology that offers immersive and interactive experiences to users. Integrating VR into your game development using Unreal Engine opens up new possibilities for creating captivating worlds and interactions. In this section, we'll delve into the basics of VR development in Unreal, covering essential concepts, tools, and best practices.

### Understanding Virtual Reality

Virtual Reality refers to a computer-generated environment that simulates a real-world experience. VR typically involves the use of a head-mounted display (HMD) and input devices like motion controllers to immerse users in a 3D environment. Unreal Engine provides robust support for developing VR applications, allowing you to create stunning and immersive experiences.

### VR Hardware and Compatibility

When developing for VR in Unreal Engine, it's essential to consider the hardware and platforms your game will support. Different VR headsets and devices have varying specifications and capabilities. Ensure that your game is compatible with the target VR platforms and that you optimize performance accordingly.

### Unreal Engine's VR Framework

Unreal Engine offers a comprehensive VR framework that simplifies VR development. This framework includes built-in support for popular VR platforms like Oculus Rift, HTC Vive, and PlayStation VR. Unreal's VR framework streamlines the setup of VR cameras, motion controllers, and interactions, allowing you to focus on content creation.

### Setting Up a VR Project

To start developing a VR project in Unreal Engine, follow these steps:

192. Create a new project in Unreal Engine, choosing the appropriate template for VR development (e.g., VR First Person or VR Third Person).

193. Configure your project's settings to match your target VR platform and hardware. Set up the correct VR plugins and input mappings.

194. Import VR assets and configure your virtual world to support VR interactions. Pay attention to scale, lighting, and performance optimization.

195. Test your VR project using a VR headset and motion controllers. Debug and iterate on your VR experience as needed.

### VR Interaction Models

VR experiences often involve complex interactions with the virtual environment. Unreal Engine provides various interaction models to handle actions like grabbing objects, pointing, and teleporting. You can use Blueprints or C++ to implement these interactions, depending on your preference and project requirements.

```cpp
// Example of grabbing an object in VR using C++
void GrabObject(UPrimitiveComponent* ObjectToGrab, USceneComponent* GrabbingH
and)
{
    // Implement grabbing logic here
    // Attach ObjectToGrab to GrabbingHand
}
```

### Performance Optimization

Optimizing performance is critical in VR development to ensure a smooth and comfortable experience for users. Consider techniques like level-of-detail (LOD) optimization, occlusion culling, and reducing complex geometry. Constantly monitor your project's frame rate to maintain VR compatibility.

### User Comfort and Best Practices

VR can be intense for some users, leading to discomfort or motion sickness. Implement comfort features like teleportation, snap turning, and vignettes to reduce potential discomfort. Follow VR design guidelines to create user-friendly interfaces and interactions.

### Conclusion

Developing VR experiences in Unreal Engine offers the potential to create immersive and engaging content. By understanding VR concepts, leveraging Unreal Engine's VR framework, and following best practices, you can embark on a journey to craft captivating VR worlds and provide users with unforgettable virtual adventures.

---

## 18.2 Designing VR Experiences and Interactions

Designing VR experiences requires careful consideration of user interactions, comfort, and immersion. In this section, we'll explore the key principles and best practices for designing VR experiences in Unreal Engine.

### User-Centered Design

VR experiences should prioritize user comfort and engagement. Keep in mind that VR can be an intense and immersive medium, so design with the user's well-being in mind.

Understand the physical limitations of VR users, such as motion sickness, and implement design elements that mitigate discomfort.

## Immersive Environments

Creating immersive VR environments is essential to captivate users. Unreal Engine's powerful graphics capabilities allow you to craft detailed and visually stunning worlds. Pay attention to scale, lighting, and textures to enhance the sense of presence and realism within the VR space.

## Intuitive Interactions

VR interactions should feel natural and intuitive. Utilize motion controllers to enable hand presence and gestures. Implement hand tracking or gesture recognition to allow users to interact with objects and the environment. Use haptic feedback to provide tactile sensations when interacting with virtual objects.

```
// Example of haptic feedback in VR using Unreal Engine
void ApplyHapticFeedback(UHapticFeedbackEffect_Base* HapticEffect, UMotionCon
trollerComponent* Controller)
{
    if (HapticEffect && Controller)
    {
        Controller->PlayHapticEffect(HapticEffect, MotionControllerHand);
    }
}
```

## Teleportation and Locomotion

VR locomotion can be challenging, as it may cause discomfort for some users. Implement teleportation mechanics or other comfortable locomotion options to move users within the virtual space. Ensure that movement feels smooth and avoids abrupt changes.

## User Interface (UI) Design

Designing UI elements for VR requires a different approach than traditional 2D interfaces. VR UI should be immersive and seamlessly integrated into the environment. Consider placing UI elements within the virtual world, using floating menus, or attaching them to the user's hand or controller for easy interaction.

## Feedback and Animation

Provide feedback to users through animations, sounds, and visual cues. For example, animate objects to react to user interactions, emit sounds when objects collide, and use particle effects to enhance the sense of immersion. Feedback enhances the feeling of agency and presence in VR.

### User Testing

User testing is crucial for VR experience design. Gather feedback from users, especially those who are new to VR, to identify pain points and areas for improvement. Conduct iterative testing to refine the VR experience and address usability issues.

### Performance Optimization

Optimizing performance is critical in VR development. Maintain a consistent frame rate to prevent motion sickness and discomfort. Utilize Unreal Engine's performance profiling tools to identify and address performance bottlenecks, such as high-polygon assets or complex physics simulations.

### Comfort Features

Incorporate comfort features into your VR experience, such as comfort mode options, vignettes during motion, and adjustable comfort settings. These features allow users to tailor their VR experience to their comfort level and reduce motion sickness.

### Testing on Different VR Platforms

Test your VR experience on various VR platforms and devices to ensure compatibility and performance. Different VR headsets may have varying specifications and input methods, so adapt your experience accordingly.

### Conclusion

Designing VR experiences and interactions in Unreal Engine requires a thoughtful approach that prioritizes user comfort, immersion, and intuitive interactions. By following best practices, conducting user testing, and optimizing performance, you can create VR experiences that captivate users and provide them with memorable virtual adventures.

---

## 18.3 VR Performance Optimization

Optimizing performance is a critical aspect of VR development in Unreal Engine. Achieving a consistent and high frame rate is essential to provide users with a comfortable and immersive VR experience. In this section, we'll explore performance optimization techniques specific to VR development.

### Frame Rate Considerations

In VR, maintaining a high and stable frame rate is paramount. A low frame rate can lead to motion sickness and discomfort for users. VR experiences often target a frame rate of 90 frames per second (FPS) or higher to ensure smooth and responsive interactions.

## Level of Detail (LOD) Optimization

Implementing LOD optimization is crucial in VR. LOD allows objects to have different levels of detail based on their distance from the user. Unreal Engine provides tools to create LODs for 3D models, reducing the rendering load when objects are distant. Apply LODs to meshes, textures, and materials to improve performance.

## Occlusion Culling

Occlusion culling is the process of not rendering objects that are entirely hidden by other objects. In VR, this technique is particularly useful for reducing the number of objects that need to be rendered in the user's field of view. Unreal Engine's occlusion culling system can automatically handle this, but you should still design your levels with occlusion in mind.

## Physics Optimization

Physics calculations can be computationally expensive. Optimize physics interactions by simplifying collision shapes, using collision layers effectively, and reducing the number of active physics objects when they are not visible or needed for gameplay.

```
// Example of reducing physics object count when not needed
if (!IsVisibleToPlayer(Object))
{
    Object->SetPhysicsEnabled(false);
}
```

## Shader Optimization

Complex shaders can impact VR performance. Use Unreal Engine's shader profiling tools to identify and optimize expensive shaders. Consider reducing the number of shader passes, utilizing mobile shaders for VR platforms, and avoiding excessive post-processing effects.

## Texture Compression

Texture sizes and formats significantly affect VR performance and memory usage. Use texture compression techniques, such as mipmapping and texture streaming, to reduce memory overhead. Additionally, limit the use of high-resolution textures where they are not necessary for close-up details.

## Dynamic Lighting and Shadows

Dynamic lighting and shadows can be resource-intensive. Minimize the use of dynamic lights and shadows in VR unless they are essential for gameplay. Consider using baked lighting and static shadows to improve performance.

## Haptic Feedback Optimization

Haptic feedback in VR controllers can enhance immersion but should be used judiciously. Avoid excessive haptic feedback, as it can be distracting and affect performance. Limit haptic feedback to actions that provide meaningful tactile cues to the user.

## Benchmarking and Profiling

Regularly benchmark and profile your VR experience to identify performance bottlenecks. Utilize Unreal Engine's built-in profiling tools to analyze frame timing and identify areas that need optimization. Test on target VR hardware to ensure real-world performance.

```python
# Example of a simple frame rate benchmarking function in Python
def benchmark_frame_rate():
    current_frame_rate = get_current_frame_rate()
    if current_frame_rate < target_frame_rate:
        return "Frame rate is below the target"
    else:
        return "Frame rate is within the target range"
```

## User Testing

Conduct user testing with a focus on performance and comfort. Gather feedback from users to identify any discomfort or performance-related issues. Iterate on your VR experience based on user feedback to ensure a smoother and more enjoyable experience.

## Conclusion

VR performance optimization is essential to deliver a comfortable and immersive VR experience. By employing techniques such as LOD optimization, occlusion culling, and texture compression, you can achieve a consistent high frame rate and create VR experiences that captivate users without causing discomfort or motion sickness.

---

## 18.4 Addressing VR Challenges

While virtual reality (VR) offers exciting possibilities, it also presents unique challenges that developers must address to create successful VR experiences. In this section, we'll explore some common challenges in VR development and discuss strategies to overcome them.

### 1. Motion Sickness

Motion sickness can be a significant issue in VR due to the discrepancy between visual and vestibular (inner ear) signals. To mitigate motion sickness, consider implementing techniques like teleportation, smooth locomotion with comfort options, and providing a fixed frame of reference when the player moves.

```cpp
// Example of teleportation implementation in Unreal Engine
void TeleportToLocation(FVector Destination)
{
    // Implement teleportation logic here
    // Move the player to the Destination location
}
```

## 2. Performance

Achieving and maintaining high frame rates is crucial in VR to prevent discomfort. To address performance challenges, use level of detail (LOD) optimization, occlusion culling, and texture compression, as discussed in the previous section. Regularly profile your VR experience to identify and address performance bottlenecks.

## 3. User Interface (UI) Design

Designing user interfaces for VR requires thoughtful consideration. UI elements should be legible and easy to interact with in a 3D space. Use 3D menus, laser pointers, or hand-tracking gestures for navigation. Test your UI with actual VR users to ensure usability.

## 4. Interaction Complexity

VR interactions can be complex due to the need for intuitive hand presence and gestures. Provide clear and concise tutorials or guidance to help users understand how to interact with the VR environment. Implement hand tracking or motion controller support to enhance interaction fidelity.

## 5. Comfort Options

Different users have varying tolerance levels for VR comfort. Offer comfort options like adjustable field of view (FOV) reduction during movement, snap turning, and vignettes. Allow users to customize these settings to match their comfort preferences.

```
// Example of FOV reduction during movement in Unreal Engine
void ReduceFOVDuringMovement(float MovementSpeed)
{
    // Implement FOV reduction logic based on MovementSpeed
}
```

## 6. Content Creation

Creating VR content can be more time-consuming and resource-intensive than traditional game development. Ensure that your 3D assets are optimized for VR to maintain performance. Utilize Unreal Engine's VR development tools and assets to streamline the content creation process.

## 7. Testing on Different VR Platforms

VR experiences must often run on multiple VR platforms with varying specifications. Test your VR application on different VR headsets and platforms to ensure compatibility and performance. Adapt your VR experience to each platform's capabilities.

## 8. User Comfort

Prioritize user comfort throughout the VR experience. Avoid rapid or unexpected movements, intense visual effects, or situations that could induce discomfort or nausea. Solicit feedback from users and iterate on your VR design to enhance comfort.

### 9. Hardware Limitations

Different VR hardware has limitations in terms of tracking accuracy, field of view, and input methods. Be aware of the hardware's capabilities and limitations when designing your VR experience. Consider offering alternative input methods to accommodate a wider range of VR devices.

### 10. Playtesting and Feedback

Regular playtesting with VR users is essential to identify and address VR-specific issues. Collect feedback on comfort, usability, and overall experience. Iterate on your VR design based on user feedback to create a more polished and enjoyable VR experience.

### Conclusion

VR development presents unique challenges, including motion sickness, performance optimization, UI design, and user comfort. By addressing these challenges through thoughtful design, testing, and optimization, you can create VR experiences that captivate users and offer a comfortable and immersive journey into virtual worlds.

---

## 18.5 Future Trends in VR and Unreal Integration

As technology evolves, so does the landscape of virtual reality (VR) development. Staying ahead of the curve and understanding future trends in VR is essential for Unreal Engine developers. In this section, we'll explore some of the anticipated trends in VR and how Unreal Engine is positioned to integrate with these developments.

### 1. Wireless VR

Wireless VR headsets are gaining popularity as they offer greater freedom of movement and convenience. Unreal Engine developers should consider optimizing their VR experiences for wireless devices, ensuring compatibility with platforms like the Oculus Quest and future wireless headsets.

### 2. Eye Tracking and Foveated Rendering

Eye-tracking technology is poised to become a standard feature in VR headsets. This technology allows for foveated rendering, where the highest level of detail is focused on the area where the user is looking. Unreal Engine is well-suited to support eye tracking and foveated rendering, optimizing performance and enhancing realism.

### 3. Realistic Avatars and Social VR

Social VR experiences are becoming increasingly popular, and users expect realistic avatars and interactions. Unreal Engine's advanced character animation and rendering capabilities make it a strong choice for creating lifelike avatars and social VR experiences. Integration with AI-driven chatbots and natural language processing is also a growing trend in social VR.

## 4. VR for Education and Training

VR is finding applications beyond gaming, particularly in education and training. Unreal Engine's versatility makes it an excellent tool for creating educational VR experiences, from historical recreations to interactive science simulations. Integration with learning management systems and analytics will be crucial in this context.

## 5. Healthcare and Therapy

VR is being used for therapeutic purposes, such as pain management, PTSD treatment, and exposure therapy. Unreal Engine's ability to create immersive environments makes it a valuable platform for healthcare applications. Future trends may include integrating biofeedback and physiological monitoring into VR experiences.

## 6. Augmented Reality (AR) and Mixed Reality (MR) Integration

The lines between VR, AR, and MR are blurring. Unreal Engine's support for AR and MR development positions it as a versatile tool for creating cross-reality experiences. Integrating AR and MR features, such as object recognition and spatial mapping, will be increasingly important.

```
// Example of AR object recognition in Unreal Engine
void OnARObjectRecognized(ARObject DetectedObject)
{
    // Implement actions based on recognized objects
}
```

## 7. Gesture and Voice Control

Gesture and voice control are becoming standard input methods in VR. Unreal Engine developers can leverage technologies like hand-tracking sensors and voice recognition to create more immersive and intuitive VR interactions.

## 8. Accessibility and Inclusivity

As VR becomes more mainstream, ensuring accessibility and inclusivity is vital. Unreal Engine should continue to support features like closed captioning, customizable controls, and assistive technologies to make VR experiences accessible to a broader audience.

## 9. Global Collaboration and Multiplayer VR

Global collaboration in VR is a growing trend, with users from around the world coming together in shared virtual spaces. Unreal Engine's robust networking capabilities make it a powerful tool for creating multiplayer VR experiences. Supporting cross-platform multiplayer and user-generated content will be essential.

### 10. AI and Procedural Generation

AI-driven procedural generation is becoming more prevalent in VR content creation. Unreal Engine can integrate AI algorithms for world generation, character behavior, and content creation. The use of AI to enhance realism and interactivity will continue to evolve.

### Conclusion

Unreal Engine's flexibility and robust features position it well for the future of VR development. As VR technology advances and new trends emerge, Unreal Engine developers can adapt and innovate, creating immersive and engaging VR experiences that push the boundaries of what is possible in virtual reality. Keeping a pulse on these trends and integrating them into VR projects will be key to staying at the forefront of VR development.

# Chapter 19: Mobile Game Development with Unreal

## 19.1 Adapting to Mobile Platforms

Mobile game development has become a thriving sector within the gaming industry, and Unreal Engine offers the tools and capabilities to create high-quality mobile games. In this section, we'll explore the fundamentals of adapting your game to mobile platforms using Unreal Engine.

### Mobile Gaming Landscape

Before diving into development, it's crucial to understand the mobile gaming landscape. Mobile devices vary significantly in terms of processing power, screen size, and input methods. Consider the target audience and platform when adapting your game.

### Performance Optimization

Mobile devices have limited processing power compared to PCs and consoles. To ensure your game runs smoothly on mobile, optimize performance rigorously. Utilize Unreal Engine's profiling tools to identify and address performance bottlenecks, such as high-polygon models and resource-intensive effects.

### Input Methods

Mobile devices rely on touchscreens or gyroscopic sensors for input. Adapt your game's controls and user interface to accommodate touch gestures, taps, swipes, and device tilting. Consider adding virtual joysticks or buttons if they enhance gameplay.

```
// Example of touch input handling in Unreal Engine
void HandleTouchInput(float TouchX, float TouchY)
{
    // Implement touch input logic here
    // Translate touch coordinates to in-game actions
}
```

### Scalable Graphics

Create scalable graphics and assets to accommodate various screen resolutions and aspect ratios. Use Unreal Engine's asset management features to automatically adapt textures and models based on device capabilities. Consider offering graphics quality settings to allow users to tailor the experience to their device's performance.

### Monetization Strategies

Mobile games often rely on monetization to generate revenue. Explore various monetization strategies, such as in-app purchases, ads, and premium pricing. Integrate monetization mechanics that align with your game's design and user experience.

### Mobile-Specific Design Considerations

Design your game with mobile-specific considerations in mind. Mobile gamers typically prefer shorter play sessions, making it essential to design levels or game loops that accommodate quick bursts of gameplay. Implement features like cloud saves to allow users to switch between devices seamlessly.

### Battery Optimization

Mobile games should be energy-efficient to preserve device battery life. Minimize CPU and GPU usage during idle moments, and optimize background processes. Implement power-saving features like screen brightness adjustment and screen timeout management within your game.

### App Store Guidelines

To publish your game on app stores, adhere to their guidelines and requirements. Familiarize yourself with the submission process, age ratings, and content restrictions. Prepare promotional materials like screenshots and app descriptions to attract users.

### Cross-Platform Development

Unreal Engine supports cross-platform development, allowing you to target multiple mobile platforms simultaneously. Utilize Unreal's project settings and platform-specific configurations to build for iOS and Android with ease.

### Performance Testing on Real Devices

Test your game on real mobile devices to ensure compatibility and performance. Emulators provide a useful development environment, but real devices may reveal unique issues. Regular testing on a range of devices is essential to provide a consistent user experience.

### Conclusion

Adapting your game to mobile platforms with Unreal Engine requires careful consideration of performance optimization, input methods, scalability, and monetization strategies. By understanding the mobile gaming landscape and adhering to best practices, you can create successful mobile games that cater to a diverse and thriving audience.

---

## 19.2 Mobile-Specific Design Considerations

When developing mobile games with Unreal Engine, it's essential to consider mobile-specific design considerations to create an engaging and enjoyable experience for your target audience. Mobile gamers have unique preferences and constraints compared to players on other platforms. In this section, we'll explore key design considerations for mobile games.

## 1. Short Play Sessions

Mobile gamers often play games in short, on-the-go sessions. Design your game to accommodate quick bursts of gameplay, allowing users to engage even when they have limited time. Implement short levels, challenges, or tasks that can be completed in a few minutes.

## 2. Touchscreen Controls

Mobile devices primarily rely on touchscreen input. Ensure that your game's controls are intuitive and responsive to touch gestures. Implement touch-based actions like tapping, swiping, and pinching for gameplay interactions. Provide visual cues or tutorials to guide players on how to use these controls effectively.

```
// Example of touch-based input handling in Unreal Engine
void HandleTouchInput(float TouchX, float TouchY)
{
    // Implement touch input logic here
    // Translate touch coordinates to in-game actions
}
```

## 3. Simplified User Interface (UI)

Optimize your game's user interface for mobile screens. Keep UI elements clear, concise, and easy to interact with using touch controls. Avoid cluttered layouts and tiny buttons that can be challenging to tap accurately on smaller screens. Use responsive design principles to adapt the UI to different screen sizes and orientations.

## 4. Offline Play

Consider adding offline playability to your mobile game. Mobile devices are frequently used in environments with limited or no internet connectivity. Allowing users to enjoy your game offline increases its accessibility and appeal.

## 5. Device Compatibility

Account for a wide range of mobile device specifications and capabilities. Test your game on various devices with different screen sizes, resolutions, and hardware configurations to ensure compatibility. Use Unreal Engine's scalability settings to adapt graphics and performance based on the user's device.

## 6. Battery Optimization

Mobile games should be energy-efficient to preserve device battery life. Minimize resource-intensive background processes and animations when the game is not in the foreground. Implement power-saving options like screen brightness adjustments and battery-friendly graphics settings.

## 7. Frequent Updates

Mobile gamers expect regular updates and content additions. Plan a content release schedule to keep players engaged and encourage retention. Updates can include new levels, characters, events, or challenges to maintain player interest over time.

## 8. Cross-Platform Play

Consider implementing cross-platform play to allow mobile gamers to connect with players on other devices. Cross-platform multiplayer can enhance the community and provide a broader player base for your game. Ensure fair competition and a level playing field among all platforms.

## 9. Performance Monitoring

Monitor your game's performance on various mobile devices using Unreal Engine's profiling tools. Identify performance bottlenecks, optimize resource usage, and maintain a stable frame rate to ensure a smooth gaming experience across different devices.

## 10. User Feedback and Iteration

Gather feedback from mobile players and use it to improve your game continually. Listen to user reviews and ratings on app stores and consider implementing player suggestions and addressing reported issues in updates. Engage with the mobile gaming community to build a loyal player base.

## Conclusion

Mobile-specific design considerations are crucial when developing games for mobile platforms using Unreal Engine. By tailoring your game to short play sessions, optimizing touchscreen controls, simplifying the user interface, and addressing device compatibility, you can create a mobile gaming experience that resonates with users and stands out in the competitive mobile gaming market.

---

## 19.3 Performance and Battery Optimization

Performance and battery optimization are critical aspects of mobile game development with Unreal Engine. Mobile devices come in various hardware configurations, and ensuring a smooth and energy-efficient gameplay experience is essential to reach a wide audience. In this section, we'll delve into strategies for optimizing both performance and battery usage in your mobile game.

## 1. Graphics Optimization

**a. Level of Detail (LOD):** Implement LOD (Level of Detail) for 3D models, textures, and materials to reduce rendering load on the GPU. This technique adjusts the level of detail based on the object's distance from the camera, optimizing performance without sacrificing visual quality.

```
// Example of LOD implementation in Unreal Engine
void ApplyLODForObject(GameObject object)
{
    // Implement LOD logic here
    // Adjust object's level of detail based on distance
}
```

**b. Texture Compression:** Use texture compression techniques such as mipmapping and texture streaming to reduce memory usage and GPU workload. Compress textures without compromising visual quality to improve performance.

**c. Shader Complexity:** Optimize shaders by reducing the number of shader passes and minimizing expensive computations. Use mobile-friendly shaders when targeting lower-end devices.

2. CPU Optimization

**a. CPU Profiling:** Utilize Unreal Engine's profiling tools to identify CPU bottlenecks. Analyze CPU usage during gameplay and optimize code responsible for AI, physics, and game logic.

**b. Multithreading:** Leverage multicore processors by implementing multithreading for tasks like AI calculations and physics simulations. Ensure thread safety and avoid race conditions in your code.

```
// Example of multithreading in Unreal Engine
void CalculateAIPathAsync(GameObject aiObject)
{
    AsyncTask(ENamedThreads::AnyThread, [=]()
    {
        // Perform AI pathfinding calculations in a separate thread
        // Update game state when calculations are complete
    });
}
```

**c. Object Pooling:** Implement object pooling to reuse game objects rather than instantiating and destroying them frequently. This reduces CPU overhead associated with object management.

3. Battery Optimization

**a. Energy-Efficient Animations:** Design animations and particle effects to be energy-efficient. Minimize the use of continuous animations and resource-intensive visual effects that drain the battery quickly.

**b. Background Processes:** Ensure that your game minimizes background processes and resource usage when it's not in the foreground. Implement pause mechanisms and reduce CPU and GPU load during idle moments.

```
// Example of reducing resource usage when the game is in the background
void OnGamePause()
{
    // Implement pause logic here
    // Reduce resource usage during pause
}
```

**c. Screen Brightness:** Allow users to adjust screen brightness within the game. Lowering screen brightness can significantly extend battery life during gameplay.

### 4. Device Compatibility

**a. Scalable Graphics:** Use Unreal Engine's scalability settings to adapt graphics quality based on the user's device. Provide options for users to adjust graphics settings to match their device's performance.

**b. Device Testing:** Test your game on a variety of real mobile devices to ensure compatibility and performance across different hardware configurations. Address device-specific issues to create a seamless experience.

### 5. Battery-Friendly Features

**a. Power Saving Mode:** Implement a power-saving mode within your game that automatically adjusts graphics settings, reduces frame rate, and limits resource-intensive features when the device's battery is low.

**b. Screen Timeout Management:** Respect the user's screen timeout settings to avoid keeping the screen active when the game is not in use, which can lead to unnecessary battery drain.

### Conclusion

Optimizing performance and battery usage is crucial for the success of your mobile game. By implementing strategies such as graphics and CPU optimization, battery-friendly features, and device compatibility testing, you can create a mobile game that not only runs smoothly but also extends the device's battery life, providing an enjoyable and energy-efficient gaming experience for players on various mobile devices.

---

## 19.4 Touch Interface Design

Designing an effective touch interface is essential for mobile games developed using Unreal Engine. Unlike traditional gaming platforms with physical controllers, mobile devices rely on touchscreens for user input. In this section, we'll explore key principles and best practices for designing a touch interface that enhances the gameplay experience on mobile.

## 1. Touch Gestures

Mobile games often use touch gestures as primary input methods. Consider the following common touch gestures and how they can be integrated into your game:

- **Tap:** Implement tapping for actions such as shooting, jumping, or selecting items. Ensure that taps are responsive and have visual feedback to confirm the action.

```
// Example of tap input handling in Unreal Engine
void HandleTapInput()
{
    // Implement tap input logic here
    // Perform the specified action when the screen is tapped
}
```

- **Swipe:** Swiping can be used for character movement, camera rotation, or scrolling through menus. Make swipes intuitive and provide visual cues to guide players.

- **Pinch and Zoom:** For games with zoomable maps or interfaces, support pinch gestures for zooming in and out. Ensure smooth zooming animations and limits to prevent over-zooming.

- **Drag and Drop:** Drag and drop interactions are suitable for inventory management or puzzle-solving. Design drag-and-drop mechanics that are easy to control and understand.

## 2. Virtual Buttons and Joysticks

When traditional physical buttons are not available, consider adding virtual buttons and joysticks to the screen. These on-screen controls should be intuitive and customizable. Allow players to adjust the position and size of virtual buttons to suit their preferences.

```
// Example of virtual joystick input handling in Unreal Engine
void HandleVirtualJoystickInput(float JoystickX, float JoystickY)
{
    // Implement virtual joystick input logic here
    // Translate joystick input to character movement
}
```

## 3. Responsive Design

Design your touch interface with different screen sizes and aspect ratios in mind. Ensure that interface elements are appropriately scaled and positioned to accommodate various devices. Use responsive design principles to adapt the UI layout dynamically.

### 4. Visual Feedback

Provide visual feedback for touch interactions. When a button is pressed or a gesture is executed, use animations, color changes, or sound effects to indicate that the action has been recognized. Visual feedback enhances the user's sense of control and engagement.

### 5. Minimize Fatigue

Consider ergonomics and player comfort when designing touch controls. Avoid placing critical buttons in hard-to-reach areas of the screen, as this can lead to hand fatigue. Keep frequently used controls within easy thumb reach.

### 6. Gestural Consistency

Maintain consistency in touch gestures and controls throughout the game. Use similar gestures for similar actions to create a predictable and intuitive user experience. Avoid introducing complex or non-standard gestures without proper guidance.

### 7. Accessibility

Ensure that your touch interface is accessible to all players. Implement customizable controls and support for alternative input methods, such as game controllers or accessibility features for players with disabilities.

### 8. Testing and Iteration

Testing your touch interface on real mobile devices is crucial. Conduct usability testing with a diverse group of players to gather feedback on the effectiveness and comfort of your touch controls. Iterate on your design based on user feedback.

### Conclusion

Designing a touch interface for mobile games in Unreal Engine requires careful consideration of touch gestures, virtual buttons, responsive design, visual feedback, and accessibility. By creating an intuitive and ergonomic touch interface, you can enhance the overall gameplay experience and make your mobile game more engaging and accessible to a wider audience of players.

---

## 19.5 Monetization Strategies for Mobile Games

Monetization is a crucial aspect of mobile game development, as it allows developers to generate revenue from their games. In this section, we'll explore various monetization strategies that you can implement in your mobile game developed using Unreal Engine.

## 1. In-App Purchases (IAPs)

In-app purchases are a popular monetization method for mobile games. You can offer virtual items, currency, power-ups, skins, or additional content for purchase within your game. Implement a virtual store where players can buy these items using real money. Ensure that IAPs enhance the gameplay experience but do not create a pay-to-win situation.

```
// Example of handling in-app purchases in Unreal Engine
void ProcessInAppPurchase(Item purchasedItem)
{
    // Implement logic to provide the purchased item to the player
    // Update the player's inventory and game progress
}
```

## 2. Ads

Integrate advertisements into your mobile game to generate revenue. There are several ad formats to consider:

- **Interstitial Ads:** Display full-screen ads between game levels or during natural breaks in gameplay.

- **Banner Ads:** Show small, non-intrusive banners at the top or bottom of the screen during gameplay.

- **Rewarded Ads:** Offer players rewards, such as in-game currency or power-ups, in exchange for watching ads. This can enhance player engagement.

## 3. Premium Pricing

Offer your mobile game as a premium product with an upfront purchase cost. Players pay a one-time fee to download and access the full game. Ensure that the game provides a complete and enjoyable experience without the need for additional purchases.

## 4. Subscription Models

Implement subscription models that grant players access to premium content, features, or ongoing updates for a recurring fee. Subscription-based monetization can provide a steady stream of revenue and encourage player loyalty.

```
// Example of managing subscriptions in Unreal Engine
void ProcessSubscriptionPurchase(SubscriptionType subscription)
{
    // Grant the player access to premium content or features
    // Handle subscription renewals and cancellations
}
```

### 5. In-Game Advertising

Integrate product placements or sponsored content within your game. Partner with advertisers to feature their products or brands in a non-disruptive and contextually relevant way.

### 6. Cross-Promotion

Cross-promote your other games or products within your mobile game. Encourage players to explore your portfolio by offering rewards or incentives for installing or engaging with other titles you've developed.

### 7. Limited-Time Offers and Events

Create limited-time events and special offers that entice players to spend money or engage with your game. These time-limited promotions can drive urgency and increase monetization during specific periods.

### 8. Data Monetization

Consider monetizing player data with their consent. Aggregated and anonymized player insights can be valuable to market researchers and advertisers. Ensure strict compliance with privacy regulations and obtain user consent.

### 9. Affiliate Marketing

Partner with affiliate programs to promote products or services within your game. Earn a commission for each successful referral or sale generated through your game's affiliate links.

### 10. Community Support

Foster a strong community around your mobile game to encourage player donations or contributions. Some players may willingly support your game's development through voluntary payments or crowdfunding.

### 11. Fair Monetization

Regardless of your chosen monetization strategy, prioritize fairness and transparency. Avoid overly aggressive monetization tactics that may alienate players. Clearly communicate the value of purchases and be responsive to player feedback and concerns.

### Conclusion

Choosing the right monetization strategy for your mobile game developed with Unreal Engine requires careful consideration of your game's genre, audience, and design. A well-balanced approach that provides value to players while generating revenue is key to long-term success. Experiment with different monetization methods, gather player feedback, and adapt your strategy to create a sustainable and enjoyable gaming experience for your audience.

# Chapter 20: Looking to the Future

## 20.1 Emerging Trends in Game Development

The world of game development is continually evolving, driven by advancements in technology and changing player preferences. In this section, we'll explore some of the emerging trends in game development that you should keep an eye on as you navigate your journey in the industry.

### 1. Virtual Reality (VR) and Augmented Reality (AR)

VR and AR technologies have been on the rise, opening up new possibilities for immersive gaming experiences. With the advent of more accessible hardware and software development kits, VR and AR games are becoming increasingly popular. Unreal Engine offers robust support for VR and AR development, making it a valuable tool for creating immersive experiences.

```
// Example of VR interaction in Unreal Engine
void HandleVRInteraction(HandController controller)
{
    // Implement VR interaction logic here
    // Detect gestures and interactions in virtual reality
}
```

### 2. Cloud Gaming

Cloud gaming services are gaining traction, allowing players to stream games from remote servers to their devices. This eliminates the need for powerful local hardware and expands the potential player base. Developers may need to adapt their games to run effectively on cloud platforms and explore new revenue models in this space.

### 3. User-Generated Content and Modding

Empowering players to create their own content and modifications for games has been a growing trend. Games that support user-generated content and modding communities can enjoy extended lifespans and enthusiastic player engagement. Unreal Engine's flexibility makes it suitable for supporting modding and user-generated content.

### 4. Artificial Intelligence (AI)

AI-driven NPCs and adversaries are becoming more sophisticated, enhancing the realism and challenge of games. Game developers are integrating machine learning and neural networks into their titles to create dynamic and adaptive AI behaviors.

```
// Example of AI behavior using neural networks in Unreal Engine
void UpdateAIWithNeuralNetwork(NPCCharacter npc)
{
    // Implement AI logic using neural networks
```

```
    // NPCs adapt and learn from player behavior
}
```

## 5. Blockchain and NFTs

Blockchain technology and Non-Fungible Tokens (NFTs) are entering the gaming space. These technologies can enable ownership of in-game assets and the creation of player-driven economies. However, they also come with unique challenges and considerations regarding security and player trust.

## 6. Cross-Platform Play and Cross-Progression

The demand for cross-platform play continues to grow. Players want to enjoy games with friends, regardless of their gaming platform. Supporting cross-platform multiplayer and cross-progression can expand a game's player base and foster a sense of community.

## 7. Sustainability and Environmental Impact

There is a growing awareness of the environmental impact of gaming. Game developers are exploring ways to reduce the carbon footprint of their creations, from energy-efficient game design to sustainable server hosting.

## 8. Accessibility and Inclusivity

Game developers are increasingly focusing on making games more accessible to a broader audience. This includes considerations for players with disabilities, such as customizable controls, text-to-speech features, and more inclusive design choices.

## 9. Live Services and Games as a Service (GaaS)

The trend of live services and Games as a Service (GaaS) continues to dominate the industry. This model involves ongoing updates, content drops, and monetization strategies designed to keep players engaged long-term.

## 10. Ethical Game Design

Ethical considerations in game design are gaining importance. Developers are scrutinizing aspects like addiction mechanics, microtransactions, and the impact of games on mental health. Ethical game design principles are being integrated to ensure player well-being.

## Conclusion

As a game developer, staying informed about emerging trends is crucial for keeping your skills relevant and your games competitive. The future of game development holds exciting possibilities, from immersive VR experiences to innovative AI-driven gameplay. By embracing these trends and adapting your approach, you can contribute to the evolving landscape of the gaming industry and continue to create engaging and impactful games.

## 20.2 Unreal Engine in the Evolving Tech Landscape

Unreal Engine has been at the forefront of game development for years, but its influence extends beyond gaming. In this section, we'll explore how Unreal Engine is positioned within the evolving tech landscape and its role in various industries and applications.

### 1. Film and Animation Production

Unreal Engine is widely used in the film and animation industry. Its real-time rendering capabilities allow filmmakers to create stunning visual effects and virtual environments. Directors can preview scenes in real-time, saving time and resources during production. Unreal Engine's virtual production tools have revolutionized the way movies and TV shows are made.

```
// Example of real-time rendering in Unreal Engine for film production
void PreviewSceneInRealTime(MovieDirector director)
{
    // Use Unreal Engine to visualize scenes and special effects
    // Make real-time adjustments to achieve desired results
}
```

### 2. Architectural Visualization

Architects and designers leverage Unreal Engine to create interactive architectural visualizations. It enables clients and stakeholders to explore buildings and spaces in real-time 3D. Unreal Engine's high-quality rendering capabilities help professionals showcase their designs effectively.

### 3. Automotive Industry

Unreal Engine is used for automotive visualization and simulation. Car manufacturers can design and visualize vehicles in a virtual environment, test autonomous driving algorithms, and create interactive showrooms for customers.

```
// Example of automotive simulation in Unreal Engine
void SimulateAutonomousDriving(UnrealVehicle vehicle)
{
    // Implement autonomous driving algorithms and test in a virtual environm
ent
    // Analyze and optimize vehicle performance
}
```

### 4. Training and Simulation

In sectors like defense and healthcare, Unreal Engine is used for training simulations. It provides realistic virtual environments for training scenarios, from military exercises to surgical simulations. Unreal Engine's fidelity is valuable for creating lifelike training experiences.

## 5. Education

Educational institutions are adopting Unreal Engine to teach game development, 3D modeling, and animation. Students gain practical experience in a powerful and industry-standard engine. It also offers opportunities for educational game development.

## 6. Virtual Museums and Exhibits

Unreal Engine is used to create virtual museums and exhibitions. Visitors can explore historical sites, art galleries, and educational exhibits from anywhere in the world. This technology has gained prominence, especially in times of limited physical access.

## 7. Therapeutic and Healthcare Applications

In the healthcare sector, Unreal Engine is used for therapeutic applications and patient education. Virtual reality therapy, medical simulations, and patient education modules are being developed to improve healthcare outcomes.

## 8. AEC (Architecture, Engineering, and Construction)

AEC professionals use Unreal Engine to visualize and present architectural and construction projects. It aids in design validation, stakeholder communication, and project coordination. Real-time collaboration features facilitate better decision-making.

## 9. Industrial Design and Manufacturing

Unreal Engine finds applications in industrial design and manufacturing. It assists in product visualization, prototyping, and testing. Unreal's real-time rendering helps manufacturers assess product designs effectively.

## 10. Art and Entertainment

Beyond gaming and film, Unreal Engine is used in the art and entertainment industry. Artists and musicians use it to create interactive experiences, virtual concerts, and immersive art installations.

## Conclusion

Unreal Engine's versatility and real-time capabilities have positioned it as a leading technology not only in the gaming industry but also in various sectors that rely on visualization, simulation, and interactivity. As technology continues to evolve, Unreal Engine is likely to play an even more significant role in shaping the way we work, learn, entertain, and experience the world around us. Developers and professionals across industries will continue to harness its power to create innovative and engaging experiences.

## 20.3 Continuing Education and Skill Development

In the rapidly evolving field of game development and technology, staying current with the latest trends and mastering new skills is essential. In this section, we'll explore the importance of continuing education and skill development for game developers using Unreal Engine.

### 1. Continuous Learning

Game development is a dynamic field where technologies, tools, and best practices evolve regularly. Unreal Engine itself receives updates and improvements that introduce new features and workflows. To stay competitive, game developers must commit to continuous learning.

```
// Example of continuous learning in game development
void LearnNewFeaturesAndTechniques(UnrealEngineVersion version)
{
    // Stay updated with the latest Unreal Engine features and documentation
    // Explore new techniques and best practices through online courses and t
utorials
}
```

### 2. Online Resources

There is an abundance of online resources available for Unreal Engine developers. These include official documentation, community forums, YouTube tutorials, and online courses. Leveraging these resources can help developers acquire new skills and troubleshoot issues more efficiently.

### 3. Official Unreal Engine Documentation

Unreal Engine's official documentation is a valuable source of information. It provides in-depth explanations, tutorials, and examples for various engine features and functionalities. Developers should refer to this documentation regularly to enhance their knowledge.

### 4. Community Engagement

Engaging with the Unreal Engine community can be highly beneficial. It allows developers to exchange knowledge, seek advice, and collaborate on projects. Participating in forums, attending user group meetings, and joining online communities can provide valuable insights and networking opportunities.

### 5. Online Courses and Certifications

Several online platforms offer courses and certifications specific to Unreal Engine. These courses cover a wide range of topics, from beginner to advanced levels. Completing such courses can validate your skills and knowledge in the engine.

## 6. Conferences and Workshops

Attending industry conferences and workshops can be a great way to learn from experts, gain hands-on experience, and network with peers. Unreal Engine-related events often feature presentations and sessions that showcase the latest advancements and techniques.

## 7. Experimentation and Personal Projects

Building personal projects and experimenting with Unreal Engine is an excellent way to develop new skills. Trying out different features, creating prototypes, and pushing the boundaries of what the engine can do can lead to valuable discoveries.

```
// Example of experimenting with Unreal Engine features
void ExperimentWithNewGameMechanics()
{
    // Create prototypes to test and refine new gameplay ideas
    // Experiment with Unreal Engine's blueprint system and scripting capabil
ities
}
```

## 8. Mentorship and Collaboration

Experienced game developers can benefit from mentorship, and newer developers can learn from more experienced peers. Collaborative projects provide opportunities for skill sharing and mentorship within the game development community.

## 9. Adapting to Emerging Technologies

As technology evolves, game developers should be open to exploring emerging technologies that complement their skill set. This includes areas like virtual reality, augmented reality, machine learning, and cloud gaming.

## 10. Soft Skills

In addition to technical skills, game developers should also focus on developing soft skills. Effective communication, problem-solving, teamwork, and project management are essential in the industry.

## Conclusion

Continuing education and skill development are not just beneficial but essential for success in the game development field, especially when using a powerful and versatile engine like Unreal Engine. By embracing a mindset of continuous learning, utilizing online resources, engaging with the community, and exploring emerging technologies, game developers can not only keep up with industry trends but also drive innovation and create exceptional gaming experiences. Whether you are a beginner or a seasoned professional, investing in your skill development is a pathway to a fulfilling and successful career in game development.

## 20.4 Joining the Unreal Developer Community

The Unreal Developer Community is a vibrant and supportive network of individuals and organizations who share a passion for Unreal Engine and game development. In this section, we'll explore the benefits of joining this community and how you can actively participate.

### 1. Access to Resources

One of the primary advantages of being part of the Unreal Developer Community is access to a wealth of resources. This includes official documentation, tutorials, sample projects, and plugins created and shared by fellow developers. These resources can significantly speed up your development process.

```
// Example of utilizing community-created plugins in Unreal Engine
void IntegrateCommunityPlugin()
{
    // Incorporate third-party plugins or assets shared by the community
    // Enhance your game with additional functionality or assets
}
```

### 2. Networking Opportunities

The Unreal Developer Community provides excellent networking opportunities. You can connect with developers from around the world, including industry professionals, indie developers, and hobbyists. Networking can lead to collaborations, job opportunities, and the sharing of valuable insights.

### 3. Community Forums and Support

Unreal Engine's official forums and community-driven platforms like Unreal Slackers are hubs for discussions, problem-solving, and knowledge sharing. When you encounter challenges or have questions, the community is often quick to offer assistance and solutions.

### 4. Showcasing Your Work

The community provides platforms for showcasing your projects and receiving feedback. Whether you're working on a personal project, a portfolio piece, or a commercial game, sharing your work can lead to recognition and valuable critique.

### 5. Learning from Others

By actively participating in the community, you can learn from the experiences and insights of others. Reading about their successes, failures, and development journeys can provide valuable lessons and inspiration for your own projects.

## 6. Contributing to Open Source

Many community members contribute to open-source projects related to Unreal Engine. You can join these efforts, collaborate on projects, or even start your own open-source initiatives. Contributing to open source not only benefits the community but also enhances your own skills.

```cpp
// Example of contributing to an open-source Unreal Engine project
void ContributeToCommunityProject()
{
    // Collaborate with other developers on an open-source project
    // Improve the project, fix issues, and contribute back to the community
}
```

## 7. Attending Meetups and Events

Local Unreal Engine meetups and user groups are organized by community members worldwide. These events provide opportunities to meet like-minded developers in person, share experiences, and participate in workshops or presentations.

## 8. Engaging with Epic Games

Epic Games, the creator of Unreal Engine, actively engages with the Unreal Developer Community. They often provide updates on the engine's development, listen to user feedback, and offer grants and opportunities for exceptional projects.

## 9. Competitions and Challenges

The community frequently hosts game development competitions and challenges. Participating in these events can motivate you to create unique projects, improve your skills, and potentially win prizes or recognition.

## 10. Giving Back

As you gain experience and expertise with Unreal Engine, consider giving back to the community. Share your knowledge through tutorials, plugins, or by helping others on forums. Being a helpful member of the community can be rewarding and fosters a positive atmosphere.

## Conclusion

Joining the Unreal Developer Community is a valuable step for any game developer using Unreal Engine. It offers access to resources, networking opportunities, support, and a platform to showcase your work. Engaging with the community can accelerate your learning, provide inspiration, and open doors to collaborative projects and career opportunities. Whether you are a novice or an experienced developer, actively participating in the community can enhance your game development journey and contribute to the growth and vitality of the Unreal Engine ecosystem.

## 20.5 Charting Your Path Forward in Game Development

As you conclude your exploration of Unreal Engine and game development, it's essential to consider your future path and goals in this dynamic field. In this section, we'll discuss some key considerations and strategies for charting your path forward.

### 1. Define Your Goals

Start by defining your career and project goals. Do you aspire to work in a particular sector, such as AAA game development, indie games, simulations, or a different industry altogether? Knowing your goals will help you make informed decisions and allocate your time and resources effectively.

### 2. Specialize or Diversify

Consider whether you want to specialize in a specific aspect of game development, such as programming, level design, art, or sound, or if you prefer to be a versatile generalist. Specialization can make you an expert in your field, while diversification can allow you to work on a broader range of projects.

### 3. Build a Portfolio

A strong portfolio is crucial in the game development industry. Showcase your best work, including personal projects, freelance work, or contributions to larger teams. Keep your portfolio up to date and tailor it to the type of work you want to pursue.

```
// Example of updating a game development portfolio
void UpdatePortfolioWithLatestProjects()
{
    // Add new projects, demos, or contributions to your portfolio
    // Highlight your skills and accomplishments
}
```

### 4. Continued Learning

Game development is an ever-evolving field. Commit to continuous learning by staying up to date with industry trends, learning new tools and technologies, and expanding your skill set. Take courses, attend workshops, and engage with the community.

### 5. Networking

Networking is essential for career growth. Attend industry events, conferences, and local meetups. Connect with professionals on LinkedIn and other social platforms. Building a network can lead to job opportunities, collaborations, and valuable insights.

### 6. Job Search and Freelancing

If you're pursuing a career in game development, actively search for job openings, internships, or freelance opportunities. Tailor your resume and cover letter to highlight your relevant skills and experiences. Freelancing can be an excellent way to gain experience and build your reputation.

## 7. Entrepreneurship

Consider the possibility of starting your game development studio or indie game project. Platforms like Unreal Engine provide accessible tools for indie developers. Entrepreneurship can offer creative freedom but also comes with its challenges in terms of funding and marketing.

## 8. Continuous Improvement

Embrace a growth mindset and focus on continuous improvement. Seek feedback on your work, learn from mistakes, and aim to become better with each project. Your ability to adapt and learn is a valuable asset.

## 9. Work-Life Balance

Maintaining a healthy work-life balance is vital for long-term success. Game development can be demanding, so prioritize self-care and ensure you have a support system in place.

## 10. Giving Back

As you progress in your career, consider giving back to the game development community. Share your knowledge, mentor newcomers, and contribute to open-source projects. Your experiences can help others on their journey.

## Conclusion

Charting your path forward in game development requires careful consideration of your goals, skills, and interests. Whether you aim to work for established studios, create your games, or explore other industries where Unreal Engine skills are valuable, staying dedicated to learning and networking will be key to your success. Remember that your journey is unique, and each step you take contributes to your growth as a game developer. Embrace the challenges and opportunities that come your way, and continue to fuel your passion for creating interactive experiences in the exciting world of game development.

www.ingramcontent.com/pod-product-compliance
Lightning Source LLC
La Vergne TN
LVHW051445050326
832903LV00030BD/3248